Social Studies Excursions, K–3

Book One: Powerful Units on Food, Clothing, and Shelter

JANET ALLEMAN and JERE BROPHY
With Contributions by Barbara Knighton

HEINEMANN
Portsmouth, NH

Heinemann
A division of Reed Elsevier Inc.
361 Hanover Street
Portsmouth, NH 03801–3912
www.heinemann.com

Offices and agents throughout the world

© 2001 by Janet Alleman and Jere Brophy

The authors and publisher wish to thank those who have generously given permission to reprint borrowed material:

"Ten Thematic Strands" from *Curriculum Standards for Social Studies: Expectations of Excellence*, Bulletin No. 89 (1994). Published by the National Council for Social Studies, Washington, DC. Reprinted by permission.

"Five Key Features of Powerful Social Studies Teaching and Learning" from *Social Education*, 57 (1993). Published by the National Council for Social Studies, Washington, DC. Reprinted by permission.

Recipes and illustrations for "Chef Combo's 'Milk Blender Special'," "Squirrel Feed," and "Chef Combo Shape House" are used courtesy of the National Dairy Council.®

Library of Congress Cataloging-in-Publication Data
Alleman, Janet.
    Social studies excursions, K–3 / Janet Alleman and Jere Brophy with contributions by Barbara Knighton.
        p.   cm.
    Includes bibliographical references.
    Contents: Bk. 1. Powerful units on food, clothing, and shelter
    ISBN 0-325-00315-7 (pbk.)
    1. Social sciences—Study and teaching (Primary).   I. Brophy, Jere E.
II. Knighton, Barbara.   III. Title.

LB1530 .A44 2001
372.83'044—dc21   00-054121

Editor: William Varner
Production: Lynne Reed
Cover design: Darci Mehall, Aureo Design
Author photographs: Elbinger Studio
Manufacturing: Deanna Richardson

Printed in the United States of American on acid-free paper
05   04   03   02   01   VP   1   2   3   4   5

To my husband, George Trumbull

—Janet Alleman

To my grandsons Mark Speier, Christian Speier, and Jered Brophy

—Jere Brophy

Contents

· ·

Series Preface

. . . .

This series contains three volumes, each of which includes detailed plans for social studies units intended for use in the primary grades. The unit plans provide a substantive content base and learning and assessment activities designed to help primary-grade teachers provide their students with a powerful introduction to social education. Like the major primary-grade social studies textbook series, these units focus on cultural universals—basic human needs and social experiences found in all societies, past and present (food, clothing, shelter, family living, communication, transportation, government, economics/money, and childhood). However, unlike the units found in the major textbook series, the units in this series are structured around powerful ideas and designed to develop those ideas in depth and with attention to their applications to life outside of school. Consequently, they are suitable for use as substitutes for, or elaborations of, units on the same topics found in the textbook series.

Such elaboration is needed because the textbooks produced for use in the early grades are primarily picture books that do not provide sufficient content to support a powerful social studies program. Concerning shelter, for example, these textbooks typically offer only a few pages that show a variety of shelter forms and make the observation that "people around the world live in many different kinds of houses." They do not attempt to explain why these different housing types exist, and the manuals that come with them do not provide guidance to teachers about how they might develop such understanding in their students. In contrast, our shelter unit explores multiple facets of this cultural universal in depth, including consideration of the geographic, economic, and cultural reasons that have led various past and present societies to develop their characteristic housing styles. Students emerge from the unit with connected understandings about how and why humans in different times and places have developed contrasting responses to their shelter needs, along with greatly enhanced knowledge about cultural, economic, and technological aspects of shelter in today's society.

The series has been developed primarily for preservice and inservice primary-grade teachers who want a more substantive and powerful social studies program than the major textbook series can support. Each volume contains plans for three instructional units intended to support instruction for forty to sixty minutes per day for three to four weeks. Units are divided into lessons that elaborate the content base in detail and include plans for learning activities, assessment tasks, and follow-up home assignments. The home assignments are not conventional worksheets but instead are activities calling for students and their parents to engage in conversations or other enjoyable activities connected to the unit topic. Along with the unit plans as such, each volume includes information about how and why the units were developed, suggestions about how teachers might adapt them to their students and local communities, and tips about planning and implementing the units from the authors and from Barbara Knighton, the teacher who has had the most experience teaching the units to her students.

Besides teachers who will use the units directly with their own students in their own classrooms, the volumes in this series should be useful to several other audiences. State- and district-level staff developers and social studies curriculum coordinators should find the volumes useful as bases for workshops and presentations on making primary-grade social studies more powerful and more in line with national and state standards. Each unit develops a network of powerful ideas (basic social understandings) about the topic and provides opportunities for students to apply these ideas in their lives outside of school. The instructional content and processes reflect the guidelines of the National Council for the Social Studies and related professional organizations.

Finally, the volumes should be useful to professors and others conducting preservice and inservice teacher education relating to social studies in the primary grades. Using materials from this series, instructors can show teachers how the cultural universals addressed in the early social studies curriculum can be developed with a focus on powerful ideas and their applications, so as to create a social studies program that reflects reform standards. Also, by assigning preservice teachers to teach one or more lessons from these units, instructors can provide opportunities for their students to experience what it is like to develop big ideas in depth and to begin to build habits of good professional practice.

Since the 1930s, there has been widespread agreement among primary-grade curriculum makers and teachers that cultural universals are appropriate topics for introducing students to social studies concepts and principles. Given this "wisdom of practice," we believe that instructors will find that the approach taken in this series (i.e., retaining the cultural universals as unit topics but developing them much more coherently and powerfully) makes more sense as a response to criticisms of the contemporary primary-grade social studies textbooks than commonly suggested alternatives that call for shifting to something else entirely (e.g., a primary focus on history or on social issues). We elaborate this point at the end of the first chapter in each volume.

Acknowledgments

· ·

The units presented in this series could not have been developed without the assistance of a great many people. Most prominent among them is Barbara Knighton, the teacher who first makes our unit plans come to life in her classroom and provides us with many suggestions for improving them. We also wish to acknowledge and thank Gina Henig, Barbara's colleague, who also has provided us with useful feedback and suggestions; the principal, parents, and students associated with the school at which Barbara teaches; Carolyn O'Mahony and Tracy Reynolds, who interviewed students before and after they experienced the units; and June Benson, who transcribed the audiotapes of the class sessions and the interviews. We also wish to acknowledge and thank the College of Education at Michigan State University for its support of the research and development that led to these units and the Spencer Foundation for its support of a related line of research on what K–3 students know (or think they know) about topics commonly addressed in early elementary social studies.

1

Background
How and Why We Developed the Units

This is the first in a series of three volumes in which we present plans for instructional units on cultural universals—basic human needs and social experiences found in all societies, past and present—designed to be taught in the primary grades (K–3). The units primarily reflect the purposes and goals of social studies, but they do include some science content. They also integrate language arts by including writing assignments and reading and discussion of children's literature. The units may be used as supplements to (or substitutes for) the primary-grade textbooks in the major elementary social studies series.

This first volume includes plans for units on food, clothing, and shelter. Volume 2 will contain plans for units on family living, communication, and transportation. Volume 3 will contain plans for units on government, economics/money, and childhood throughout history and across cultures. Each unit has been developed to stand on its own as an independent module, so there is no inherent order in which they need to be taught.

The units have been taught successfully to first and second graders, and they can be adapted for use in kindergarten and third grade. This is because all students, even kindergartners, have had a variety of personal experiences with cultural universals and are ready to learn more. At the same time, however, what primary-grade students know (or think they know) about these topics is spotty, mostly tacit, and frequently distorted by misconceptions, so even third graders can to benefit from opportunities to learn most of what is included in these units. In schools where the complete set of units is taught, the primary-grade teachers will need to coordinate their planning to determine which units will be taught at which grade level.

The Need for a Powerful Content Base in Early Social Studies

In most American elementary schools, the primary-grade social studies curriculum addresses three major goals: (1) socializing students concerning prosocial attitudes and behavior as members of the classroom community; (2) introducing them to map concepts and skills; and (3) introducing them to basic social knowledge drawn mostly from history, geography, and the social sciences. Even though all three of these instructional goals and related content emphases are featured in state and district curriculum guides for elementary social studies, they are not equally well addressed in the resource materials commonly made available to elementary teachers. The major textbook series generally do a good job of providing appropriate content and learning activities for developing students' map concepts and skills. They are more variable in what they offer as a basis for socializing students as citizens of the classroom community (and subsequently, successively broader communities).

A good selection of ancillary resources is available to support primary-grade teachers' planning of experiences designed to help their students learn to interact respectfully, collaborate in learning efforts, resolve conflicts productively, and in general, display prosocial attitudes and democratic values in their behavior as members of the classroom community. Unfortunately, good instructional resources are not readily available to support primary-grade teachers' efforts to help their students develop basic knowledge about society and the human condition. There is widespread agreement among critics of the major elementary social studies series that the content presented in their primary-grade texts is thin, trite, and otherwise inadequate as a foundation for developing basic social understandings. (These criticisms are reviewed in detail in Brophy & Alleman, 1996, and in Larkins, Hawkins, & Gilmore, 1987.)

The social studies curriculum for the elementary grades is usually organized within the expanding communities sequence that begins with a focus on the self in kindergarten and gradually expands to address families in Grade 1, neighborhoods in Grade 2, communities in Grade 3, states and geographic regions in Grade 4, the United States in Grade 5, and the world in Grade 6. However, the categories in this expanding communities sequence refer primarily to the levels of analysis at which content is addressed, not to the content itself. That is, although there is some material on families in first grade, on neighborhoods in second grade, and on communities in third grade, the topics of most instructional units are the human social activities that are carried on within families, neighborhoods, and communities. These activities tend to be structured around cultural universals (food, clothing, shelter, communication, transportation, government, etc.).

Despite problems with the textbook series, we believe that the cultural universals traditionally addressed in the primary grades provide a sound basis for developing fundamental social understandings. First, they are basic to the human condition. Human activities relating to these cultural universals account for a considerable proportion of everyday life and are the focus of much of our social organization and communal activity. Furthermore, children begin accumulating direct personal experiences with most cultural universals right from birth, so by the time they begin school, they have developed considerable funds of knowledge and experience they can draw upon in constructing understandings of social education concepts and principles.

If cultural universals are taught with appropriate focus on powerful ideas and their potential life applications, students should develop basic sets of connected understandings about how the social system works; how and why it got to be that way over time; how and why it varies across locations and cultures; and what all of this might mean for personal, social, and civic decision making. The units in this series provide a content base capable of supporting this kind of powerful social studies teaching.

As we've noted, such a content base is needed because it is not provided in the major publishers' elementary social studies textbook series. The primary-grade texts in these series (especially the K–2 texts) are better described as picture books than textbooks. Their pages often contain rich collages of color photos relating to the unit topic, but these photos are accompanied by little or no text—a sentence or two at most. The photos are potentially useful as instructional resources if students are induced to process them with reference to powerful ideas, but the texts typically do not convey such ideas to students. Nor do the accompanying manuals convey them to teachers or provide guidance concerning how the photos might be used as bases for powerful social studies teaching.

For example, a lesson on shelter might have several pages of photos showing a variety of past and present homes (tipis, longhouses, pueblos, yurts, igloos, jungle huts, stilt houses, log cabins, castles, mansions, high-rise apartment buildings, and various forms of modern family homes). However, the text on these pages might say little or nothing more than, "People all around the world live in many different kinds of homes." Students will not get much out of exposure to such collages unless they are helped to process what they are seeing with reference to powerful ideas (in this case, ideas that will help them appreciate the reasons why the different kinds of homes were constructed by the people who built them). Thus, for example, the students might learn that the Native

Americans who built tipis did so because they packed up periodically to follow the buffalo and needed portable housing; that the Eastern woodlands tribes had plentiful supplies of wood to use to build their longhouses, whereas the Southwestern desert tribes had to bake adobe bricks to build their pueblos; that rice farmers in many parts of the world have to build their homes high on poles because they live in marshes or flood plains that support rice farming; or that high-rise apartment buildings are found in large cities because a premium on centrally located space creates pressures to build up instead of out. With exposure to ideas such as these, students can appreciate photo collages on homes as illustrations of human adaptability to time and place in meeting shelter needs. In contrast, students who are only shown the collages are likely to see nothing more than photos illustrating that some people build strange, exotic, or even bizarre homes for no apparent reason.

Teaching Cultural Universals for Understanding, Appreciation, and Life Application

Our development of instructional units on cultural universals has been guided by several sets of principles. One set reflects an emerging consensus about what is involved in teaching school subjects for understanding, appreciation, and life application. Reviews of research on such teaching (e.g., Good & Brophy, 2000) suggest that it reflects the following ten principles:

1. The curriculum is designed to equip students with knowledge, skills, values, and dispositions that they will find useful both inside and outside of school.
2. Instructional goals focus on developing student expertise within an application context and with emphasis on conceptual understanding of knowledge and self-regulated application of skills.
3. The curriculum balances breadth with depth by addressing limited content but developing this content sufficiently to foster conceptual understanding.
4. The content is organized around a limited set of powerful ideas (basic understandings and principles).
5. The teacher's role is not just to present information but also to scaffold and respond to students' learning efforts.
6. The students' role is not just to absorb or copy input but also to actively make sense and construct meaning.
7. Students' prior knowledge about the topic is elicited and used as a starting place for instruction, which builds on accurate prior knowledge but also stimulates conceptual change if necessary.

8. Activities and assignments feature tasks that call for critical thinking or problem solving, not just memory or reproduction.

9. Higher-order thinking skills are not taught as a separate skills curriculum. Instead, they are developed in the process of teaching subject-matter knowledge within application contexts that call for students to relate what they are learning to their lives outside of school by thinking critically or creatively about it or by using it to solve problems or make decisions.

10. The teacher creates a social environment in the classroom that could be described as a learning community, featuring discourse or dialogue designed to promote understanding.

These principles emphasize focusing instruction on big ideas that are developed in depth and with attention to their applications. In identifying big ideas to feature in our units, we sought an appropriate balance among the three traditional sources of curriculum: (1) knowledge of enduring value (including but not limited to disciplinary knowledge); (2) the students (their needs, interests, and current readiness); and (3) the needs of society (the knowledge, skills, values, and dispositions that our society would like to see developed in future generations of its citizens).

Teaching for Conceptual Change

Related principles come from research on teaching for conceptual change. Students' prior knowledge about topics sometimes includes naive ideas or even outright misconceptions that can cause the students to ignore, distort, or miss the implications of new information that conflicts with their existing ideas. Teachers who are aware of common misconceptions can plan instruction to address these directly. This involves helping students to recognize differences between their current beliefs and the target understandings, and to see the need to shift from the former to the latter. Such instruction is often called *conceptual change teaching*.

Kathleen Roth (1996) developed an approach to conceptual change teaching that she applied to science and social studies. She embedded the conceptual change emphasis within a more comprehensive "learning community" model of teaching school subjects for understanding. This approach emphasizes eliciting valid prior knowledge that instruction can connect with and build upon, not just identifying misconceptions that will need to be addressed. Our instructional units were designed accordingly.

These efforts also were informed by a series of studies that we conducted on K–3 students' knowledge and thinking about cultural universals. These studies yielded a great deal of information about accurate prior knowledge that most students are likely to possess as they begin each unit, as well as about important knowledge gaps and common naive ideas or misconceptions that will need to be addressed during the instruction.

These findings are noteworthy because some proponents of alternative curricula have claimed that there is no need to teach about cultural universals in the primary grades because children learn all that they need to know about them through everyday experiences. This claim was made in the absence of relevant research. Our studies speak directly to this issue.

We have found that the knowledge about cultural universals that children accumulate through everyday experiences is limited, disconnected, and mostly tacit rather than well articulated. Also, it frequently is distorted by naive ideas or outright misconceptions. We do not find this surprising, because most of children's experiences relating to cultural universals are informal and do not include sustained discourse structured around key ideas. In any case, it is now clear that primary-grade students stand to benefit from systematic instruction about these topics. A summary of our key findings concerning each of the cultural universals is included in the introduction to its corresponding instructional unit.

NCSS Standards

Our unit development efforts also were informed by two definitive standards statements released by the National Council for the Social Studies (NCSS) during the 1990s: one on curriculum and one on teaching and learning. The curriculum standards are built around ten themes that form a framework for social studies (see Figure 1). The publication that spells out these standards elaborates on each theme in separate chapters for the early grades, the middle grades, and the secondary grades, listing performance expectations and potential classroom activities that might be used to develop the theme (National Council for the Social Studies, 1994). The NCSS subsequently sponsored publication of a collection of readings that illustrate how the ten themes might be addressed in elementary social studies teaching (Haas & Laughlin, 1997), and a survey of children's literature published in the 1990s that relates to these themes (Krey, 1988).

Along with its curriculum standards, the NCSS released a position statement identifying five key features of powerful social studies teaching and learning (see Figure 2). The publication that elaborates on these five key features frames them by stating that social studies teaching is viewed as powerful when it helps students develop social understanding and civic efficacy (National Council for the Social Studies, 1993). Social understanding is integrated knowledge of the social aspects of the human condition: how these aspects have evolved over time, the variations that occur in different physical environments and cultural settings, and emerging trends that appear likely to shape the future. Civic efficacy is readiness and willingness to assume citizenship responsibilities. It is rooted in social studies knowledge and skills, along with related values (such as concern

Ten themes serve as organizing strands for the social studies curriculum at every school level (early, middle, and high school); they are interrelated and draw from all of the social science disciplines and other related disciplines and fields of scholarly study to build a framework for social studies curriculum.

I. Culture

Human beings create, learn, and adapt culture. Human cultures are dynamic systems of beliefs, values, and traditions that exhibit both commonalties and differences. Understanding culture helps us understand ourselves and others.

II. Time, Continuity, and Change

Human beings seek to understand their historic roots and to locate themselves in time. Such understanding involves knowing what things were like in the past and how things change and develop—allowing us to develop historic perspective and answer important questions about our current condition.

III. People, Places, and Environment

Technological advancements have ensured that students are aware of the world beyond their personal locations. As students study content related to this theme, they create their spatial views and geographical perspectives of the world; social, cultural, economic, and civic demands mean that students will need such knowledge, skills, and understandings to make informed and critical decisions about the relationship between human beings and their environment.

IV. Individual Development and Identity

Personal identity is shaped by one's culture, by groups, and by institutional influences. Examination of various forms of human behavior enhances understandings of the relationships between social norms and emerging personal identities, the social processes that influence identity formation, and the ethical principles underlying individual action.

V. Individuals, Groups, and Institutions

Institutions exert enormous influence over us. Institutions are organizational embodiments to further the core social values of those who comprise them. It is important for students to know how institutions are formed, what controls and influences them, how they control and influence individuals and culture, and how institutions can be maintained or changed.

VI. Power, Authority, and Governance

Understanding of the historic development of structures of power, authority, and governance and their evolving functions in contemporary society is essential for emergence of civic competence.

VII. Production, Distribution, and Consumption

Decisions about exchange, trade, and economic policy and well-being are global in scope, and the role of government in policy making varies over time and from place to place. The systematic study of an interdependent world economy and the role of technology in economic decision making is essential.

VIII. Science, Technology, and Society

Technology is as old as the first crude tool invented by prehistoric humans, and modern life as we know it would be impossible without technology and the science that supports it. Today's technology forms the basis for some of our most difficult social choices.

Continues

FIGURE 1 Ten Thematic Strands

IX. Global Connections

The realities of global interdependence require understanding of the increasingly important and diverse global connections among world societies before there can be analysis leading to the development of possible solutions to persisting and emerging global issues.

X. Civic Ideals and Practices

All people have a stake in examining civic ideals and practices across time, in diverse societies, as well as in determining how to close the gap between present practices and the ideals upon which our democracy is based. An understanding of civic ideals and practices of citizenship is critical to full participation in society.

Source: National Council for the Social Studies. (1994). *Curriculum Standards for Social Studies: Expectations of Excellence* (Bulletin No. 89). Washington, DC: Author.

FIGURE 1 (Continued)

Meaningful

The content selected for emphasis is worth learning because it promotes progress toward important social understanding and civic efficacy goals, and it is taught in ways that help students to see how it is related to these goals. As a result, students' learning efforts are motivated by appreciation and interest, not just by accountability and grading systems. Instruction emphasizes depth of development of important ideas within appropriate breadth of content coverage.

Integrative

Powerful social studies cuts across disciplinary boundaries, spans time and space, and integrates knowledge, beliefs, values, and dispositions to action. It also provides opportunities for students to connect to the arts and sciences through inquiry and reflection.

Value-Based

Powerful social studies teaching considers the ethical dimensions of topics, so that it provides an arena for reflective development of concern for the common good and application of social values. The teacher includes diverse points of view, demonstrates respect for well-supported positions, and shows sensitivity and commitment to social responsibility and action.

Challenging

Students are encouraged to function as a learning community, using reflective discussion to work collaboratively to deepen understandings of the meanings and implications of content. They also are expected to come to grips with controversial issues, to participate assertively but respectfully in group discussions, and to work productively with peers in cooperative learning activities.

Active

Powerful social studies is rewarding but demanding. It demands thoughtful preparation and instruction by the teacher, and sustained effort by the students to make sense of and apply what they are learning. Teachers do not mechanically follow rigid guidelines in planning, implementing, and assessing instruction. Instead, they work with the national standards and with state and local guidelines, adapting and supplementing these guidelines and their instructional materials in ways that support their students' social education needs.

The teacher uses a variety of instructional materials, plans field trips and visits by resource people, develops current or local examples to relate to students' lives, plans reflective discussions, and scaffolds students' work in ways that encourage them to gradually take on more responsibility for managing their own learning independently and with their peers. Accountability and grading systems are compatible with these goals and methods.

Students develop new understandings through a process of active construction. They develop a network of connections that link the new content to preexisting knowledge and beliefs anchored in their prior experience. The construction of meaning required to develop important social understanding takes time and is facilitated by interactive discourse. Clear explanations and modeling from the teacher are important, but so are opportunities to answer questions, discuss or debate the meaning and implications of content, or use the content in activities that call for tackling problems or making decisions.

Source: National Council for the Social Studies. (1993). "A Vision of Powerful Teaching and Learning in the Social Studies: Building Social Understanding and Civic Efficacy." *Social Education, 57,* 213–223.

FIGURE 2 Five Key Features of Powerful Social Studies Learning

for the common good) and dispositions (such as an orientation toward confident participation in civic affairs).

Along with publishing the statement on powerful teaching, the NCSS has made available a multimedia teacher education resource. It is a professional development program that includes print materials and videotapes for use by district-level staff developers working with teachers to revitalize local social studies programs (Harris & Yocum, 1999).

In developing our units, we did not begin with these NCSS standards. Instead, we began with lists of powerful ideas that might anchor networks of social knowledge about the cultural universal under study. As unit development proceeded, however, we used the NCSS content and teaching standards as guidelines for assessing the degree to which the unit was sufficiently complete and well balanced. No individual lesson includes all of the ten content themes and the five features of powerful teaching, but all of these content and process standards are well represented in the plans for the unit as a whole.

We have found that units planned to develop connected understandings of powerful ideas consistently meet the NCSS standards (as well as state standards). Our units include embedded strands that address history, geography, economics, culture, government, and decision making. However, the units were developed as pandisciplinary (or perhaps we should say, predisciplinary), integrated treatments of the topic, not as collections of lessons organized around the academic disciplines treated separately.

Key Characteristics of the Units

In summary, we emphasize teaching for understanding (and where necessary, conceptual change) by building on students' prior knowledge and developing key ideas in depth and with attention to their applications to life outside of school. The unit plans provide a basis for three to four weeks of instruction, depending on the topic and the degree to which the teacher includes optional extensions. All of the units feature six common components:

1. The units begin with focus on the cultural universal as experienced in contemporary American society, especially in the students' homes and neighborhoods. (This includes eliciting students' prior knowledge and helping them articulate this mostly tacit knowledge more clearly.) Early lessons use familiar examples to help students develop understanding of how and why the contemporary social system functions as it does with respect to the cultural universal being studied.

2. The units consider how the technology associated with the cultural universal has evolved over time. Lessons on this historical dimen-

sion illustrate how human responses to the cultural universal have been influenced by inventions and other cultural advances.

3. The units address variation in today's world in the ways that the cultural universal is experienced in different places and societies. Along with the historical dimension, this geographical/cultural dimension of the unit extends students' concepts to include examples different from the ones they view as prototypical. This helps them to place themselves and their familiar social environments into perspective as parts of the larger human condition (as it has evolved through time and as it varies across cultures). In the language of anthropologists, these unit components "make the strange familiar" and "make the familiar strange" as a way to broaden students' perspectives.

4. The units include physical examples, classroom visitors, field trips, and, especially, children's literature selections (both fiction and nonfiction) as input sources.

5. The units include home assignments that call for students to interact with parents and other family members in ways that not only build curriculum-related insights but engage the participants in enjoyable and affectively bonding activities.

6. The units engage students in thinking about the implications of all of this for personal, social, and civic decision making in the present and future, in ways that support their self-efficacy perceptions with respect to their handling of the cultural universal throughout their lives. Many lessons raise students' consciousness of the fact that they will be making choices (both as individuals and as citizens) relating to the cultural universal under study. Many of the home assignments engage students in decision-making discussions with other family members. These discussions (and later ones that they often spawn) enable the students to see that they can affect others' thinking and have input into family decisions.

Our units address many of the same topics traditionally taught as part of the expanding communities curriculum. However, they are designed to be far more powerful than the ostensibly similar units found in contemporary textbooks. They focus on the elementary and familiar in that they address fundamental aspects of the human condition and connect with experience-based tacit knowledge that students already possess. However, they do not merely reaffirm what students already know. Instead, they help students to construct articulated knowledge about aspects of the cultural universal that they have only vague and tacit knowledge about now. They also introduce students to a great deal of new information, develop connections to help them transform scattered items of information into a network of integrated knowledge, and stimulate them to apply this knowledge to their lives outside of school. For more information about the rationale underlying the units, see Brophy and Alleman (1996).

Developing the Unit Plans

In developing unit plans, we began by generating a list of big ideas about the cultural universal that might become the major understandings around which to structure the unit. The initial list was developed from three major sources: (1) social studies education textbooks written for teachers, standards statements from NCSS and other social studies–related professional organizations, and the writings of opinion leaders and organizations concerned with education in history, geography, and the social sciences; (2) ideas conveyed about the cultural universal in elementary social studies texts and in fictional and nonfictional literature sources written for children; and (3) our own ideas about which aspects of the cultural universal are basic understandings that students could use to make sense of their social lives. As we developed and discussed this basic list of key ideas, we revised it several times. In the process, we added some new ideas, rephrased existing ones, combined those that appeared to go together, and sequenced them in a way that made sense as a list of lesson topics for the unit.

Once we were satisfied with the listing and sequencing of big ideas, we began drafting lesson plans. We elaborated the big ideas in considerable detail and considered ways in which they might be applied during in-class activities and follow-up home assignments. We also shared tentative plans with Barbara Knighton and other collaborating teachers. Barbara critiqued what was included and contributed specific teaching suggestions, such as identifying places where she might bring in some personal possession to use as a prop, read a children's literature selection that we had not considered, or add a learning activity.

Sequencing the Lessons

Typically, a unit begins with consideration of the cultural universal as it is experienced in the contemporary United States, and especially in the homes and neighborhoods of the students to be taught. Subsequent lessons bring in the historical dimension by considering how human response to the cultural universal has evolved through time. Later lessons bring in the geographical, cultural, and economic dimensions by considering how human response to the cultural universal has varied in the past and still varies today according to local resources and other aspects of location and culture. Still later lessons bring in the personal and civic efficacy dimensions by involving students in activities calling for them to consider their current and future decision making with respect to the cultural universal and to address some of the social and civic issues associated with it. Finally, a review lesson appears as a conclusion to the unit.

Looking across the unit as a whole, the sequence of instruction:

1. Begins by building on students' existing knowledge, deepening it, and making it better articulated and connected (to solidify a common base of valid prior knowledge as a starting point).
2. Broadens their knowledge about how the cultural universal is addressed in the context most familiar to them (contemporary American society).
3. Extends their knowledge to the past and to other cultures.
4. Provides opportunities to apply what they are learning to present and future decision making as individuals and as citizens.
5. Concludes with a review.

Our Approach Compared to Alternatives

We have noted that our response to the widely recognized content problem in primary-grade social studies is to retain cultural universals as the unit topics but develop these topics much more thoroughly than they are developed in the textbook series, and with better focus on big ideas. Others have suggested different responses. We briefly mention the major alternative suggestions here, both to explain why we do not endorse them and to further explain our own position.

Cultural Literacy/Core Knowledge

E. D. Hirsch, Jr. (1988) proposed cultural literacy as the basis for curriculum development. He produced a list of more than five thousand items of knowledge that he believed should be acquired in elementary school as a way to equip students with a common base of cultural knowledge to inform their social and civic decision making. We agree with Hirsch that a shared common culture is needed, but we question the value of much of what he included on his list of ostensibly important knowledge. Furthermore, because it is a long list of specifics, it leads to teaching that emphasizes breadth of coverage of disconnected details instead of depth of development of connected knowledge structured around powerful ideas.

Subsequently, educators inspired by Hirsch's book have used it as a basis for developing the CORE Curriculum, which encompasses science, social studies, and the arts. The social studies strands are built around chronologically organized historical studies, with accompanying geographical and cultural studies. First graders study ancient Egypt and the early American civilizations (Mayas, Incas, Aztecs). Second graders study ancient India, China, and Greece, along with American history up to the Civil War. Third graders study ancient Rome and Byzantium, various

Native American tribal groups, and the thirteen English colonies prior to the American Revolution. Because it is divided by grade levels and organized into World Civilization, American Civilization, and Geography strands, the CORE curriculum is a considerable improvement over Hirsch's list of assorted knowledge items as a basis for social studies curriculum in the primary grades. However, it focuses on the distant past. We think that cultural universals have more to offer than historical chronicity as a basis for introducing students to the social world. Also, we believe that an approach that begins with what is familiar to the students in their immediate environments and then moves to the past, to other cultures, and to consideration of the future constitutes a better-rounded and more powerful social education than an exclusive focus on the past that is inherently limited in its applicability to students' lives outside of school.

History/Literature Focus

Kieran Egan (1988), Diane Ravitch (1987), and others have advocated replacing topical teaching about cultural universals with a heavy focus on history and related children's literature (not only historical fiction but myths and folktales). We agree with them that primary-grade students can and should learn certain aspects of history, but we also believe that these students need a balanced and integrated social studies curriculum that includes sufficient attention to powerful ideas drawn from geography and the social sciences. Furthermore, we see little social education value in replacing reality-based social studies with myths and folklore likely to create misconceptions, especially during the primary years when children are struggling to determine what is real and enduring (vs. false/fictional or transitory/accidental) in their physical and social worlds. Thus, although fanciful children's literature may be studied profitably as fiction within the language arts curriculum, it is no substitute for a reality-based social studies curriculum.

Issues Analysis

Many social educators believe that debating social and civic issues is the most direct way to develop dispositions toward critical thinking and reflective decision making in our citizens (Evans & Saxe, 1996). Some of them have suggested that primary-grade social studies should deemphasize providing students with information and instead engage them in inquiry and debate about social policy issues. We agree that reflective discussion of social issues and related decision-making opportunities should be emphasized in teaching social studies at all grade levels. However, we also believe that a heavy concentration on inquiry and debate about social policy issues is premature for primary-grade students whose prior knowledge and experience relating to the issues are quite limited.

In this first chapter we have presented the rationale for our approach to primary-grade social studies, identified six key components that are common to all of our units, and described how we develop the units and assess their effectiveness through classroom tryouts. In Chapter 2 we will share experience-based suggestions about how to prepare to teach the units and bring them to life in your classroom.

2

Implementation
Preparing for and Teaching the Units

Preparing to Teach the Units

Based on our experiences with Barbara Knighton and other teachers, we suggest the following as steps that you might take in planning to incorporate our units into your curriculum. (Barbara also has some tips to pass along, which she does in the introductions to each unit and each subsequent lesson.)

Initial Planning and Scheduling

We suggest that you begin by reading through the unit several times to familiarize yourself with its goals, resources, content, and activities. Then begin making plans for how to fit the unit into your schedule; how to gather the needed instructional resources and arrange for potential classroom visitors or field trips; and how to adapt the unit to your grade level, your students' home cultures, and your local community.

We have organized each unit as a series of "lessons," but you should expect considerable variation in the time needed to complete these lessons. The content and activities that we have included within a given lesson are grouped together because they develop a common set of connected big ideas, not because they are expected to take a particular amount of time to complete. Some lessons may require two or three class sessions (or more, if your sessions are very short).

To maximize the coherence of the units, we recommend that they be taught forty to sixty minutes each day, five days per week, for three to four weeks. This probably exceeds the amount of time that you ordinarily allocate to social studies as a daily average, although you probably allocate at least that much time to science and social studies combined. If you are not doing so already, we recommend that you adopt a practice followed by Barbara and many other primary-grade teachers: Instead of teaching both science and social studies each day for twenty to thirty minutes, alternate these subjects so that you teach only social studies for three to four weeks for forty to sixty minutes per day, then shift to science for the next three to four weeks for forty to sixty minutes per day. This will simplify your instructional planning and classroom management, as well as make it possible for you to provide your students with more sustained and coherent instruction in both subjects.

Adapt Plans to Your Students

You should also consider whether the plans might need to be adapted to suit your grade level. If you teach in kindergarten or first grade, you may want to omit or plan substitutes for certain activities, especially those that call for writing. (Alternatively, you could provide extra support for your students' writing, such as posting words they are likely to want to use but not know how to spell.) If you teach second or third grade, you may want to plan some application activities that go beyond those currently included in the unit. You are in the best position to judge what to teach your students about the topic and how they might best apply what they are learning in and out of school. However, in making any changes or additions to the unit plans, keep the major goals and big ideas in mind.

Think about ways to adapt or enhance the unit to connect it to your students' home cultures and to resources in your local area. Do some of your students' parents work in occupations related to the cultural universal? If so, this might provide opportunities for fruitful classroom visits (by the parents) or field trips (to their work places). Do some of your students come from cultures that feature traditional artifacts related to the cultural universal (ethnic foods, clothing items, etc.)? If so, you might invite these students or their parents to bring the items to class and explain them. Are there stores, factories, museums, government offices, historical landmarks, and so forth located in your area that relate to the cultural universal? If so, you might exploit these potential resources by obtaining information or materials from them, by arranging for people who work there to visit your class, or by arranging for your class to visit the sites. When your class is receiving a presentation from a parent or other visitor, or is visiting a site, you can use your own comments and questions to help guide the presentation and connect it to the unit's big ideas. (If possible, provide presenters with a list of these big ideas ahead of time.)

Gather Resources

You will need to gather the resources needed to teach the unit. Most of these are materials already available in the classroom or common household items that you can bring from home, but some are children's literature books that you will need to purchase or borrow from a library. If you are unable to obtain a recommended book, you may wish to search for a substitute, enlisting the help of local librarians if possible. Before including a book in your plans, however, read through it to make sure that it is suitable for use with your students and worthwhile as a resource for developing one or more of the unit's big ideas. Also, consider how you will use the book:

ly certain parts?

h, or should you try to get a copy for each

copy, will you leave the students in their
show illustrations, or will you gather them
d group on a rug and show the illustrations
you read?
some designated place following the reading
dents can inspect it?

pplementing or substituting for the chil-
ntified as resources for the unit, we have a
d on our experiences to date. First, chil-
deos, CD-ROMs, and other multimedia
as content vehicles and as ways to connect
motions. Nonfictional children's literature
ut how and why things work as they do
cross cultures. Fictional sources are more
emotions, as in reading and discussing
or about a child who volunteers at a soup
kitchen.

urrent Check-Outs summary for BIDARD CH
     Mon Mar 02 14:59:34 CST 2009

ARCODE: r0126826267
ITLE: Social studies excursions, K-3 /
UE DATE: Mar 16 2009

ARCODE: r0125573552
ITLE: Caldecott connections to social s
UE DATE: Mar 16 2009

However, not all children's literature selections that are related to a unit's topic are appropriate as instructional resources for the unit. For example, we originally intended to use the book *A House Is a House for Me* (Hoberman, 1978) to introduce the unit on shelter. The book seemed ideal for this purpose because it offers cleverly written and illustrated material on the different forms of "houses" lived in by people, animals, or even inanimate objects. As the book progresses, however, the material becomes more and more fanciful in applying the term *house,* to the point that we became concerned about communicating misconceptions: "A box is a house for a tea bag; a teapot's a house for some tea. If you pour me a cup and I drink it all up, then the teahouse will turn into me." We decided that even though this book was topic-related, it was not support-ive of our instructional goals. (It is better suited to language arts goals than to social studies goals.)

Problems such as these frequently lead us to drop children's literature selections from our unit plans. In some cases their deficiencies are obvious (e.g., content or illustrations that are so dated as to be misleading, or that focus on the exotic and convey ethnic stereotypes instead of helping students to appreciate cultural variations as intelligent adaptations to time and place). However, some deficiencies are more subtle and recognized only when problems occur as they are used during class (e.g., the language is too difficult or fanciful, or the content or illustrations tend to derail the class from key ideas into side issues). When such problems appear in nonfictional selections, some of the books still can be used by presenting their most useful parts and omitting the rest. However, fictional selections usually have to be either read all the way through or omitted entirely.

Add Learning Activities

You also may wish to supplement or substitute for some of the learning activities or home assignments included in the unit plans. We believe that any activity considered for inclusion in a unit should meet all four of the following basic criteria: (1) goal relevance; (2) appropriate level of difficulty; (3) feasibility; and (4) cost effectiveness. Activities have goal relevance when they are useful as means of accomplishing worthwhile curricular goals (i.e., intended student outcomes). Each activity should have a primary goal that is important, worth stressing, and merits spending time on. Its content base should have enduring value and life-application potential. This criterion is typically met when the activity is useful for developing one of the big ideas that anchor the unit's content base.

An activity is at the appropriate level of difficulty when it is difficult enough to provide some challenge and extend learning, but not so difficult as to leave many students confused or frustrated. You can adjust the difficulty levels of activities either by adjusting the complexity of the activities themselves or by adjusting the amount of initial modeling and explanation and subsequent help that you provide as you engage the students in the activities.

An activity is feasible if it can be implemented within whatever constraints apply in your classroom (space and equipment, time, student readiness, etc.). An activity is cost effective if the learning or other benefits expected to flow from it justify its costs in time and trouble for you and your students and in foregone opportunities to schedule other activities.

In selecting from activities that meet these primary criteria, you might consider several secondary criteria that identify features of activities that are desirable but not strictly necessary:

1. Along with its primary goal, the activity allows for simultaneous accomplishment of one or more additional goals (e.g., application of communication skills being learned in language arts).

2. Students are likely to find the activity interesting or enjoyable.

3. The activity provides an opportunity to complete a whole task rather than just to practice part-skills in isolation.

4. The activity provides opportunities for students to engage in higher-order thinking.

5. The activity can be adapted to accommodate individual differences in students' interests or abilities.

Along with these criteria, which apply to individual activities, we suggest additional criteria for the set of activities for the unit taken as a whole:

1. The set should contain a variety of activity formats and student response modes (as another way to accommodate individual differences).

2. Activities should progressively increase in levels of challenge as student expertise develops.

3. Students should apply what they are learning to current events or other aspects of their lives outside of school.

4. As a set, the activities should reflect the full range of goals identified for the unit.

5. Where students lack sufficient experiential knowledge to support understanding, learning activities should include opportunities for them to view demonstrations, inspect artifacts or photos, visit sites, or in other ways to experience concrete examples of the content.

6. Students should learn relevant processes and procedural knowledge, not just declarative or factual knowledge, to the extent that doing so is important as part of developing basic understanding of the topics.

The key to the effectiveness of an activity is its cognitive engagement potential—the degree to which it gets students thinking actively about and applying content, preferably with conscious awareness of their goals and control of their learning strategies. If the desired learning experiences are to occur, student involvement must include cognitive engagement with important ideas, not just physical activity or time on task. In short, the students' engagement should be minds-on, not just hands-on.

If an activity calls for skills or response processes that are new to your students (e.g., collaboration within a pair or small group, writing in a journal) you will need to provide them with modeling and instruction in how to carry out these processes and with opportunities to practice doing so. In this regard, we recommend that you introduce new processes or skills in the context of applying already-familiar content. Young learners often become confused if they are asked to cope with both new content and new skills at the same time (or they become so focused on trying to carry out the activity's processes successfully that they pay little attention to the big ideas that the activity was designed to develop).

The success of an activity in producing thoughtful student engagement with important ideas depends not only on the activity itself but on the teacher structuring and teacher-student interaction that occur before, during, and after it. Thus, an important part of making an activity successful as a learning experience is your own:

1. Introduction of the activity (communicating its goals clearly and cueing relevant prior knowledge and response strategies).
2. Scaffolding of student engagement in the activity (explaining and demonstrating procedures if necessary, asking questions to make sure that students understand key ideas and know what to do before releasing them to work on their own, and then circulating to monitor and intervene if necessary as they work).
3. Handling of debriefing/reflection/assessment segments that bring the activity to closure (during which you and the students revisit the activity's primary goals and assess the degree to which they have been accomplished).

For more information about designing or selecting learning activities, see Brophy and Alleman (1991).

Plan Your Assessment Component

We view assessment as a basic component of curriculum and instruction that should be an ongoing concern as a unit progresses, not just as something to be done when the unit is completed. Also, the goals of assessment should include generating information about how the class as a whole is progressing in acquiring the intended learnings and about ways in which curriculum and instruction may need to be adjusted in the present or future, not just generating scores that will provide a basis for assigning grades to individual students.

You might begin by assessing your students' prior knowledge before you start teaching the unit. You can use some or all of our interview questions for this purpose (these are provided in the introduction to each unit), or else formulate your own questions. Such preassessment will provide you with useful information, both about valid prior knowledge that you can connect with and about gaps, naive ideas, and misconceptions that you can address specifically as you work through the unit. It may suggest the need for additional physical artifacts, photos, or other props or visuals, or for more extensive explanations of certain points than you had anticipated providing.

To promote accomplishment of this broad assessment agenda, we have embedded informal assessment components within most lessons, and we have included a review lesson at the end of each unit. However, you may want to add more formal assessment components, especially if your students will be participating in state- or district-wide social studies testing. Also, you may want to include relatively formal assessment (i.e., tests that carry implications for grading) as a way to communicate high expectations for student engagement and effort in social studies activities and as a way to convey to students and their parents that you consider social studies to be just as basic a curricular component as language arts, mathematics, and science.

In any case, we recommend that you focus on the major goals and big ideas when planning a unit's assessment components. This includes affective and dispositional goals, not just knowledge and skill goals. It may require you to use alternative forms of assessment instead of—or in addition to—conventional tests. In this regard, bear in mind that a great deal of useful assessment information can be gleaned from your students' responses to ongoing in-class activities and home assignments. These responses frequently will indicate that certain points need reteaching or elaboration because several students are confused about them. For more information about assessment in elementary social studies, see Alleman and Brophy (1997, 1999).

Prepare the Parents

Most of the lessons include home assignments calling for students to interact with parents or other family members by discussing some aspect of how the cultural universal is experienced or handled within their family (and then recording some key information on a brief response sheet to be returned to class and used as data in follow-up discussion). It will be important to alert the parents to this feature of the social studies units and elicit their cooperation in completing the home assignments and seeing that their children return the data sheets the next day. If your school schedules parent orientation meetings early in the school year, this would be a good time and place to explain the social studies program to them in person. In any case, before beginning your initial unit, send the parents an informational letter (see Figure 3). Subsequently, in sending home the data retrieval sheets for individual home assignments, be sure to include sufficient information to enable parents to know what to do as they interact with their child to accomplish the assignment successfully.

Some teachers become concerned when they hear about our home assignments. However, we have found that most parents not only cooperate by taking the time needed to complete the requested activities with

Dear Parents,

This year we are taking part in a new exciting way to learn social studies. Our units of study will be based on cultural universals. A cultural universal is something that is common to children around the world, such as food, clothing, or shelter. By using the cultural universals, we are able to help children first connect the learning to their own lives and then learn more.

Within each unit, we will look at the many parts of the cultural universal and how it ties to important social studies topics like history, careers, geography, economics, and more. Our hope is to have students who are more excited and motivated to learn about the world within their reach and far away.

Our first cultural universal unit will be food. During this unit, we will be starting with the basic food groups and the building blocks of nutrition to build students' beginning knowledge. Then we will have several lessons about farms and growing food around the world, as well as processing food. We will also learn about inventions, careers, economics, and more.

As parents, you will be asked to contribute your knowledge in this area as well. Some home assignments might involve recipes, logging your family's eating habits, or even interviewing food workers. Another way to help with our learning is to ask your child often about our food lessons and share your own thoughts about the topics we discuss.

If you have any questions about this unit or the cultural universals, please feel free to drop me a note or call. Thank you for your help in making this unit successful.

Mrs. Knighton

FIGURE 3 Model Letter to Parents

their children, but enjoy doing so, see the activities as valuable, and express considerable enthusiasm for them. There are several reasons for this. First, the assignments do not require any special preparation or demanding work from the parents. Mostly, they involve family members in activities that are nondemanding for the parents, interesting and informative for the children, and enjoyable for both (e.g., talking about how the family came to live where it does; locating the furnace and talking about how it works; inspecting clothing labels to note where the garments were manufactured; or talking about what relatives, friends, or neighbors do in jobs relating to the cultural universal under study).

In addition to personalizing the unit's content and providing additional opportunities for students to construct understandings of it and communicate about it, these home assignments engage the parents and children in conversations that support family ties and enhance their appreciation for one another. The children learn many things about their parents' past lives and decision making that help them know the parents more fully as individuals, and the parents learn a lot about their children's ideas, interests, and capabilities. Parents commonly report that these interactions have helped them (and other family members, such as older siblings) to develop enhanced respect for their child's insights and reasoning abilities, and that interests that the child expressed during these interactions subsequently led to other shared activities. When you communicate with parents about the home assignments, do so in ways that encourage them to look forward to experiencing these interesting and emotionally satisfying interactions with their children, not just to "helping them with their homework."

Theory and research on learning suggest that exposure to new information is of most value to learners when it leads them to construct understandings of big ideas that are retained in forms that make them easily accessible for application in the future. This is most likely to occur when learners have opportunities not just to read or hear about these big ideas but to talk about them during interactions with others. The home assignments embedded in our units create important extensions to the discourse that occurs in the classroom by providing opportunities for your students to engage in additional knowledge construction at home during content-based interactions with parents and other family members.

The home assignments allow students to connect what they learn in social studies class to their lives outside of school. We want students to be able to use the social knowledge and skills they are learning whenever these are applicable. Doing this consistently requires, along with accessible knowledge and skills, self-efficacy perceptions and related beliefs and attitudes that orient students toward drawing on their social learning and using it to inform their thinking and decision making about personal, social, and civic issues. Our home assignments (and the subsequent topic-related interactions that they tend to engender) will help both your students and their family members to appreciate the students' developing capabilities for engaging in informed discussions about the social world, reasoning about the trade-offs embedded in potential alternative courses of action, and developing plans or making decisions accordingly. Typically, self-efficacy perceptions become enhanced as students begin to discover and appreciate their own growing expertise and as family members begin to display increased respect for their knowledge and informed opinions.

For more information about out-of-school learning opportunities in social studies, see Alleman and Brophy (1994).

Arrange for Pairing With Older Students

A few of the suggested in-class activities call for pairing your primary-grade students with intermediate-grade students who come to your class for the occasion and act as mentors, helping your students to meet the activity's requirements. Pairing with older mentors is especially helpful for kindergarten or first-grade students whose writing skills are limited. During these activities, the mentors help the younger students to generate and clarify responses to questions, then record the responses. Ideally, each pair of students will engage in sustained conversation about the questions, and the older students will develop and explain their own answers to the questions along with helping the younger students to do so.

Both groups of students typically benefit from these pair activities. The older students tend to enjoy and take satisfaction in helping the younger students to develop their thinking, and the younger students benefit from the presence of a partner who provides both needed assistance in carrying out the activity and an authentic and responsive audience for their ideas. An added bonus is that the warm affective tone of these interactions tends to carry over and contribute to a positive interpersonal climate in the school as a whole.

If you want to include these mentor/pair activities, you will need to make arrangements with one or more intermediate-grade teachers. (Ordinarily it is best to work with a single intermediate-grade class, both to simplify the planning involved and to make it possible for the same pairs of students to work together throughout the year.) Initially, this will require explaining the general purpose and nature of these activities and negotiating agreement on a general plan. Subsequently, prior to the implementation of each pair activity, the teachers will need to prepare their respective classes for participation by explaining (and, perhaps, modeling or role-playing) what will be accomplished during the activity and how each of the participants is expected to fulfill his or her role.

Establish a Social Studies Corner or Learning Center

If you have room in your classroom, we recommend that you develop a social studies corner or interest center. At minimum, this should include a wall display of key words, photographs, student products, and so forth connected to the unit topic, along with a collection of related books and other materials that students can inspect during free times in class or take home at night. Ideally, the social studies area would be a more complete learning center, equipped with a table, some chairs or a rug, maps and a globe, and physical artifacts for students to inspect; activities for them to complete; or opportunities for exploration or enrichment using print materials, CD-ROMs, or other learning resources. The area should also include materials previously used during lessons that your students might wish to inspect at their leisure, such as children's literature selections or photos or artifacts that connect people, events, places, or institutions in your community to the cultural universal under study.

Because each of our units includes a historical dimension, we recommend that you display a time line along one of the walls of your classroom.

The units typically address human responses to the cultural universal "long, long ago" (cave dweller days), "long ago" (seventeenth or eighteenth centuries, or Native American/pilgrim/pioneer days), and "today" (especially in the contemporary United States). Your time line might be composed of connected sheets of construction paper that stretch for five to fifteen feet horizontally, with key words and photos or symbols depicting developments in human responses to each cultural universal that characterized each of these three time periods (and perhaps others in between, such as the early twentieth century).

Additional items can be added to the time line (on a new row) each time a new social studies unit is taught. These can be occasions for looking across units to revisit some of the big ideas, especially common threads such as development over time and variation across locations and cultures in human response to cultural universals. Ideas about what to display on the time line can be found in the historical text and charts included in each unit.

Teaching the Units

Our units are built around featured big ideas that are elaborated in some detail, sometimes in language that you might use to present information to your students. This format makes these sections easier to follow by eliminating phrases such as "Explain to your students that . . ." However, their script-like appearance is not meant to imply that you should use them as scripts by reading or reciting them to your students. They are meant only as background information to inform your lesson planning. Ordinarily, you should explain or elicit this information as you develop the content with your students, but not read or recite it directly from our lesson plans. You will also need to adapt the material to your students and your local situation by placing it into a context that includes your own and your students' experiences, photos and artifacts from your local community, and references to current events and local connections.

In the process, bring the unit to life by showing or telling your students about your own past or present involvements with the cultural universal (e.g., "My favorite play clothes are _____"; "Here's a photo of me when I dressed up for a special occasion—I was the flower girl for my aunt's wedding when I was six years old"). Barbara Knighton uses this personalized approach to great advantage in her classroom. Her students are fascinated to learn details about her personal life and background, and the modeling she provides as she shares this information encourages her students to share productively about topic-relevant aspects of their own lives. This kind of sharing also enhances the authenticity and life-application potential of the material, especially when the teacher explains the reasons for personal decisions (e.g., about where to live, whether to buy or rent, etc.).

Another way for you to personalize and communicate enthusiasm for the content is to share your own responses to the in-class activities and home assignments. This will provide you with additional opportunities for modeling engagement with the big ideas and contributing responses that will stimulate your students' thinking. In this regard, it is important to make sure that your students carry out the home assignments in collaboration with their parents or other family members and bring back the completed data sheets the next day, and that you follow up by displaying the data and leading the students through a discussion of its meanings and implications (typically at the beginning of the next day's social studies period). Students should understand that you view the home assignments as an integral part of social studies, that you expect them to complete the assignments faithfully and return the data sheets the next day, and that the information on these data sheets will be reviewed and discussed as part of the next lesson.

In developing unit content with your students, you will need to find an appropriate balance between showing/telling key ideas, trying to elicit these ideas through questioning, and providing opportunities for your students to discover them through their engagement in activities and assignments. Traditional ideas about teaching emphasized transmission approaches in which teachers (or texts) do a lot of explaining and students are expected to remember or copy this input and retrieve it later when answering recitation questions or filling out worksheets. More recent ideas about teaching emphasize social constructivist methods, in which teachers focus more on asking questions and leading discussions than on showing/telling, and students are expected to collaborate in constructing knowledge as they discuss issues or debate alternative solutions to problems.

Exclusive reliance on transmission approaches is unwise because it bores students and unwittingly encourages them to emphasize low-level rote memorizing strategies instead of processing what they are learning more actively. However, exclusive reliance on social constructivist approaches also is unwise. It can be inefficient and confusing, especially if the students do not have much accurate prior knowledge and therefore end up spending a great deal of their class time carrying on discussions that are based on false premises and laced with naive ideas and misconceptions. Counterproductive discussions of this kind often occur when primary-grade students (who are still undergoing cognitive development) are prematurely asked to discuss topics about which their prior knowledge is limited, poorly articulated, and distorted by naive ideas or misconceptions. Consequently, we recommend that you begin most units and lessons with instruction designed to establish a common base of accurate knowledge (relying more heavily on showing and telling at this stage) and then gradually shift into more emphasis on questioning and discussion as students' expertise develops.

Even when doing a lot of showing and telling to establish a common base of knowledge, however, try to avoid extended "lecturing." Use more of a narrative (storytelling) style to develop explanations, and spice your presentations with frequent references to examples from your own life, your students' lives, or current events. Also, break up extended "teacher talk" segments and keep your students actively involved by asking questions, pausing to allow students to discuss a point briefly with partners or table-mates, or asking them to indicate understanding (or readiness to provide an example) by raising their hands, touching their noses or ears, and so on. Bear in mind that although your students usually will lack articulated knowledge about the topic, they will have personal experience with many of its aspects. You can keep making connections to this experience base as you develop big ideas, both to enhance the meaningfulness of the content for your students and to keep them actively involved as the lesson progresses.

On days when you will be making a home assignment, be sure to leave enough time at the end of class to go over the assignment with your students. Explain and model how they should present it to their families and show how they might respond to one or two of the questions on the data sheet. Your students should go home feeling confident that they know what the assignment requires and how they (working with family members) will respond to it.

Also, do the home assignment yourself. This allows you to bring something to the table the next day when you summarize and lead discussion of the data. In addition, it communicates through modeling the importance of the home assignments and some of the thinking involved in applying social studies learning to our lives outside of school; it alleviates potential concerns about invasion of privacy (because you are sharing your life, too); and it helps your students and their families to get to know you as a person in ways that promote positive personal relationships.

Unit 1: Food

Introduction

· ·

To help you think about food as a cultural universal and begin to plan your teaching, we have provided a list of questions that address some of the big ideas developed in our unit plans (see Figure 4). The questions focus on what we believe to be the most important ideas for children to learn about food. These include its basic nature (as a source of energy), changes in food production and consumption over time, foods eaten in different places and cultures, reasons for cooking and preserving food, healthy food versus junk food, the origins of various food types, and the economics of food production.

To find out what primary-grade students know (or think they know) about these questions, we interviewed more than two hundred students in Grades K–3. You may want to use some or all of these questions during preunit or prelesson assessments of your students' prior knowledge. For now, though, we recommend that you jot down your own answers before going on to read about the answers that we elicited in our interviews. This will sharpen your awareness of ways in which adults' knowledge about food differs from children's knowledge, as well as reduce the likelihood that you will assume that your students already know certain things that seem obvious to you but may need to be spelled out for them.

If you want to use some of these questions to assess your own students' prior knowledge before beginning the unit, you can do this either by interviewing selected students individually or by asking the class as a whole to respond to the questions and recording their answers for future reference. If you take the latter approach, an option would be to embed it within the KWL technique by initially questioning students to determine what they <u>k</u>now and what they <u>w</u>ant to find out, then later revisiting

1. People all over the world eat food. Is that just because they like to, or do they need food? . . . Why? . . . What does food do for us?

2. What is food? . . . How is food different from other things that are not food? . . . What does food have that other things don't have? . . . Are there things we eat that are not food?

3. Scientists talk about different food groups. Have you heard of food groups?

4. Think about the foods that people ate about 80 years ago, around 1920. Do we have foods today that they didn't have in 1920? . . . Why didn't they have _____ back then?

5. Back then, did they eat some foods that we don't eat today? . . . Why don't we eat _____ today?

6. Are there some countries where people eat different foods than we eat? . . . What do they eat that we don't eat? . . . What do we eat that they don't eat?

7. Think about Japan. Do the Japanese people eat different foods than we do? . . . What things do the Japanese people eat that we don't eat? . . . What things do we eat that the Japanese people don't eat?

8. Some foods that we eat now were brought here to America by people who came from other countries. What are some of these foods that were brought here from other countries?

9. American people eat a lot of beef, but Chinese people eat a lot of chicken. Why is that?

10. American people eat a lot of bread, but Chinese people eat a lot of rice. Why is that?

11. We eat some foods raw, but we cook meats and many vegetables before we eat them. Why do we cook these foods? . . . How does cooking make these foods better for us to eat? . . . What does cooking do to these foods?

12. We eat many vegetables and most fruits raw. Why don't we cook these foods?

13. We put many foods in the refrigerator to keep them cold. Why do we do that?

14. Before electricity was discovered, people didn't have refrigerators. Where did they keep their foods then? . . . How did they preserve foods to keep them from spoiling? . . . How did this keep foods from spoiling?

15. Some foods keep for a long time in bottles or cans without spoiling. Why is that?

16. Certain foods are healthful and nutritious. What are some of these foods that are especially good for you? . . . Why are these foods good for you?

17. Other foods—often called junk foods—are not very healthful or nutritious. What are some of these junk foods? . . . Why are these foods not so good for you?

18. Let's talk about how we get different foods. We'll start with applesauce. How is applesauce made? . . . Tell me more about that—how do they get from apples to applesauce? . . . What's the first step? . . . Then what?

19. How is cheese made? . . . How do you get from milk to cheese? . . . Tell me more about that—what's the first step? . . . Then what?

20. How is bread made? . . . How do you get from wheat to bread? . . . Tell me more about that . . . What's the first step? . . . Then what?

21. How is the meat in a hamburger made? . . . How do you get from cows to hamburger meat? . . . What's the first step? . . . Then what?

22. Many farmers raise crops, but others raise animals. For example, some farmers raise chickens. Why do these farmers raise chickens? . . . What do we get from chickens?

23. Some farmers raise cows. What do we get from cows?

24. Some farmers raise pigs. What do we get from pigs? . . . What do we call that meat?

25. Some farmers raise sheep. What do we get from sheep? . . . Do we get meat from sheep? . . . What do we call this meat we get from sheep?

26. A pound of cereal costs more than a pound of apples. Why is that?

27. It costs more to eat a meal in a restaurant than it does to have the same meal at home. Why is that?

28. Many farmers grow corn. Tell me about the steps that farmers go through to grow corn. . . . What does the farmer do next? How does the farmer plant the corn? . . . What does the farmer do after the corn is planted? . . . Does the farmer have to do anything else besides watering the corn? . . . What does the farmer do when the corn is ready? . . . After the corn is picked and taken away, what does the farmer do before planting next year's crop?

29. There are lots of farmers here in Michigan, but there are not many farmers up in Alaska. Why not?

30. How is farming today different from farming one hundred years ago?

31. What are some inventions that have helped farmers?

32. Long ago, most people had to be farmers in order to produce enough food to feed everyone. But today, only a few farmers produce all the food we need. Why is that?

FIGURE 4 (Continued)

their answers and recording what they learned. An alternative to preassessing your students' knowledge about topics developed in the unit as a whole would be to conduct separate preassessments prior to each lesson, using only the questions that apply to that lesson (and perhaps adding others of your own choosing).

Children's Responses to Our Interviews

All of the students understood that food is a basic need. They typically said that we need food to avoid starvation or to grow and be healthy. However, they struggled to define food or distinguish it from nonfood. Only 15 percent described food as a source of energy. Others said that food items have taste and nonfood items have no taste or a bad taste, that foods have juice or seeds inside them, or (reasoning circularly) that what we eat is food and it is food because we eat it. Common confusions and misconceptions included the ideas that pills or vitamins are food, that solids are food but liquids (including soup) are not, that food includes only what is good for you (so that candy and ice cream are not included), or that the concept subsumes foods commonly consumed in the United States but not unconventional energy sources such as bugs, flowers, clover, horses, or sunflower seeds. Most students had yet to learn that the essential characteristic of food is that it provides energy and that this definition subsumes a much broader range of foods than the subset with which they were familiar.

The students had difficulty comparing the food eaten around 1920 with the food eaten today. Most knew or guessed that there were some differences, but many of these could not cite specific examples or were incorrect if they did. Commonly expressed valid ideas included: some modern foods were not available then because the concept, recipe, or technology (e.g., pizza ovens) needed for them hadn't been invented yet or because the ingredients were not available locally and transportation had not developed to the extent that it has today. Common confusions included thinking of the 1920s as pioneer times, talking about differences in ways that food was obtained (e.g., hunting game or picking berries in the forest) rather than about the food itself, and identifying as unavailable foods that actually were available then (e.g., corn, jelly, peanut butter, eggs, beer, soda). Some students also suggested that certain foods were eaten in 1920 but are not eaten today (e.g., porridge, buffalo, dinosaur, corn bread).

When asked to compare food eaten in the United States with items consumed in other countries, most students identified one or more differences (not always correctly), but few could even suggest reasons for these differences. They characterized Americans as eating traditional "meat and potatoes" meals, fast foods, junk foods, fruit and vegetables, and cereal. Only about 25 percent could name specific foods eaten elsewhere, mostly in China, Italy, or Mexico (e.g., rice, pasta, tacos). When asked about Japan, the students tended to suggest that the Japanese eat foods such as rice or fish but not pizza or spaghetti, fruits and vegetables, candy, or processed foods common in the United States.

When asked why American people eat a lot of beef but Chinese people eat a lot of chicken, 30 percent could not respond, and most of the rest attributed the differences to personal or cultural taste preferences. Only eleven students indicated that the Chinese raise more chickens and the Americans raise more cattle, and only three that the United States has more open space suitable for cattle raising. The students similarly struggled to respond to the next question about why the Americans eat a lot of bread but the Chinese eat a lot of rice. Again, most could not respond beyond positing differences in taste preferences, and those who did generate explanations often had to "reach" considerably to do so (e.g., rice is easier to eat with chopsticks, the Chinese lack knives to spread things on bread, the Chinese do not know about bread). Eight students did suggest that it is easier to grow wheat in the United States but easier to grow rice in China, but none could explain why.

The students' responses to questions about food in the past and in other cultures frequently communicated presentism (a tendency to disparage the past by emphasizing what it lacked compared with today) and chauvinism (a tendency to value what is familiar over what is unfamiliar). These response patterns indicate the need to help students appreciate unfamiliar technologies and cultural practices as intelligent adaptations to place and time, and to avoid dismissing them as inexplicably bizarre or as evidence of moral or intellectual deficiencies.

Most students explained the need for cooking in terms of softening certain foods to make them easier to eat or heating them to make them taste better. Fewer than 25 percent indicated that eating certain foods raw could make people sick, and only seven percent specifically indicated that cooking kills germs or bacteria.

When asked why we refrigerate certain foods, half of the students spoke of keeping them from getting stale or rotten. The other half gave responses that did not include spoilage: some foods taste better when cold, would melt if not kept cold, and so forth. When asked why foods can be kept in bottles or cans without spoiling, about half could not respond and some of the rest could only offer dubious explanations (e.g., that cans and bottles are cold or that there is liquid in them). However, fifteen students did say that bottles and cans are closed so that no air can get in them, and five indicated that no bacteria can get in. In general, the students understood that steps need to be taken to prevent food from becoming decayed, but only a small minority understood the role of bacteria in spoiling food.

Several questions asked the students to indicate healthful versus unhealthy foods and explain the differences between them. Most students correctly identified fruits, vegetables, and other nutritious foods as "good for you" and candy, chocolate, soda, ice cream, and other snack foods as "junk foods." Their explanations were accurate as far as they went, although they were not grounded in scientific concepts: good foods keep you healthy, make you strong, make you grow, give you energy, and contain vitamins, minerals, proteins, and other "healthy stuff" but not fats or sugars; junk foods have little or none of these healthy things in them, contain a lot of sugar and fat, and are likely to give you cavities and make you fat, sick, or hyperactive.

Students were asked about the origins and processes involved in making several common foods that vary in the degree to which they undergo transformations as they are converted from raw materials into the final product. When asked how applesauce is made, more than two-thirds mentioned the key step of crushing apples into mush, and many added other steps such as cutting the apples, removing the peel and core, or adding ingredients such as sugar or cinnamon. Only twenty students, however, noted the need to cook the apples.

More than half understood that cheese comes from cows or milk, but only a few could offer explanations of how it is made, and most of these were vague (e.g., you leave the milk sitting for a long time, you add something to it). The exception was a first grader who said that you have to separate the curds and whey and then take the whey and "squeeze it into a big ball."

Concerning bread making, about 30 percent couldn't respond, and many of the others could only say that it is made from grain, from dough, or in machines. However, twelve students spoke of grinding wheat into flour, twenty-seven spoke of mixing flour with milk and other ingredients, and twenty-nine spoke of baking the resulting dough.

When asked where the meat in a hamburger comes from, about half could not respond, and about 40 percent said from cows. In addition (or instead), about 35 percent said from pigs, chickens, turkeys, or other animals. Few students showed detailed knowledge of the origins and production processes involved in creating these four foods. On the other hand, there were few detailed misconceptions. Typically the students were unable to respond, generated an answer that was vague but valid as far as it went, or conveyed a relatively minor misconception (e.g., hamburger is made from ham).

When asked why farmers raise chickens, cows, pigs, and sheep (respectively), the students indicated good knowledge and very few misconceptions. They said that chickens are raised for meat and eggs, cows for beef and milk products, pigs for pork/bacon/ham, and sheep for meat and wool. Although most were aware of cattle and pigs as meat sources, very few mentioned the hides of these animals as leather sources. In contrast, when talking about sheep, the students were much more likely to mention wool (and the fabrics made from it) than meat, and only two used the specific terms *lamb* or *mutton*.

No student gave a clear explanation of why a pound of cereal costs more than pound of apples, although eight said that cereal needs to be made but apples can be picked, five said that cereal has more (or more expensive) stuff in it (e.g., sugar), and fifteen said that cereal comes in a box. Of the rest, thirty-four were unable to respond and thirty-eight said that there are more pieces of cereal in a pound than there are apples (reminiscent of many of the naive conceptions discovered by Jean Piaget in his experiments on conservation in children's thinking). Other responses included the ideas that the cereal box has a toy in it, cereal lasts longer than apples, more people buy cereal than apples, and cereal is better for you. Clearly, only a minority of students had even a general idea about why a pound of cereal would cost more than a pound of apples.

The second economic question asked why it costs more to eat a meal in a restaurant than it does to have the same meal at home. A majority of the students either could not respond or else made statements that did not include explanations (e.g., you pay for food at the restaurant but food at home is free). Only about 28 correctly explained that the cost of the meal in the restaurant includes money to pay the people who work there. Other responses either communicated only part of this idea (e.g., people at the restaurant make the food) or offered explanations that were incorrect or irrelevant (e.g., there is a greater selection of dishes and you can eat more at the restaurant, food at restaurants is better than the food you eat at home, restaurants are public places and people like to eat out, the surroundings are special, the people at the restaurant have already bought the food). Responses to these two economics questions indicated that most of the students had either no knowledge or only the beginnings of knowledge that part of the cost of an item is the cost of the labor required to produce it, and that ordinarily each of the people involved at each step in the process must be paid (ultimately by the people who purchase the final product).

The students generally showed good knowledge and few misconceptions about the steps that farmers go through to grow corn. Majorities mentioned planting seeds, watering them, waiting for the plants to grow, and then harvesting the corn. Smaller numbers mentioned other steps in the process such as weeding, raking, or hoeing the soil; shucking or cleaning the corn; selling it or taking it to a store; and consuming it. Some who made the latter response seemed to think that farmers grow corn principally for their own consumption rather than as a cash crop.

To assess their knowledge of the effects of climate and geography on farming, students were asked why there are many farmers around Michigan but not so many in Alaska. About a third could not respond, and another third said that it is too cold in Alaska for crops to grow or for animals to survive. Most of the rest mentioned that there is cold or snow in Alaska, but did not directly connect this to the survival of plants or animals. A few suggested other explanations, such as that not as many people live in Alaska, there are many predators such as wolves or bears there, or there is not enough sunlight.

The interview concluded with three questions on developments in farming over time. When asked how farming today is different from farming one hundred years ago, about 40 percent were unable to respond. Of the rest, a majority said that farmers then did not have the machines that farmers have today, so farming was more difficult. Other comments included notions that back then people hunted but did not have farms, farms were smaller, and farmers did not have the range or quality of plants or animals that we have now.

When asked to identify some inventions that have helped farmers, almost a third could not respond, and five students incorrectly named horses or cows as inventions. However, the rest were able to name one or more inventions, including tractors, plows, planting and harvesting machines, hand tools such as pitchforks or shovels, generic machines or motors, sprinklers and manure spreaders, and improved seeds, fertilizers, and other technologies.

The students struggled with the final question about why most people in the past had to be farmers in order to produce enough food to feed everyone but today a few farmers produce all of the food we need. More than half could not respond, and many others made irrelevant observations, such as that today we buy food from stores, we enjoy a greater variety of foods, farmers have more animals, or crops grow faster. Thirty students showed glimmerings of understanding when they responded that farmers today have more equipment, farms are bigger now, or farmers have more knowledge. Nevertheless, despite good knowledge about machines and other inventions that have improved farming over time, no student was able to articulate the key idea that improved technology multiplies what a farm worker is able to accomplish in a day. Thus, K–3 students can profit from instruction on this and other examples of how technology multiplies worker output.

Overview of Food Unit—Barbara Knighton

Food seems to be a favorite with everyone. It's easy to get your students interested in this topic, and they will eagerly await the lesson. Having actual food samples helps to make the lessons fun and meaningful. Also, continue throughout the lesson to help students make connections to their own world and the foods they eat.

Sponge activities fit in with this unit particularly well. If you have a few extra minutes, you can ask students to talk one at a time or with a partner about a recent meal. Give them a focus question related to the most recent lesson, such as, "Turn to your partner and talk about breakfast. Make a list of everything that needed to be refrigerated."

Parent involvement is extra important with this unit. You can begin by asking parents to help supply the food needed for each of the lessons. Another way to get them involved—and save you work—is to have a parent organize and publish the recipe book from the second lesson.

You will want to send a letter home briefly outlining the learning for this unit. This would be a great time to ask for the recipe book volunteer. Also, mention the upcoming lesson about special family and ethnic foods. When parents know ahead of time, it's easier for them to plan, and you get a better response.

The home assignments work very well with this unit. No matter what busy lives our students have, they must eat every day. I find that if I include discussions about the home assignments in the next day's lesson, more students will bring the assignments back. The information that you get makes interesting graphs, class books, and bulletin boards. It doesn't matter how you share the information, but make sure that you take the time to do it.

Finally, be sure to keep the big ideas in mind as you teach. The more often you come back to those ideas in different discussions and in different ways, the more students will begin to internalize them. Don't allow yourself to get overinvolved with specific details of the lesson and miss the important ideas. Especially focus on the fact that the functions of food are the same for everyone but people meet those needs in many varied ways.

Lesson 1

Functions of Food

Resources

- Bulletin board that depicts the functions of food or drawings and words indicating what specific food groups do for you (to be placed along the outside of the various sections of the food pyramid)
- Food pyramid—large poster from Dairy Council (contact your state Dairy Council)
- Large blank pyramid
- Food cutouts to place on the large food pyramid
- Sample foods
- Blank food pyramid for home assignments
- Food pyramid (in color) to be taken home (available from the Dairy Council)
- Two pounds of granulated sugar
- Photos of children representing various cultures and places in the world
- Trays with foods representing United States, China, and Mexico
- Three transparencies depicting the food pyramid (use for analyzing the three lunches)
- Copies of Figure 5: Food Pyramid Worksheet (for home assignment)

Children's Literature

Cook, D. (1995). *Kids' Multicultural Cookbook*. Charlotte, VT: Williamson.

Dibble, L. (1993). *Food and Farming*. New York: Dorling Kindersley.

Kindersley, B., & Kindersley, A. (1995). *Children Just Like Me*. New York: Dorling Kindersley.

King. V. (1994). *What's for Dinner?* Bothell, WA: The Wright Group.

Lynn, S., & James, D. (1997). *What We Eat*. Chicago: World Book.

General Comments

Prepare a bulletin board with visuals (pictures, labels, cutouts) that will be addressed during the next several weeks. Here are some sample questions that could be included:

Why do we need food?

What foods are healthy to eat?

Where does food come from?

Why do people choose different kinds of food?

How did people long ago get their food?

Why do we need to eat different kinds of foods?

What are your family's special foods?

How do climate and physical features of the land influence the
types of foods we eat?

How does culture influence what people eat?

What are some of the foods that we eat that weren't available long
ago?

General Purposes or Goals

To help students understand and appreciate: (1) the functions of food; (2) the food pyramid and how various foods contribute to keeping us healthy; (3) the diversity of foods that people eat, based on what is available (physical features of the land and climate) and cultural differences/preferences; and (4) the choices that are made for satisfying the need for food.

Main Ideas to Develop

- Food is a basic need.
- Food gives us energy and provides us with the nutrients needed to build strong and healthy bodies.
- Some foods are especially healthful and nutritious (those on the pyramid).
- People around the world tend to eat foods from the same basic food groups. However, the foods may look quite different due to culture and geography. They also may taste different due to seasonings that people from different parts of the world prefer.

Teaching Tips from Barbara

You might want to do the first lesson in two days. It provides a solid frame of reference for other lessons. It also makes great connections to science and health. When you do the same lunches from around the world, don't push the multicultural connection. Instead, focus on the functionality of food and the pyramid, no matter where the food is from. You will spend more time on worldwide foods later. Another interesting activity for this lesson is to have your students tally the food groups for a day's worth of food choices.

Starting the Lesson

Pose questions regarding the functions of food: Why do we need food? Why do we need a variety of foods? After preliminary discussion of these questions, launch the unit by showing the class the bulletin board that has been started depicting the functions of food. Read the questions and elicit student responses/speculations. Write them on 3″ × 5″ cards and attach them to the bulletin board. Periodically during the unit, refer to the questions and student responses and "check out" their accuracy. Encourage students to expand the responses as understanding and application develop.

Use the following information as introductory material for each category of the food pyramid that establishes functions of food. Encourage the students to bring pictures to add to the appropriate categories over the next few weeks. As more information becomes available in visual and written/oral forms, encourage students to share their knowledge and experiences.

Suggested Lesson Discussion

Food protects us from the heat and cold, builds strong bones, keeps our muscles strong, and helps keep our hair, blood, and teeth healthy. Some foods help our eyes, help our skin heal, help prevent diseases, and help us digest what we eat. All foods give energy.

We need food so that our bodies will work. Food gives us energy and helps us grow. Food is needed to grow hair, fingernails, bones, and teeth, and for healing cuts. There are many different kinds of foods to choose from. To keep our bodies fit and healthy, we need to eat different kinds of foods. No one food contains everything our body needs. Eating too much of some kinds of food but not enough of other kinds is not good for us.

Look at the food pyramid (see Figure 5, on page 46). The foods at the top should be eaten in small amounts and sparingly. The foods below the top should be eaten daily. Eating a balanced diet helps keep your body healthy. Fats and oils, sugar, and sweets should be eaten in small amounts. Some fat is needed to keep your body warm and protect your bones and organs, but too many fats and oils, like those in bacon, butter, and hot dogs, can make you fat and slow you down. Too much sugar in your diet is also harmful. Years ago, people ate about two pounds of sugar in a year. [Show a two-pound container of sugar.] Now, some people eat that much every week. It tastes good, but it does not help you grow!

[After giving the students a brief overview of the pyramid, conduct an interactive discussion by building a class food pyramid together. Using a collection of food cutouts, have students place them in the appropriate categories as you discuss them. Explain that many foods can supply the needed nutrients of a given category. Have students place drawings and words along the outside of the pyramid explaining what foods in that category do for you.]

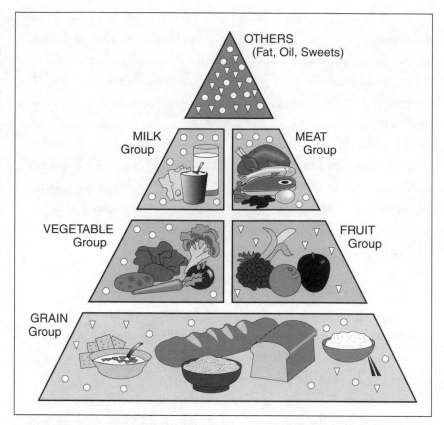

FIGURE 5 Food Pyramid Worksheet

Cheeses, milk, yogurt, eggs, meat, fish, beans, poultry, and nuts are at the next level of the pyramid. Animals provide us with meat and fish. We drink milk from cows (or goats and sheep), and we eat eggs laid by hens. Milk is turned into many other foods, including yogurt and cheese. Eggs are prepared in several different ways and are used in a variety of foods, such as pancakes, breads, and cookies. The foods at this level of the pyramid give you protein, which helps keep your muscles firm and helps build healthy hair and blood. The milk, cheese, and yogurt give you calcium, which helps build strong bones and teeth.

Fruits and vegetables are at the next level of the pyramid. These foods contain lots of raw materials (vitamins) that your body needs to grow. Your body needs thirteen different vitamins. Each one does a special job. Vitamin A helps your eyes adjust to the dark. Vitamin C helps your skin heal and helps prevent colds and other illnesses. Fruits and vegetables also contain lots of fiber—"rough stuff" that helps you digest your food. Therefore, fruits and vegetables are very nutritious and provide very good snacks.

Some fruits and vegetables grow in faraway places (bananas, kiwi); however, many grow in our country during the growing season [give local examples]. During the winter, they need to be shipped from warm places, where they grow year-round. Some fruits grow on tall trees (apples); some grow on low bushes or vines (berries, grapes). Some vegetables grow above ground (lettuce, peas, beans) and some grow beneath the ground (potatoes, carrots). Some are leaves (spinach) and some are roots (carrots). Some taste better raw while others taste better cooked.

The bottom part of the food pyramid is grain foods—bread, cereal, rice, and pasta. Farmers grow grain crops in huge fields. Wheat is a very important grain in our country. It provides much of the flour used in making bread. Wheat is also used to make pasta and different kinds of cereal. Rice, oats, and corn are other grains used for making cereal and bread. Farmers raise these grain crops and sell them to companies that make the food products. Eaten as cereal, bread, pasta, and so on, grains provide us with energy that our body can use right away.

People's diets usually emphasize the grains that are most readily available—those grown and processed locally during the growing seasons or those that can easily be transported from where they are grown. However, diets also are influenced by geography. For example, rice grows in warm places and needs lots of water. It is an important grain in some parts of Asia, where people eat it at every meal.

Explain that most of us eat foods from each of these groups at meals—breakfast, lunch, dinner, and that you're going to look at lunches that you might eat if you were a student living in Mexico, in China, and in the United States.

Locate each of these three countries on the globe and on the world map. Review the fact that people around the world tend to eat foods from the pyramid; however, the foods may look different due to culture and to geography and climate. For example, all over the world, people eat grains. The type varies due to soil, rainfall, length of growing season, etc. They also may taste different due to seasonings that people from different parts of the world prefer.

Show and examine the following three lunches, indicating that all foods in the lunches belong to the food groups.

USA	CHINA	MEXICO
Hamburger on whole wheat bun with lettuce, tomato, salt, and pepper; carrot and celery sticks; banana; Rice Krispies™ treat; milk	Rice with chicken and vegetables; string beans; ginger and soy seasoning; fruit with ginger; sweet rice cookie; tea	Taco (corn meal) with lettuce, tomato, chicken, hot pepper seasoning; avocado; puff pastry; hot chocolate

As a class, analyze what is in each lunch. (First, make sure that every student can identify each item.) Then as a class, analyze each lunch. Decide which food group (or groups) is represented by the item. Use a transparency depicting the food pyramid, and make tally marks in the appropriate categories. Decide if the lunch is healthy. Review the idea that people from different cultures tend to eat balanced meals that include foods from the same food groups, but the specific foods that they eat differ. Also, make the point that most of the foods illustrated in the lunches are found locally, although some are shipped. Climate and physical features of the land determine what can be grown locally.

Explain that money available to spend also affects what we eat. Generally, foods that come from other places cost more than those grown locally, due to preservation and transportation costs. For example, American people eat a lot of beef because we raise a lot of cattle, and Chinese and Mexican people eat a lot of chicken. The chicken is prepared differently because different spices are used. Explain that people in the United States also eat chicken, and beef is available in other countries as well. Culture and personal preference also affect what we eat for lunch.

Optional   Provide students with sample foods representing the main categories of the food pyramid. Have them identify the foods and the categories that they represent.

Activity

At the conclusion of the discussion, give the students the opportunity to play a game. Give each student a paper food item (from the Dairy Council). The object of the game is for the students to determine which group the item belongs to, be ready to stand up when the food group is called, and explain why the item belongs in that group. Stress the importance of reading labels on packages to determine the ingredients, noting that many foods represent more than one food group. Also, point out that processing makes some foods less healthy (e.g., potatoes are healthy, french fries are unhealthy).

If time permits, provide simple scenarios about geography and culture using pictures depicting children from around the world. Ask students to draw foods, select foods from the collection of cutouts, or respond verbally to indicate what the children might eat based on where they live, and why. For example, African children living in hot wetlands eat bananas, manioc, and vegetables; Swiss children living on rolling, grassy hillsides where summers are cool eat cheese, milk, and vegetables.

Underscore the idea that today, with modern means of communication and transportation, most foods are available throughout the world—for a price. Those that are produced locally and are the most plentiful tend to cost less than those that are shipped in from other places or are in short supply.

Activity

Ask students to put their heads together at their tables, quietly share the most interesting ideas they learned from the lesson, and then signal when they have at least two ideas. Elicit responses from each table. Record the ideas on newsprint and have the class read them aloud.

Summarize

Wherever people live in the world, they need food. The kinds of food that are most nutritious include dairy products, eggs, meat, beans, poultry, nuts, fruits, vegetables, and grains. The lower you go on the food pyramid, the more servings (per day) you should have.

- Food has several functions. It gives us energy and helps us grow. It is needed to grow hair, fingernails, bones, teeth, and so on.
- These functions are universal across time and cultures.
- The most nutritious foods are included in the food pyramid.
- The lower you go on the food pyramid, the more servings (per day) you should eat.
- People all over the world tend to eat foods from the basic food groups.
- These foods may look quite different, based on how they are prepared. The preparation of foods, including the seasonings that are used, may vary due to cultural preferences.
- Most foods are available throughout the world. Those that are produced locally usually are plentiful and tend to cost less than those that shipped in from other places.

Assessment

Provide each student with a copy of the food pyramid and food cutouts. Have the students place a favorite food that represents each category on the pyramid and explain the functions of each category by drawing pictures or using words and placing them on the outside of the pyramid beside each category. Have the total group complete a journal entry for the class book that focuses on the functions of food (e.g., "We need small amounts of fats and sugars because _____"). Send a copy of the entry (that includes all food categories and functions) home with each child to be read to his or her family.

Home Assignment

Have students review what they learned in school about the functions of food by reading the class journal entry to their families. Then, using the food pyramid worksheet (Figure 5), have them tally the number of servings in each category that family members ate during a given day. Discuss whether the meals were balanced. Did family members eat more servings of foods at the lowest level of the pyramid and fewer servings of foods at the highest level? Encourage the students to return the completed assignment to the classroom for an upcoming discussion focusing on "Our Eating Habits."

Dear Parents,

We encourage your child to read the class journal entry focusing on the functions of food. Then, using the food pyramid worksheet (attached), identify and tally the number of servings in each category that family members ate during a given day. Discuss whether the meals were balanced. Did family members eat more servings of food at the lowest level of the pyramid and fewer foods at the highest level? Please have your child return the completed assignment so that it can be used in an upcoming discussion focusing on "Our Eating Habits."

Sincerely,

FIGURE 6 Model Letter to Parents

Lesson 2

Choices: Snacks

Resources

- Snack examples from the United States, Japan, and Mexico (or other countries that reflect the cultural diversity of the class or your own cultural background)
- Pictures of children from the countries being discussed
- Globe
- Pictures illustrating nutritious and non-nutritious (junk food) snacks—both solid and liquid
- Samples of nutritious snacks (e.g., peanut butter/celery; island smoothie made of milk, banana, and orange or pineapple juice) and a sandwich made of yogurt, cucumber, olive oil, seasoning, and pita bread
- Samples of cereals—sugar-coated and unsweetened
- Bread—white and wheat
- Samples of grains (e.g., wheat, corn, rice) and flour
- Samples of not-so-nutritious snacks (e.g., popcorn made with butter and salt, french fries, candy bar)
- Samples of nutritious and junk liquid drinks
- Individual food pyramids for each pair of students (from Dairy Council)
- Food cutouts (from Dairy Council)
- Large food pyramid poster (from Dairy Council)

Children's Literature

Cook, D. (1995). *Kids' Multicultural Cookbook*. Charlotte, VT: Williamson Publishing Co.

National Dairy Council. (1995). *Chef Combo's Fantastic Adventures*. Rosemont, IL: Author.

Seixas, J. (1984). *What It Is, What It Does*. New York: Greenwillow Books, William Morrow & Co.

General Comments

To demonstrate the value of the home assignment, share your own response to it. Underscore the ideas that we all make choices and that geography, climate, economics, culture, and personal preferences often influence these choices. As we learn more about nutritious foods, we can make more intelligent choices, ensuring that the various food groups are represented in the proper amounts (use a large blank food pyramid to tally the students' responses). At the conclusion of the recording activity, have the students look at the food pyramid poster and count the recommended number of items to be eaten daily from each category.

In this lesson, students will learn about the value of snacks and the range of snack foods available, and they will acquire knowledge about what constitutes a healthy snack.

General Purposes or Goals

To develop an understanding and appreciation of: (1) the opportunities each of us has to make intelligent choices about the foods we eat at both meal and snack times; and (2) the different food choices we make based on our culture, geographic location, climatic conditions, and economic situation.

Main Ideas to Develop

- People's choices about the foods they eat are influenced by food availability (geographic location and climatic conditions), money availability, personal preferences, and cultural values.
- Snacks are "small meals" or food eaten between meals. When our bodies are growing, we may need the extra nutrients and calories (fuel) provided by snacks. Snacks are a part of a healthy diet if you choose them carefully.

Teaching Tips from Barbara

This lesson is usually very meaningful for students. Often kids have more control over their snack choices than they do over meals. They also love trying out the healthy recipes. This can be a nice tie into math with fractions and doubling. We've had mixed success with the snack recipe books. You definitely need to promote it well to get a good response.

Starting the Lesson

Have students share their observations about family food choices as they relate to the food pyramid. Use a large blank food pyramid and record each student's responses. At the conclusion of each counting by category, pose questions to the class such as: How many students ate enough healthy foods from the grain group? How many need to eat more? Did most of us eat enough grains yesterday? Did most families eat more foods from the bottom of the pyramid than the top? Do most families eat balanced meals? Why? Why not?

Suggested Lesson Discussion

This lesson will focus on snacks—small meals or food eaten between meals. Since your bodies are growing, they may need the extra nutrients and calories (fuel) provided by snacks. Snacks are a part of a healthy diet if you choose them carefully. Good snacks contain nutrients and fiber. They do not have too much sugar, fat, salt, or harmful additives. They will give you energy. Energy is measured in calories. Fruits, nuts, seeds, eggs, bread, peanut butter, and raw vegetables are good snacks. [Show pictures or actual examples of good snacks.] Show pictures of children in various parts of the world and sample snack foods that they might eat based on geographic and cultural factors. Point out the locations on the world map or globe.] If you were a student in Japan, you might eat rice crackers/cakes or noodle soup for a nutritious snack. Rice is a plentiful grain in Asia and rice cakes, crackers, and some noodles are made from the rice grain. If you lived in Central America—Honduras, for example— you might have a banana for a snack because bananas are plentiful in many parts of Central America. If you lived in Mexico, you might have guacamole made from avocados (alligator pear—classified as a fruit) with tortilla chips made from corn. Avocados and corn grow well in Mexico due to its climate, amount of rainfall, and length of growing season. Modern transportation and communication have made it possible for the foods used in these snacks to be shipped anywhere in the world, so the snacks could be enjoyed anywhere by people who were able to pay for them (bananas cost more here than in Central America; avocados cost more here than in Mexico; both are even more expensive in Japan).

We've talked about nutritious snacks that are available to us, as well as those that are commonly eaten by children around the world. Some-times people choose foods that are not nearly as good for them, because they like the taste. Children in the United States often choose candy bars, french fries, or packaged cakes and cookies. These are junk food snacks. While it's a good idea to have a snack when you are hungry, it's not a good idea to fill up on junk foods to the point that you do not have room for the nutritious foods that your body needs. [Conduct an interactive discussion, and as you describe each snack food, have the students decide if it should have a green checkmark and belong inside the pyramid, or a red checkmark and belong on the edge—or outside—of the pyramid because it is not a particularly nutritious example.]

What about sugar-coated cereal? [Examine a box of cereal. Read the label.] It's often half sugar and only half cereal. Don't be fooled by the name or fancy colors. Unsweetened cereals are better for you.

What about white bread? [Examine a loaf of white bread. Read the label.] It is made from bleached flour from which the germ and bran have been removed. Most of the nutrients in flour are found in the germ and bran. Better choices than white bread would be multigrain bread or bread made from whole grain. [Show grains.] Plants such as wheat, oats, and barley have an "ear" of grain on each stem. Each grain is protected by a husk. Inside the husk is the seed. The seed can be ground into flour. [Show flour.]

What about popcorn? [Show popcorn.] It's made from the corn grain, so it is a healthy food. It becomes junk food when a lot of butter/salt are added (a small amount is considered acceptable).

What about french fries? [Show french fries.] French fries are strips of potato cooked at high temperatures in oils or fats. As a result, the nutrients are cooked out of them and fat soaks in. Salt is usually added, too. As a result, potatoes that started out as *good* food become junk food.

What about chocolate candy? [Show a candy bar and read the label.] It has oils and caffeine in it, and it's mostly sugar. A candy bar has about seven teaspoons of sugar. Sugar is bad for your teeth. The bacteria that live in your mouth feed on the sugar and turn it into acid, which causes tooth decay. When you do eat sugar, get it out of your mouth afterward by brushing your teeth.

We've talked about some nutritious snacks and shown how nutritious foods can become junk foods when we add lots of sugar, fat, and salt to them. We've also examined solid foods such as candy bars that are mainly junk.

There are also liquid snacks that need to be considered. Milk is the best liquid snack unless you are allergic to it. You also can use milk to make a shake, but this is less nutritious because shakes have sugar, flavoring, and fat from the ice cream. Fresh fruit juices are nutritious snacks. However, when you drink frozen, canned, or bottled juices, be sure to read the label first. If it says "pure juice, no additives or preservatives," you will not be drinking junk food. [Show nutritious and junk liquid drinks.] Imitation fruit drinks are mostly sugar and water. Soda and other soft drinks are also mostly sugar and water. Caffeine is sometimes added. It's a drug you don't need, especially near bedtime (it can keep you from sleeping). Some soft drinks have no sugar ("diet" drinks). They are "artificially sweetened" with chemical additives. [Show artificially sweetened drink—and read the label.] However, these diet drinks also have no food value (calories). Drinking them doesn't harm you by filling you with junk foods, but it doesn't provide you with any nutrition either.

Junk food usually tastes good. In fact, many people think it tastes better than nutritious foods. Don't be tricked! Base your food and snack choices on the facts you've learned. Use the food pyramid as a guide for your decisions.

Most people eat/drink some junk food. While small amounts of it are not harmful, large amounts of junk food may cause you to:

- Get sick easily
- Feel tired a lot
- Not grow as tall as you would otherwise
- Grow too fat
- Develop cavities in your teeth

Activity

Ask students to think about all of the possibilities for nutritious snacks that they could choose. Have students work in pairs using the food cutouts to select nutritious snack foods that obviously fall into the pyramid's categories. If time permits, encourage them to add other nutritious snacks (not represented by the existing cutouts). They might want to cut out or draw pictures at home and add to their visual representation of nutritious snacks. The end product should be posters representing nutritious snacks.

After a brief discussion focusing on the idea that we have the opportunity to make intelligent choices, have the class make and sample a few nutritious snacks (e.g., celery filled with peanut butter or light cream cheese, a Caribbean island smoothie (shake made of milk, bananas, and orange or pineapple juice), or tzatzizi from Greece (dip made of plain yogurt, cucumber, olive oil, and seasoning) spread on pita bread. Discuss as a group that many of these snacks come from local products; however, some of their ingredients need to be shipped from other parts of the United States or other countries. Snack foods produced in our local area in season tend to cost less. Processed snacks tend to cost more than foods eaten in their natural form. For example, a banana would tend to cost less than a fruit smoothie.

Optional   You might want to spend an additional class period making and sampling nutritious snacks that the students could make with minimal adult supervision. Students should be encouraged to sample all of the nutritious snacks unless they have known allergies. [This information should be available on the students' health cards.] Point out the distinction between not liking something and getting sick as the result of eating it. For this lesson, parental assistance would be useful.

The National Dairy Council has recipes with illustrations especially prepared for use with young children (Figures 7A–7C). We have included three that we have used in the classroom: Milk-Blender Special (nutritious drink); Squirrel Feed (snack for student consumption); and Chef Combo's Shape House (sandwich). We suggest that to conserve time, the teacher (or adult assistants) premeasure the ingredients and precut shapes for material that will be used in sandwiches.

Provide each student with a copy of each recipe just prior to preparing each snack. Encourage the students to read the recipe along

MILK BLENDER SPECIAL

EQUIPMENT:

Blender   Measuring   Knife
cup

INGREDIENTS:

1 cup   5 strawberries   ½ ripe
milk   banana

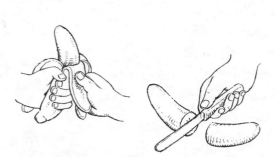

1 Peel the banana
and cut it in half.

2 Combine all ingredients
in the blender.

3 Mix until frothy.

4 Enjoy.

FIGURE 7A Milk Blender Special

√ COOXBrock

SQUIRREL FEED
RECIPE CARD #1

1 Put 4 spoons of cereal in a cup.

SQUIRREL FEED
RECIPE CARD #2

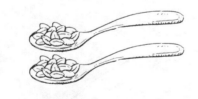

2 Add 2 spoons
of peanuts.

FIGURE 7B Squirrel Feed

SQUIRREL FEED
RECIPE CARD #3

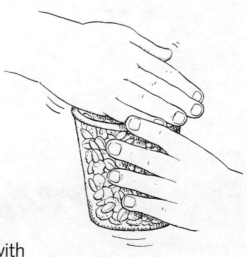

3 Add 1 spoon of
sunflower seeds.

SQUIRREL FEED
RECIPE CARD #4

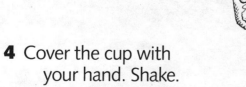

4 Cover the cup with
your hand. Shake.

CHEF COMBO'S
SHAPE HOUSE
RECIPE CARD #1

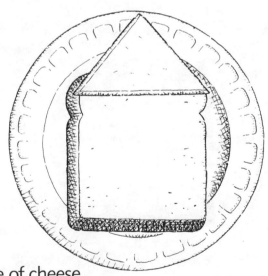

1 Place 1 slice of bread
on a plate.

CHEF COMBO'S
SHAPE HOUSE
RECIPE CARD #2

2 Place a triangle of cheese
over the bread for the roof.

FIGURE 7C Chef Combo's Shape House

CHEF COMBO'S
SHAPE HOUSE
RECIPE CARD #3

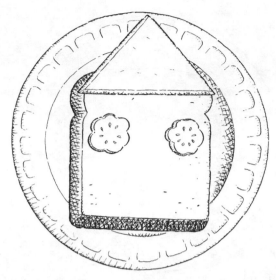

3 Add 2 pickles for windows.

CHEF COMBO'S
SHAPE HOUSE
RECIPE CARD #4

4 Add 1 strip of meat for a door.

with you, and as a class, determine what foods are being used and where they fit on the pyramid. Introduce the term *ingredients*—things that go into making certain foods. Other points to be made during the conversation:

- Snacks are "small meals" or foods eaten between meals.
- Snacks are a part of a healthy diet if we choose them carefully.
- Some foods that we can have as snacks are healthy (e.g., popcorn, potatoes) until we add ingredients that make them unhealthy (e.g., buttered popcorn, french-fried potatoes, sugar added to strawberry/banana drink or to squirrel food). This is usually because we add too much from the "other" group on the food pyramid.

Summarize

Children all over the world tend to enjoy snacks. The most nutritious snacks are made from dairy products, eggs, beans, nuts, fruits and vegetables, and grains. Some snacks are eaten in the natural form such as fruit; other snacks are made from processed ingredients (e.g., dip from yogurt and cucumbers). When we select snacks that are made from several ingredients, we need to be sure that all of the ingredients are good for us. While small amounts of junk foods are okay, large amounts can cause us to get sick more easily or to feel tired a lot.

Assessment

Here is a list of snacks (see Figure 8). As the teacher reads the examples aloud, the students should mark either N or J on the line beside the word (N = nutritious; J = junk food).

Discuss the students' responses, underscoring the importance of eating nutritious snacks most of the time. Then have the class prepare a group journal entry describing what snacks are, why we need to select nutritious ones most of the time, and how geography, climate, economics, culture, and personal preference influence our choices.

Home Assignment

Encourage students to discuss with their families their favorite nutritious snacks and bring a recipe for one of them to school. Make sure the family name is on the recipe. The class will compile a recipe book of nutritious snacks (invite a parent to assist).

_____ 1. Hot fudge sundae

_____ 2. Fruit cup (apples, peaches, grapes)

_____ 3. Vanilla pudding with whipped cream

_____ 4. Chocolate chip cookies

_____ 5. Popcorn with lots of butter and salt

_____ 6. Chocolate candy bar

_____ 7. Toast with peanut butter

_____ 8. Carrot sticks

_____ 9. Yogurt

_____ 10. Banana

FIGURE 8   Student Response Sheet

Dear Parents,

Our class has been discussing nutritious snacks and the opportunities each of us has to make intelligent choices about them. We encourage you to have a conversation with your child about this topic. Also, we would appreciate it if your family would send its favorite snack recipe to school. Our class is planning to make a recipe book of nutritious snacks.

Sincerely,

Figure 9 Model Letter to Parents

Lesson 3

Changes in Food Over Time

Resources
- Time line for bulletin board
- Pictures depicting how food was secured long, long ago (cave dwellers), long ago (pioneers), and today
- Samples of local foods enjoyed by pioneers (e.g., corn, corn pudding, squash, berries, etc.)
- Basket of food items that were not available during pioneer days, but that we can have today because of technologies, modern means of transportation, and communication

Children's Literature
Kalman, B. (1982). *Food for the Settler*. New York: Crabtree.

Miller, J. (1993). *Native Americans*. Danbury, CT: Children's Press, Grolier.

McGovern, A. (1992). *If You Lived in Colonial Times*. New York: Scholastic.

Walker, B. M. (1979). *The Little House Cookbook*. New York: Harper-Collins.

General Comments
The intent of this lesson is to develop a sense of wonder and interest in how people have acquired food over time. Students will step back in time and sample foods enjoyed by people many years ago. They will come to realize how much easier it is to get food today and how most Americans enjoy an abundance of food choices.

General Purposes or Goals
To develop an understanding and appreciation of: (1) how securing food has changed over time; and (2) how modern preservation, transportation, and communication methods have enhanced the variety of foods available to us.

Main Ideas to Develop

- People very long ago hunted, foraged (gathered), and fished for food. Then they began to domesticate animals (they became herders). Later, people began to raise their own crops.
- Farming has changed over time. Early farmers often were able to raise only enough food for their own families.
- In the past, people's diets reflected the availability of local foods. This pattern still exists to some extent, but modern transportation has allowed choices to be expanded.
- Food sources, food presentation, food preparation, and food processing have changed dramatically over time.

Teaching Tips from Barbara

Again, food samples help to make this lesson meaningful. I chose wild rice for gathering, venison for hunting, homemade jam and jerky for preserving, and corn bread for pioneer food. My students were very fascinated with the hunting information in this lesson. They asked many questions. Be prepared to deal with philosophy questions about hunting as good/bad or fair/not fair.

Starting the Lesson

Discuss the home assignment. Explain that long, long ago people lived in caves or simple huts. To get food, they hunted animals and gathered plants (which included wild fruits and nuts). [As you share the "story" of changes in food over time, use a time line and add pictures or drawings illustrating key points. You might don a hat or a simple costume to represent each of the time periods—long, long ago (cave people), long ago (Native Americans, pioneers), and today. An option is to make a time line on a white board and add words and sketches as you share the story. You might want to show examples of food—especially the less familiar ones—as your share the story.

Use Table 1 as a guideline. It compares the various foods that were available during the three broad time periods. At the end of the "story," the class might fill in a similar chart and discuss how food has changed over time.]

TABLE 1 Time Period Comparison Chart

CAVE PEOPLE'S FOODS	PIONEER FOODS	OUR FOODS TODAY
1. Meat from wild animals that were hunted	1. Meat from wild animals that were hunted (deer, moose, bear)	1. Meat from animals raised on farms and ranches
2. Wild fruits	2. Wild fruits	2. Orchard-grown fruits
3. Nuts	3. Nuts	3. Nuts
4. Edible plants	4. Edible plants	4. Edible plants
5. Fish	5. Fish, wild poultry	5. Fish, domesticated poultry
	6. Beans	6. Beans
	7. Squash	7. Squash
	8. Potatoes	8. Potatoes
	9. Tomatoes	9. Tomatoes
	10. Sunflower seeds	10. Sunflower seeds
	11. Corn	11. Corn
		12. Frozen fruits/vegetables
		13. Fresh fruits (apples, bananas)
		14. Fresh vegetables (broccoli, peas)
		15. Fast foods
		16. Processed foods (pasta, potato chips)

Suggested Lesson Discussion

As time passed, some people continued to gather plants and hunt and fish for their food. In America, Native Americans learned how to grow crops such as beans, squash, potatoes, tomatoes, sunflowers, and many kinds of corn. Later they got horses from the Europeans who had come to settle in America, so instead of just hunting nearby buffalo on foot, they were able to move around and follow the buffalo. As a result, buffalo meat became highly valued.

The first pioneers lived off the land and ate many of the same foods as the cave dwellers. Meals might include wild berries, nuts, edible plants, meat from animals that they hunted (deer, rabbits, squirrels, etc.), and fish caught in a nearby stream. They ate the foods that were available by hunting and foraging. Soon they learned from the Native Americans how to plant crops that would grow well on the land. These crops included corn, squash, potatoes, and tomatoes (see chart). The pioneer families would clear some land, usually near a stream or river (so that they would have a source of water for drinking, cooking, and washing), build a house (log cabin), and plant some crops. Besides raising crops, they continued to hunt and fish. Some of the pioneers brought chickens and geese (to provide eggs), pigs, and other domesticated animals to America, and over time, these were readily available. Gradually, the pioneers began to grow more crops and raise more animals than they needed, so they would trade them for clothes, tools, or other supplies. Soon open-air markets sprang up. Later, small shops were built, and clusters of shops became small villages.

The pioneers worked very hard. They had few tools and no modern conveniences. The only jobs available to most of them were working the land (planting, cultivating, watering crops, harvesting), hunting, fishing, preparing meals, fetching water from streams or wells, preserving foods for future use, and so on. Often the pioneers worked together. They had work parties known as *bees*. Corn husking, threshing (harvesting), and apple bees were often held. For example, an apple bee was a special event at harvest time. A family would invite its neighbors to peel and core all the apples from the crop. They would cook these apples to soften them, then make applesauce and apple butter (preserves). Or, instead of cooking them, they would place the cored apples (usually sliced) in the sun to dry so they would last a long time. Sometimes they would take the bruised apples and crush them for juice. They were very careful not to waste anything.

Preserving Food   The pioneers learned to preserve other foods so they could eat them throughout the year. Remember, they had no refrigerators or freezers! The easiest way for them to preserve meat was to dry it and make pemmican. They cut the meat into thin strips and dried them slowly in the sun or wind or near a fire. When the meat was dried, it was stored in strips or pounded into a powder with a stone. The powder was mixed with other foods, such as berries, for extra flavor. Pemmican could be kept for a long time. The drying method sealed in the meat's juices. Pemmican was sometimes served with scrambled eggs. Water could be added to make an instant soup or stew.

Fish were dried in much the same way as meat. Each fish was cleaned, scaled, and boned. It was wiped dry and laid on a board. After being salted, the fish would be washed and hung out to dry. Some fish were smoked after they were dried.

Animals were usually butchered in the early winter. The scraps were used to make sausages. If the settlers wanted to be sure of a meat supply during the warm months, they pickled the fresh meat. (Pickling was made of sugar, salt, and saltpeter.)

Another, but more difficult, preservation method was potting. The meat or fish had to be pounded into a paste, then mixed with spices, put in a pot, and covered with lard (so the mixture was sealed). The paste would later be added to vegetables to make stews.

Pickling was also used to preserve fruits and vegetables. Cucumbers, onions, and melons were put into wooden barrels and covered with brine. Brine was a mixture of water, vinegar, salt, and spices. Placing vegetables in this mixture would preserve them for a long time.

Fruits were preserved by making them into jams and jellies. Sweeteners such as honey and sugar were mixed with fruit, cider, and cinnamon. The mixture was sealed in a crock. Melted mutton fat was used as the seal. Then a piece of leather or an animal bladder would be stretched over the crock to keep out dust.

Many fruits and vegetables would last the entire winter when they were stored in root cellars built under houses or into the sides of hills. Root cellars were deep in the ground below the frost line, so that foods wouldn't freeze in winter yet also would stay cool in the summer. Other foods often kept in the root cellars included cider, pickled meat, pickled vegetables, fruit preserves, and eggs.

Spring houses and ice houses also were used to keep foods fresh and cool. Spring houses were small sheds built over cold springs. Butter and cream in crocks and jugs could be put directly into the cold water. Some pioneers lowered food in pails into their water wells to keep food cold. Other pioneers used ice houses. (Ice houses were built half above and half below the ground and had good drains. Ice was cut and carried from the river in winter. The ice was packed with sawdust.) Of course, in winter the pioneers could put their food outside their houses to keep it cold, but this ran the risk of having wild animals eat the food. In summary, the pioneers were able to use certain remarkable inventions and preservation processes to keep foods from spoiling, even though they didn't have refrigerators, freezers, vacuum-sealed cans, or bottles.

If you were a child during pioneer times, you could have eaten the same foods as a cave dweller; however, you would have had much more variety in your diet because your family would have learned from the Native Americans how to grow crops. [Show basket of foods available. Have students sample nuts, berries, cornbread, and corn pudding.] You would have probably eaten lots of corn because the land (plains) and climate (cool spring with lots of moisture, rain throughout the summer with lots of hot sun, and a warm, dry fall) created ideal conditions for the corn crop.

There were relatively few tame animals such as cows, so as a pioneer child, you wouldn't have had much milk. Instead, you would have drunk water and fruit juices such as cider from apples.

As time passed, some people were able to get more land. Tools and machines were invented that made the work easier. People learned how to raise more plants and animals. Because people did not have to spend all their time hunting, fishing, and growing crops, some of them got other jobs—making and repairing tools, making shoes and clothes for other people, preserving food for other people, and so on. Their work-places became shops, and soon little villages and towns sprung up.

After a while, not only were there markets, but people opened restaurants where they made and served food. Gradually, people devel-oped modern machines and appliances. For example, refrigerators and freezers became available. People learned how to freeze and vacuum-pack foods. Modern means of transportation and communication allowed us the luxury of getting foods from all over the world. [Show examples.] As time went on, fewer and fewer people were needed to farm (because of the machinery and equipment to help with the work), and more people moved to towns and cities to do other jobs. Lots of people began working in the food industry, and as a result we have many, many foods available today that were not available to the cave dwellers and pioneers. [Show basket of food items including frozen, canned, and fresh foods.]

Today we still have all the foods that were available to cave dwellers and pioneers. However, due to other foods now available—and the ease in getting them—few of us eat many of the foods eaten in earlier times. [Refer back to Table 1.] We get most of our foods by shopping at the supermarket and by going to restaurants. Foods found in the market come from all over the world due to modern transportation and commu-nication. [Some of your students' families may have gardens and some of your students may live on farms. If so, talk about crops that thrive locally and explain why.]

Many people were needed to farm in the past. Most early farmers spent all of their time working on their small farms. They grew only enough for their families. Today, because of modern equipment and technology, only a few people are needed to farm large plots of land. Large amounts of crops can be harvested and used to feed many more people besides those who farm.

Activity

Underscore the idea that it takes fewer people to do farm work today because we have large, modern machines to do the work. Ask twelve students in the class to line up in a row. Emphasize that in the past it took twelve people to do the work on a farm that requires only one farmer today—so all of the other people can do other jobs: teachers, office workers, inventors, scientists, and so on.

Alternatively, have students work in pairs. Hold up a food item or a picture of it. Then ask students to determine where it fits on the chart. Have them signal by placing their hands on their heads to determine that they are ready to respond, giving reasons for their answers.

You could also divide the class into three groups: cave dwellers, pioneers, and people today. Show a food and have students decide if their group would have had that food available. Allow thirty seconds for the groups to confer. Then have spokespersons for each group share their answers, giving reasons for their responses.

As a fourth option, give each table group a blank time line and an envelope of cutout food items. Have each group place the items on the appropriate places on the time line. Then have each group provide an explanation regarding how the foods were secured during each of the time periods.

Summarize

Turn back to Table 1 to compare food changes over time. Formulate key observations:

Food variety and availability have been greatly expanded over time. In the past, families had to spend much more time securing, processing, and preserving foods for consumption than we do today.

The changes have been dramatic. As a result, much less time is needed to provide a family with access to healthy meals every day, and most of us enjoy a rich range of food choices that were not available in the past.

Assessment

In collaboration with one or more students, role-play for the class a family from each period. In role, talk about securing food during cave dweller times, pioneer days, and today (or have the students verbally describe how food was secured during those time periods). What foods most likely were included? Why did the families make the choices they did? After each enactment, have the students explain the trade-offs that the family faced and what they did to overcome the challenges. Finally, brainstorm all of the ways of getting food and then ask all students to decide which way they prefer and why. Use the headings from Table 2 to graph their responses.

TABLE 2 Ways of Securing Food: Our Preferences

	HUNT	FORAGE	GROW CROPS	RAISE ANIMALS	SHOP FOR FOOD	EAT AT RESTAURANT
Number of Students						

Home Assignment

Encourage each student to explore with family members what foods they have at the evening meal that are available to them only because of modern means of preserving foods or transporting them from other parts of the country or world. Each student should bring the list to class to share with peers. A master list will be compiled (see Figure 10).

Foods Not Available to Families Long Ago (During Pioneer Times)

1. Steak
2. French fries
3. Broccoli
4. Banana cream pie
5.
6.
7.
8.

Place a star by those foods that come from far away.

Today we talked about the history of food. We learned that many of the foods we eat are not grown or produced nearby. They are part of our meals only because of modern means of preserving foods and transporting them from other parts of the country and the world. Discuss the foods that you eat tonight and decide which were not available to the pioneers and which had to be transported here from somewhere else. Make a list at the bottom of this sheet and return it to school. Reading the labels can help!

A. Foods we ate that were not available to the pioneers:

1.

2.

3.

4.

5.

B. Foods that had to be transported here:

1.

2.

3.

4.

5.

FIGURE 10 History of Food

Lesson 4

Changes in Farming Over Time

Resources
- Time line for unit
- Pictures and drawings depicting changes in farming over time (post on time line as "story" unfolds)
- Pictures of modern-day American farming equipment
- Pictures of farming in developing parts of the world where much of the farm work continues to be done by hand

Children's Literature
Halley, N. (1996). *Farm*. New York: Alfred A. Knopf.

Walsh Belleville, C. (1984). *Farming Today Yesterday's Way*. Minneapolis: Carolrhoda.

General Comments
This lesson explores the changes in farming that have occurred over time and will continue into the future. It is intended to engender a sense of appreciation regarding the past, wonder about the future, and excitement regarding the possibility that all of the class members have the capacity to invent a machine or a process that could change farming practices in the future.

General Purposes or Goals
To develop: (1) understanding and appreciation of the changes in farming that have occurred over time; (2) a sense of efficacy in realizing that any member of the class could invent a machine or process that could change farming practices in the future; and (3) understanding and appreciation of modern technology and its role in making food products available.

Main Ideas to Develop
- Farming has existed for a very long time. In the past, it was very hard work because most of the labor was done by hand.
- Farming has undergone major changes since pioneer times.
- New methods for producing (seeds), growing (irrigation and rotation), caring for (spraying with pesticides), and harvesting (combines, pickers, dryers) crops have been developed.
- Modern technology enables farmers to produce more food than they need for their own families, so they can sell it and use the money (income) to buy things that they can't produce themselves.

Improved technology also multiplies what a farm worker is able to accomplish in a day, so a small percentage of the population produces enough food to feed the whole country.

- There are places in the world, even today (usually developing countries) where most of the farm work is done by hand, sometimes with simple tools.

Teaching Tips from Barbara

I used the same time line to teach all three of the history lessons. I found it worked best just to switch colors and add the new farming information. This lesson was good for showing how the basics of economics caused the changes in farming. An increase in demand required an increase in supply. Also, people living on farms began to want things they couldn't produce, and they sold some of their food to get those things. In our state, we are required to teach these basics of economics, even to first graders.

Starting the Lesson

Share and discuss the results of the home assignment. Then show a picture of farming long ago.

Suggested Lesson Discussion

Farming began more than ten thousand years ago in the Middle East. It started when people discovered that certain grasses growing in the region produced edible seeds. [Show pictures from *Farm* by Ned Halley and point out the time period "long, long ago" on the time line. As you tell the story of the changes in farming over time, you might consider using a time line and having students add pictures as changes occur. Another possibility is to use a time line drawn on a white board, and as you tell the story, add drawings yourself to represent the changes.]

The Native Americans introduced farming to this continent. [Point out "long ago" on the time line.] They taught the pioneers what they had learned about raising crops that were unfamiliar to them because they didn't exist in Europe. The earliest farmers did all the work by hand using very simple/crude tools to loosen the soil, dig holes for the seeds, and so on. They also harvested the crops by hand. Early farmers had small plots of land and raised only enough crops for their families. They grew their own fruits and grains, and they raised farm animals. They also gathered roots and berries that grew in the forest (foraging). They used most parts of the crops or animals (for example, they couldn't eat corn stalks, so they chopped them up and fed them to animals). [Describe the general steps in growing crops, adding pictures to Table 3. You may wish to bring the class outside and demonstrate the steps of farming long ago using available hand tools.]

TABLE 3 Steps in Farming Long Ago

1. Dig up the ground to loosen it
2. Rake the ground to smooth it evenly
3. Plant the seeds
4. Water the plants by hand (if rain didn't fall)
5. Pull the weeds
6. Harvest the crops
7. Preserve the foods

The farmers' families worked long hours preparing the soil, planting the crops, watering the plants if enough rain didn't fall, pulling weeds, harvesting crops, preserving foods for the winter, plowing the land in preparation for the next year's crops, and so on. They depended on the land for survival and planted crops that were suited to the local soil, terrain, and climate. Their work was labor intensive and low in technology. At first, they did all of the work by hand, with the help of a few hand tools.

One of the most important pieces of equipment for the early farmer was the plow. The first farmers used tree branches or antlers from deer to break the ground, which was difficult and labor intensive. The first plow was not much more than a pointed stick. Later, a plow made of iron with a flattened blade was developed. It sliced a furrow into the topsoil and flipped it over. Today's plows are based on the same principle. [Show pictures on pp. 12–13 of *Farm* by Ned Halley. Place pictures depicting changes in the plow on the time line.]

Another process that farmers use in preparing the land for planting is harrowing. The harrow breaks the heavy clods of earth into small crumbs and provides a level surface for planting seeds. Early farmers beat the ground with hand tools. The first harrows were tree trunks or cylindrical stones pulled by oxen or horses. [Show pictures on pp. 114–115 of *Farm* by Ned Halley.] Today's harrows still operate on the same principles as rakes.

Once the soil has been prepared, it is time to plant. Before planters (machines) were invented, seed was scattered on the fields by hand. Much of this seed was lost because birds would eat it before it was covered or because it would fall among weeds that would grow and choke out the crops. Later the seed drill was invented. [Show pictures on pp. 16–17 in *Farm* by Ned Halley.] The first seed drills (planters) were pushed by hand; later they were pulled by animals. Today, much-improved planters are pulled by tractors. Some seed is even sown by airplane. [Copy pictures that depict changes over time from Halley or other sources. Place the pictures on a time line.]

Early farmers depended almost entirely on natural rainfall. Most had very small plots of land, so they could water by hand if necessary.

They had no scientific ways to fight off the main natural enemies of crops: wildlife, insects, weeds, and diseases. However, they did invent some fascinating ways to keep the pests away. For example, realistic wooden models of birds that made lots of noise as air (wind) circulated were suspended from poles or trees in fields by farmers hoping to keep real birds away from their crops. The motion and the noise were supposed to frighten real pests. Clappers, rattles, and noisemakers were given to children, who were sent out in all kinds of weather to keep the pests away. Later, scarecrows were used as an economical means of trying to frighten away birds. Often you'll see these today in gardens.

Modern science aids farmers in keeping away these enemies with chemical sprays. However, these are very expensive, and often the chemicals can have harmful effects on animals, plants, and people. [Show pp. 18–19 of *Farm* by Ned Halley.]

After spending lots of time and—in modern times, money—to care for and protect the plants, it's time for the harvesting. From the earliest times until the last 100 years or so, sickles and scythes were used. [Show pp. 20–21 in *Farm* by Ned Halley.] Harvesting could be exhausting work in the late summer heat. Once the crop was ready, it had to be harvested quickly, however, because of the need to keep the crop dry. Rain could ruin the crop, so the reapers (cutters) were followed by people who tied the corn or wheat into bundles and stood them together to dry in the sun. Once dried, they were piled in large stacks or placed in a barn to await threshing (separating the grain from the stalks). [Show pp. 20–25 in *Farm* by Ned Halley.] In the early days, the grain was knocked off the stalks by wooden tools and tossed in the air to get rid of the light waste (which would blow away). The straw or stalks were used for animal feed, roofing, hats, and baskets. The grain was used for food (bread, puddings, etc.), used for seed, or sold to buy other things not produced on the farm.

By about 1800, engines/machines were invented to do many tasks that farmers had been doing by hand using simple tools. At first, they were powered by horses, later by steam, and today by gas and electricity. These changes took away lots of work from many farm laborers, who were no longer necessary. Today, one worker driving a harvester can harvest (separate grains from chaff) in one hour the amount of wheat that it took twelve workers a whole day to harvest by hand. The first harvester, called a *repeating machine*, was invented by an American farmer named Cyrus McCormick in about 1840. [This is a place where you might want to add the biography of McCormick. It could be a powerful lesson in literacy.] The machine worked like a giant pair of scissors. It had a revolving reel that pressed the stalks of wheat against a fixed blade and sheared them off. The principle behind the mechanical harvesters has remained the same ever since, even though they've undergone many changes. [Show pp. 10–11 in *Farm* by Ned Halley.] Harvesters were pulled by horses at first, then by tractors. Today, they are self-propelled. [Show pictures on pp. 26–27 in *Farm* to illustrate.]

Tractors were invented about 1920 and are still used for a range of jobs on today's farms. The most powerful ones can pull very heavy loads—greater than one hundred horses can pull. [You might discuss horsepower as a measure of engine capacity here.] Today in America, most farms are large and most of the work is done using machines (see Table 4).

Modern equipment is available, and new developments continue to appear, but these machines cost a lot of money and are not affordable for all farmers around the world. There are places where farms are still small, most if not all of the crop is used by the family, and farmers have little money. These farmers use primitive equipment and do most of the work by hand. [Show pictures of such farming, for example, in Southeast Asia.]

[Review the changes in farming practices and equipment that have occurred over time (see Table 5).] Long ago, most people had to be farmers in order to produce enough food to feed everyone. Today a few farmers produce all the food we need. Then spend a few minutes speculating about the future, engendering a sense of efficacy (the idea that any member of the class could invent a machine or process that could improve farming practices).

TABLE 4 Steps in Farming Today

Plow the ground	(pull the plow by tractor)
Harrow the ground	(pull the harrow by tractor)
Plant the seeds (corn, wheat)	(pull the seed drill by tractor or sew the seed by airplane)
Water the plants (if necessary)	(pump the water to the fields by machine)
Weed the plants by using a cultivator	(pull the cultivator by tractor)
Spray the plants for insects and diseases, if necessary	(pull the sprayer by tractor or attach sprayer to an airplane)
Harvest the crops	(pull a machine by tractor or use a self-propelled machine such as a reaper, combine, or corn picker)

TABLE 5 Changes in Farming Over Time

Farming done by hand	Farming done with simple tools	Farming done with simple tools and equipment pulled by horses	Farming done with tools and equipment pulled by steam tractors	Farming done with tools and equipment, powered by gas tractors and self-propelled machines

Bigger and faster machines are being developed. So are machines designed to do more processes all at once. For example, perhaps someday one machine will be able to harvest the grain and process the grain into flour. [Elicit ideas from students regarding possible future inventions.]

Activity

Have students work in pairs to make plans/design a machine or process that could change farming practices in the future. Then share and discuss the results as a class.

Summarize

Farming practices continue to change over time. However, large farm machinery costs a lot of money and isn't affordable for people who raise crops only for their own use. Anyone could invent a machine or process that could change farming in the future.

Assessment

Provide each student with a time line and copied words, drawings, or pictures from library sources that represent long, long ago; long ago; today; and the future. Have students determine the appropriate sequencing and attach the pictures to the time line correspondingly. Then ask them to share with their peers at their tables what they have learned about farming over time.

Elicit individual/group responses and capture these in a group journal entry. Give each student a copy of the group response and encourage them to read it aloud to at least one family member.

Home Assignment

After your student reads the group journal entry to at least one family member, the family will discuss possible inventions that could revolutionize farming. Ask the family to provide a paragraph describing the invention. Drawings should be encouraged. Have students return the descriptions to class for sharing during the following lesson.

Dear Parents,

We would encourage your child to read the group journal entry that describes what our class learned about farming and the changes that have occurred over time. Then as a family, discuss possible inventions that could revolutionize farming. Together, please write a paragraph describing the inventions to be shared in our class. Drawings are encouraged.

Sincerely,

FIGURE 11 Model Letter to Parents

Lesson 5

Development of the Food Industry

Resources
- Display of inventions in the food industry
- Examples of foods prepared, preserved, and packaged in new ways (e.g., frozen dinners, vacuum-packed cans, dried food, airtight caps, bottled beverages, etc.)
- Pictures of pioneer kitchen and modern kitchen
- Time line of long, long ago; long ago; today; future (use it as a bulletin board)
- Table 6: Comparing Jelly Making: Past and Present
- Table 7: Development of the food industry
- Homemade grape jelly and Welch's Grape Jelly

Children's Literature
Halley, N. (1996). *Farm*. New York: Alfred A. Knopf.

Kalman, B. (1990). *The Kitchen*. New York: Crabtree.

National Geographic Society. (1977). *How Things Are Made*. Washington, DC: Library of Congress.

Phillips, S. (Ed.). (1993). *Food and Farming*. New York: Dorling Kindersley.

Ventura, P. (1994). *Food*. Boston: Houghton Mifflin.

General Comments
The intent of this lesson is to stimulate students' curiosity regarding the "food world" and the range of modern methods for preparing, preserving, and packaging foods that we enjoy (that were not available to cave dwellers and pioneers) as a result of science, and to engender a sense of efficacy about future inventions that students might contribute.

General Purposes or Goals
To: (1) develop understanding and appreciation of the variety of new methods that have become available (and were not available to cave dwellers and pioneers) for growing, preparing, preserving, and packaging foods and how we benefit from these inventions and innovations; (2) develop a sense of efficacy in realizing that anyone in the class could develop a product or process that could change the food industry of the future; and (3) realize that with every new benefit, there's a price to be paid (e.g., opportunity, cost).

Main Ideas to Develop

- New methods for growing, preparing, preserving, and packaging foods continue to be developed and refined over time. Examples include freezing, vacuum packing, preservation, air-tight cans and bottles, and controlled temperatures. Now, besides our basic nutritional needs, food processors cater to our wants and add to our comfortable lifestyle. New forms of food have become available. Examples include microwave dinners and low-fat snacks.

- People today have many more choices in the foods we eat than did cave dwellers and pioneers. Many people are involved in providing us with these choices. We pay for the choices that are available to us as a result of modern inventions and technology.

Teaching Tips from Barbara

Students were very interested in discussing changes from recent years, especially the past thirty years. As I went through the lesson, I found that they were most interested in discussing the changes that I remembered from my childhood, including the invention of the microwave, new kinds of prepared foods, and increased shelf life for foods. As mentioned previously, sharing information about yourself can boost interest and help students make connections. Another possible home assignment for this lesson is to have students interview their parents or grandparents about something that has changed in food during their lifetime.

Starting the Lesson

Begin the lesson by reviewing the home assignment and underscoring the importance of science in changing products and processes. Then, pique the students' interest by showing them a display of inventions in the food industry, eliciting questions and ideas. Use the time line to help them connect to the idea that these are recent innovations that did not exist during pioneer times (long ago). (See Table 7, page 86.) Show pictures of a pioneer kitchen and today's kitchen, noting the changes (e.g., refrigerators, microwave ovens, bread makers, etc.). Then examine new methods for growing, preparing, preserving, and packaging foods. Use an interactive discussion technique laced with photos, pictures, and examples of foods most commonly associated with the methods. Have students take turns locating the appropriate photo, picture, or food, and pass it around.

Suggested Lesson Discussion

Growing In places with cool climates, there's not usually enough heat to grow delicate or tropical vegetables. Now, however, special hothouses with glass or clear plastic walls have been designed so that farmers can grow almost any crop. This is because the temperature inside a hothouse can be controlled. Hothouses are useful even in warm places because they allow farmers to grow crops all year instead of just during the warmer seasons. For example, some vegetables that can grow out of doors only in summers now can be grown year round. This enables us to eat them fresh all year, instead of having to eat only canned or frozen versions "out of season."

However, farmers must spend money to have temperature-controlled environments for their crops. They pass on their costs, so foods grown in hothouses usually cost more.

Another scientific invention is the water garden. Some vegetables now can be grown without soil. The plants are carefully supported and supplied with water that is automatically mixed with plant food. This way of growing plants is called *hydroponics*. Tomatoes can be produced this way. Our benefit is the opportunity to have tomatoes any time of the year. However, another cost is that scientists haven't been able to figure out how to make these tomatoes as sweet, juicy, and full of flavor as the ones grown in summer gardens. [Show pictures from pp. 38–39, *Food and Farming*.]

Preserving

Freeze-Dried Food Suppose you are going on a weeklong camping trip deep in the woods and you need to take along food for the whole trip. How could you keep it fresh? Some foods spoil if they are not kept cold. Canned foods would be too heavy to carry. The best choice would be freeze-dried food. [Show examples.] It's light in weight—90 percent lighter than fresh food—and it can last a very long time without refrigeration.

To use freeze-dried food, you just add water. [Show example to illustrate.] The food soaks up the water like a sponge. In just a few minutes, the dried food returns to its original shape and color. Freeze-dried foods include everything from beans to beef stew. They are used by soldiers and astronauts. [Invite students to speculate as to why this is.]

The process for freeze-drying is first cooking, then freezing, the food. Next, the water is removed. Then the food is put into an air-tight package. When this package is opened and water is added, the dish is ready for a hungry camper. [Show the process; see pp. 50–51 of *How Things Are Made*.]

Drying Long ago, some fruits, such as apples, and fish/meats were laid out to dry in the sun in order to preserve them for meals during the long winter months. Today, we still dry certain foods. However, this is done under controlled conditions (e.g., sanitary and quality standards), and the foods then are packaged in appealing and protective ways. Examples include apples, raisins, pears, peaches, and beef jerky.

Freezing   Between 1830 and 1840, an English inventor patented an ice-making machine. In about 1877, the public first had a chance to sample beef, fish, and poultry that had been frozen for six months. The production of ice meant the opening of a global market, because ice could be used to keep foods from spoiling while they were being transported. Meat, for example, could be exported to other parts of the world from the Western United States and Argentina, where huge herds of cattle are raised (in areas that feature thick grasses and availability of grains for food). Over the years, freezing methods have improved, and more and more foods are frozen and shipped around the world.

Canned Foods   In the 1800s, canned goods came into the picture when it was discovered that sealing food inside metal cans would keep the food longer and make it easy to transport. The challenge was how to keep the food inside the can from spoiling. At first, it was believed that this could be done by removing air from the can before it was sealed. Later, it was discovered that high temperatures are needed to soften certain foods and kill off the bacteria in food. The first cans were heavy and hard to open— the first can opener hadn't been invented yet. In the early days, only soldiers, explorers, and others who carried their food supply used cans. As canning became more advanced, canned foods became mass-produced and readily available.

Preparing   To illustrate the modern methods for preparing foods, grape jelly will be used. The pioneers made jelly from the berries they found in the woods. They would squeeze out the juice and then cook it with sugar. Jars would be sterilized and hot jelly was poured into them. Animal bladders and animal fat (tallow) were used as sealers. [Show pictures from Kalman depicting a pioneer woman making jelly.]

The process has changed dramatically. [The picture story on pp. 20–27 of *How Things Are Made* can be used to illustrate the changes.]

Today, grapes for grape jelly are grown in bunches on vines, mostly on grape farms called *vineyards*. The grapes are picked (harvested) in the fall by a harvester. The grapes fall into long troughs on the harvester and then drop from a tube at the side of the machine into large crates. When a crate is full, the farm worker operating the harvester stops. Truck drivers take the crates of grapes to the jelly factory, where the inspector looks at the samples to make sure they are ripe. Then a forklift operator lifts each crate and dumps the grapes into a long rectangular funnel called a *hopper*.

The hopper funnels the grapes into pipes that flow into a room inside the jelly factory. As the grapes are pumped through the pipes, they begin to get crushed. Paddles push them through holes just big enough for grapes and juice to flow through. The crushed grapes flow into a big vat, leaving behind stems and leaves. As the grapes are heated, they get softer and separate from the skins and seeds. The juice is heated until it almost boils, and then it's quickly chilled until it almost freezes. This process, which kills bacteria, is known as *pasteurization*.

The juice is refrigerated until it's time to make a batch of jelly. Then juice is pumped into big kettles and cooked. Sugar and pectin (thickener) are added, it's cooked some more, and finally it is pumped into jelly jars. As the jars are covered, they undergo a process known as *vacuum sealing*—the air is sucked out. This preserves the jelly for a very long time, so until the jelly jar is opened, it does not need refrigeration.

The sealed jars are sent along a conveyor belt, labels are pasted on them, and samples are randomly picked off the line to test for flavor and to make sure the jars are properly sealed. The finished products are then packed into cardboard boxes, loaded on trucks, and shipped to stores. Preparing jelly today is a much more sophisticated process than it was in the time of the pioneers; much more is produced and it can be preserved for long periods of time. What other advantages are there? Are there any disadvantages?

As a class, compare in three columns the steps in making jelly (see Table 6).

[You may also wish to divide the class into three groups to plan and enact one of the three scenarios: grape jelly prepared in pioneer days, grape jelly prepared at home today, or grape jelly prepared in a factory today. Discuss the advantages and disadvantages. Elicit the help of student mentors to assist the groups.]

Packaging Foods   Today we have a range of ready-made foods (e.g., frozen dinners attractively packaged, special dietary meals, box lunches, fast-food carry-out restaurants, etc.). There's a high need for these because in many families, both parents (or where there's a single parent) work outside the home and have limited time for food preparation. Packaged foods and fast foods provide today's families with the opportunity to enjoy a range of foods without having to spend much time in food preparation. However, this entails costs: these foods often contain additives to make them look more attractive and/or keep longer, and they tend to be more expensive (so the family saves time but spends more money).

These foods cost more because they are factory processed; many workers are required to clean, trim, cook, and freeze them where they are manufactured. Then they must be transported to the store, where many of them need to be refrigerated or kept in freezers. They are packaged attractively and advertised on TV and in newspapers. All of these things cost money, and those costs are passed on to the consumer.

TABLE 6 Comparing Jelly Making: Past and Present

GRAPE JELLY PREPARED IN PIONEER DAYS	GRAPE JELLY PREPARED AT HOME TODAY	GRAPE JELLY PREPARED AT A FACTORY TODAY
1. Pick and clean fruit by hand.	1. Pick and clean fruit by hand or buy fruit at the supermarket and clean it.	1. Pick and clean fruit by machine. Transport it to the factory.
2. Prepare juice by squeezing fruit (place in cloth and squeeze by hand).	2. Prepare juice by squeezing fruit (using a hand or small machine-operated squeezer).	2. Prepare juice by squeezing it in large machine. Keep juice refrigerated until time to make a batch of jelly.
3. Add sugar to juice and cook.	3. Add sugar to juice and cook. Use a candy thermometer to test.	3. Add sugar to juice and cook. Use an electronically sensitive thermometer to check the temperature.
4. Heat stone jars or crocks.	4. Sterilize jars and cooking utensils.	4. Sterilize jars.
5. Fill stone jars or crocks with jelly.	5. Fill sterilized jars with jelly.	5. Pump hot jelly from kettle to filler and into jelly jars.
6. Seal the jars or crocks with letter paper soaked in brandy or brushed egg white. Cover with fat (tallow) or a moist animal bladder.	6. Seal the jars with paraffin.	6. Vacuum seal the jars.
		7. Label, pack, and ship.

Large-Group Activity

As a means of reviewing all of the changes in the food industry over time, have the class complete a blank chart to create something like Table 7. Underscore the ideas that people who lived long, long ago and long ago were very resourceful and creative. They were able to make very intelligent adaptations to place and time.

Activity

Have students in pairs or at tables brainstorm all the methods for growing, processing, and preserving fruits, vegetables, and other foods that we have available to us that were not available to cave dwellers and pioneers. Have students signal when they have identified a modern development. Compile the list on chart paper. As a class, generate specific examples (mark beside the method) to illustrate each method or process. Post the results of the group activity. Then, create some unique circumstances in which processing and preservation methods need to be considered. Have

TABLE 7 Development of the Food Industry Across Time

LONG, LONG AGO (CAVE DWELLERS)	LONG AGO (PIONEERS)	TODAY (US)
Hunted, fished, gathered food for the day	Hunted, fished, and gathered food for the day, at first. Soon learned to grow crops	Hunt, fish, gather mostly only as a sport/recreation
Probably dried some foods and in cold weather, temperature would keep meat for several days	Dried foods (pemmican, fish)	Grow crops
		Hydroponics
		Dried foods (meat, fruits, vegetables)
		Freeze drying
	Pot (pound meat or fish to paste, add water)	Pot (bouillon)
	Pickled (water, vinegar, salt, spices, vegetables, fruits, meats)	Pickled (cucumbers, green beans, mushrooms—many varieties)
	Stored food in root cellars, spring houses, ice houses	Freezing (fruits, vegetables, meats, ice cream—many varieties, TV dinners, etc.)
	Preserved in sugar and salt—cook/seal jelly, jams, vegetables	Preserve in cans or in sugar/salt: jams, jellies, meats, vegetables, many varieties
		Buy many mass-produced foods

each small group decide what type of food they would purchase under the circumstances and explain the reasons for their responses. Examples:

1. The family is going camping for a week.
2. The parents have limited time and can go to the store once every two weeks.
3. The family only has time for a quick meal at home before going to a sporting event.
4. Family members enjoy cooking at home and have plenty of preparation time for a nutritious meal.

Optional Predict changes for the future. We are going to be a part of it, so it's up to us to observe, read, and look at trends in order to bring about changes.

Suggested Lesson Discussion

In the farming arena, we have scientists improving plants that will grow bigger, be resistant to disease, and produce more seeds/fruits. Animals are being studied so that future breeds will grow faster, be more resistant to disease, and have more pleasant-tasting meats.

Maybe someday we'll be able (when in a hurry) to swallow a capsule that will fill us up for a few hours and contain all the nutrients of a balanced lunch. Maybe we'll have edible plates (i.e., cleverly packaged food on a plate—the plate itself being a "processed" vegetable). Who knows what else? [Brainstorm as a class about the possibilities. List the responses and then have students individually draw a picture—and be prepared to discuss it—that represents a process or product that could change the food industry in the future.]

Summarize

The food industry has developed dramatically over time. We have many more choices than did cave dwellers and pioneers. However, these choices cost money. New food products and methods of growing, preparing, preserving, and packaging foods continue to be developed and refined.

Assessment

Have each student select a favorite food that was not available in pioneer times, describe how it is prepared, explain why it was not available in the past, and explain why it costs more money today. Signal with "thumbs up" when the response is ready for sharing.

As a class, prepare a journal entry focusing on the food developments over time. Encourage sharing with an older adult.

Optional   Have students create stories about food. Select one of the following: Life as a cave dweller and foods I probably would have eaten; life as a pioneer child and foods I probably would have eaten; life today and foods I probably would eat if I lived in a rural area in Tanzania, China, or Indonesia. Have upper-grade mentors help with the story writing.

Home Assignment

Encourage the student to read to family members the class journal entry on developments in the food industry. Families should discuss what examples of modern food preparation, preservation, or packaging are represented in their meal and complete the form shown in Figure 12. Students should be prepared to share with the class.

In our evening meal, we had the following examples of modern inventions in the food industry:

Food item: _____

How was it prepared? _____

_____

Food preservation: _____

Describe: _____

How was it preserved? _____

_____

Food packaging: _____

Describe the package: _____

_____

Our grandparents didn't have _____

_____

_____

_____

because it hadn't been developed.

FIGURE 12 Modern Food Developments

Lesson 6

· ·

Types of Farming

(Note: You will probably want to extend this lesson over several days.)

Resources

- Photos of grain farms (wheat and corn), cattle ranches, dairy and poultry farms, and fruit and vegetable farms (often called truck farms)
- Time line displayed on bulletin board
- Products from the farms visited
- U.S. and world maps depicting farm sites
- Table 9: Food Sources and Food Products
- Table 10: Farm Types Comparison Chart
- Pictures of modern farm implements

Children's Literature

Dibble, L. (Consultant). (1993). *Food and Farming*. New York: Dorling Kindersley.

Fowler, A. (1994). *Corn—on and off the Cob*. Chicago: Children's Press.

Halberstadt, H. (1996). *The American Family Farm*. Osceola, WI: Motorbooks International.

Halley, N. (1996). *Farm*. New York: Alfred A. Knopf.

Jones, G. (1995). *My First Book of How Things Are Made*. New York: Scholastic.

General Comments

As this lesson is launched, use the globe to show the students where the earliest farming began. Then transition to the time line, explaining when/how pioneers got into farming. Farming began more than ten thousand years ago in the Middle East. It started with the discovery that certain grasses growing in the region produced edible seeds that could be planted again to grow a new crop. Growing grasses was easy, and the people long, long ago probably didn't know how to grow anything else. People began to clear and cultivate the land. They also learned to tame the cattle, goats, and sheep that roamed wildly across the land. Unlike the hunters and gatherers that came before them, farmers stayed in one place and formed farming settlements. Farming produced surplus food, freeing more and more people from the struggle of finding enough to eat and allowing them to pursue other occupations.

Over the years, farming has changed a lot with the inventions of new equipment. It has become highly mechanized in parts of the world where farmers have large plots of land and enough money to pay for the new processes and products.

Farmers of the past and even today usually grow the crops and raise the animals that do well in certain kinds of climates, certain soils, and on certain types of land. During these three lessons, students will be taken on imaginary mini-trips to learn about several different kinds of farms: grain and cattle farms, chicken and dairy farms, and fruit and vegetable farms. You may want to explore additional options related to the backgrounds of your students. If you decide to take a field trip to a farm, be sure to think through the goals and the major understandings to be acquired as you plan the trip.

General Purposes and Goals

To develop an understanding and appreciation of: (1) the diversity of farm types influenced by climatic conditions and land forms; (2) natural resources and their importance in raising food for people all over the world; (3) modern transportation and communication systems that make it possible for people to live far away from where the food they eat is produced; and (4) the types of farms—and workers—that provide us with the variety of foods that are needed to keep us healthy.

Main Ideas to Develop

- Food comes from many different kinds of farms. Farmers usually grow certain crops and raise certain animals that do well in the climate and on the kinds of land (plains, grasslands) found in their locale.
- The natural resources of good soil, clean air, rain, and warm sunshine help farmers all over the world to raise food for people in our communities.
- Some people live far away from where their food is produced.

TABLE 8 Food Sources and Food Products*

TYPES OF FARMS INCLUDED IN LESSONS

Wheat	—Bread, cereal, flour for pasta
Corn	—Bread, cereal, corn chips
Beef Cattle	—Beef, veal, hamburger
Dairy Cattle (cows)	—Milk, cheese, yogurt, ice cream
Poultry (chickens, geese, ducks, turkeys)	—Chicken meat, etc.; eggs
Fruit	—Cherries, apples, peaches, grapes
Vegetables	—Peas, beans, cabbage, onions

OTHER TYPES OF FARMS NOT INCLUDED

Pigs	—Pork, ham, sausage, bacon
Sheep	—Lamb, mutton
Fish, other seafood	—Sole, trout, crab, lobster, shrimp

*During the next three lessons, refer to Table 8: Food Sources and Food Products and Table 9: Farm Types Comparison Chart. Have students complete the tables as a part of each day's summary.

Teaching Tips from Barbara

This lesson lends itself very well to constructivist teaching methods. However, you must first find out students' misconceptions about farms and directly address them. Although my students are from the Midwest, they didn't understand that farms have different purposes. Most had a classic view of a farm with all kinds of animals and crops. After clearing up that misconception, it was much easier to use the books to chart different types of farms. A great art connection is to have the students create murals depicting different kinds of farms. Families enjoyed this home assignment (choosing a type of farm to live on), but be sure to include a list of choices along with a student-generated description of each one.

TABLE 9 Farm Types Comparison Chart

FARM TYPE	WHEAT	CORN	BEEF CATTLE	DAIRY	POULTRY	FRUIT/VEGETABLE
Land	Good soil, flat land	Good soil, flat land	Rolling plains	Rich soil, rolling hills	Doesn't matter if they live in controlled environment	Flat land, rich soil
Weather	Plenty of rainfall early in growing season; dry, hot weather just before harvesting	Plenty of rainfall early in growing season. Lots of sunshine	Beef cattle survive in very cold to quite hot weather conditions	Warm sunshine, cool summers	Doesn't matter if they live in controlled environment	Mild to hot depending on crop
Tools	Plow to prepare soil Planting machine Harvester/ combine/baler	Plow to prepare soil Harrow Planter (seeder) Corn picker Corn sheller	Helicopters and trucks are sometimes used to herd the animals	Milking machines	Machines that create controlled environments, feed the chickens	Pickers (machines) used for some vegetables. Others must be picked by hand.
Products	Cereal, breads, cakes, pasta, pastries (all made from flour)	Cereal, canned corn, taco shells, corn oil	Meat—steak, roast	Milk, butter, cheese, yogurt, cottage cheese, ice cream	Chicken, duck, goose meat, turkeys, eggs	Carrots, lettuce, oranges, grapefruit

Starting the Lesson

Begin the lesson by reviewing the home assignment.

Optional   Have the class meet imaginary farm children who will help conduct the tours. Select upper-grade mentors to be tour guides and present some of the content. Another option is to locate Web sites or CD-ROMs that illustrate life on the various farms. To bring these farm types to life and to maintain a high interest in the content, be sure to use lots of pictures and photos. Videotape clips would also be valuable.

Suggested Lesson Discussion

During the next several days, we are going to take an imaginary trip to several different kinds of farms. The visits will include a grain farm and beef cattle ranch, dairy and poultry farms, and fruit and vegetable farms (sometimes referred to as truck farms).

Many people in our world live on farms. We need farms because most of our food comes from them. You may wonder, "How do farmers decide what to produce?" Often, their location (where they live) and the climate help them decide. Farmers choose to grow crops or raise animals that do well in their location and climate.

Wheat   On this imaginary trip, we will visit two grain or cereal farms. While there are several types, we will take a look at two—wheat and corn. What all grains have in common is that they are cereals or grasses and we eat their seeds. Different grain crops require different climatic conditions, are cared for and harvested in different ways, taste different, and are made into different products. [Using a U.S. map, locate the site of a wheat farm in Kansas. Meet an imaginary child who will assist with the tour. Show a picture of a wheat farm and show a stalk of wheat. Point out places in the United States and the world where there are large crops of wheat.]

Wheat needs good soil, flat land, plenty of rainfall early in its growing period, and dry, hot conditions before it is harvested. Wheat farmers use machines to help with the work. One machine prepares the soil for planting by breaking it up with a plow. Another machine plants the seeds and covers them. The seeds then take root and produce a wheat plant. When the wheat is ripe, the farmer harvests it. Long ago, many people and animals were needed to harvest the wheat. Today, the family uses one or two big machines called *combines*. Combines cut the wheat, separate the grain from the straw, blow the grain into wagons that are attached to the combine, and drop the straw on the ground. Later, another machine picks up the straw and ties it into bundles that are used for animal bedding.

The wheat is sold to companies that use it to make cereal, bread, cakes, pastries, pasta, and so on. Wheat is so important that it is called a *staple food*. In fact, 35 percent of the world's people have wheat as the main food they eat every day. Not all places in the world have good climates for raising wheat; however, it can be shipped anywhere in the world for a price. Sometimes it is shipped as grain, but often it is first processed into flour or changed into food products that are then marketed and sent throughout the world. [Show wheat products such as bread, cereal, and pastas.]

Corn More corn is grown on American farms than any other food. [Show a picture of a corn plant and a sample of corn in its husk. Use the globe and world map to show places where corn does well.] Native Americans were the first people to raise corn. They called it *maize*. The Native Americans taught the pioneers and other settlers who came to America how to raise corn.

In early spring, the farmer prepares the soil by plowing it and then raking it with a harrow. [Show pictures of farm implements.] Usually, in late April or early May, the farmer plants the kernels of corn using a seeder pulled by a tractor. [Show seeder.] The machine puts the seeds into the ground. Soon the seeds sprout with the help of soil, moisture, and nutrients. Farmers hope for a lot of sunshine to help the corn grow, but sometimes they have to water their corn crop (using machines) to make sure that it also gets enough moisture. Gradually, the corn grows over the summer. "Knee-high by the Fourth of July" is a farm saying.

Today, a cornstalk usually grows to be at least seven feet tall by late summer. In some places it might grow as tall as twenty feet. One ear of corn (sometimes two) grow on each stalk. The ears are covered with husks. Under the husks are cobs covered with row after row of kernels. The silky threads on the ears are called *cornsilk*. [Show example.]

Farm families used to gather for parties called *husking bees* to remove the husks from the ears. Today, we have modern machines that plant, harvest, husk, and even shell the corn. Some corn is made into foods such as popcorn, canned corn, corn flakes, or taco shells. [Show examples.] Most of the foods that are made from corn or other grains involve changing the grain in some way (e.g., crushing it to make flour, mixing the flour with other ingredients, and then baking or frying the mixture).

Ranching On another type of farm (often known as a *ranch*), farmers raise sheep and cattle. Both cattle and sheep ranchers raise these animals primarily to sell for meat, although sheep ranchers may keep their animals longer to sell their wool year after year. Sheep meat is called *mutton* and *lamb*. Cattle meat is called *beef*. It is often made into steak, roast, or hamburger. This is done in packing plants that often are located great distances from the farms. The finished products (cuts of beef) are also shipped long distances. [Show a chart that explains and illustrates the various animals and the products they provide.]

Ranches are usually found in parts of the world where it is warm for at least most of the year but there is also enough moisture for grasses to grow. Usually there are open spaces where the ranchers allow the animals to graze. Sheep can climb hills easier than cattle can, so sheep ranches are often found in more hilly and rocky areas.

[Locate ranches on a world map or globe. Locate Texas on a U.S. map. Introduce the class to an imaginary Texas rancher's child. Point out that we often associate ranches with Texas, Oklahoma, and parts of New Mexico, as well as Australia and Argentina.] In the past, we often linked cowboys with ranches and thought of cattle as being raised in wide-open spaces. As the pioneers claimed the land and started putting up barbed-wire fences to mark the edges of their property, the cattle/sheep trails were blocked. It became much harder to drive (herd) the animals across the open land. Today, if we were to visit one of these large plains areas, we might find cowboys on horses guiding these animals across the land to new grazing areas. We might also find farmers (ranchers) in trucks or helicopters herding the animals. [Show picture of cattle ranch.]

Not all cattle farms have wide-open spaces. In fact, many have huge fenced pastures, and some even raise their cattle in feedlots or large closed areas. These cattle are fed corn and grains so they can fatten quickly and be ready for market. From the feedlots, the cattle are shipped by train to meat-packing centers, where the animals are slaughtered. [Show example of slaughter house.] The many varieties of meats are prepared and sent by refrigerated trucks, trains, and sometimes airplanes to warehouses and supermarkets. [Show examples of products from beef cattle, such as steak or hamburger.] Of course, the more preparation that has to be done to the food and the farther the meat plant is from the consumer, the more expensive the product usually is. For example, steaks from beef cattle in Australia [point to Australia on the world map] would tend to cost more than steaks from cattle raised in the United States.

Ranchers work to keep their animals healthy and free of diseases. They raise the animals as a cash crop to sell to people who want them for the meat. They use the money to buy things they need for their families.

Dairy   We will now travel to a dairy farm in Wisconsin [show on a map]. This is one of many places in the world where we find lots of dairy farms because the moist, cool summers there produce rich grasses on the rolling hills, and these grasses provide a good diet for cows. Feeding under these conditions, cows produce lots of milk that in turn is made into a range of dairy products that are shipped to many parts of the country. [Indicate the extent to which dairy farms are found in your area and note that they can be found in many parts of the world, such as Switzerland. Point out on a globe or world map.] Large numbers of dairy farms are found where the most favorable climatic conditions exist.

This dairy farm in Wisconsin has land with rich soil, clean air, and warm sunshine, all favorable conditions for growing good grass, which cows need to eat in order to produce lots of milk. Usually dairy cows need to eat other foods as well, such as hay and silage (ground-up grain), in order to provide large quantities of milk. The climate of Wisconsin is also conducive to producing these other foods for the cows.

On this dairy farm, cows are raised to produce or make milk, which is sold to make milk products such as whole milk, two-percent milk, skimmed milk, butter, cheese, yogurt, cottage cheese, and ice cream.

On this dairy farm, there is lots of work to do. One major job is to milk the cows early in the morning and then again at the end of the day. The cows are brought in from the pasture. Each cow goes to her regular place to be fed and wait her turn for milking. In the past, milking was done by hand, but today it is done by machine [show pictures]. The milk is poured from the milking machine into large cans, which are taken to the milk house. There the milk is stored in a very large tank, which keeps it cool until it is picked up by the milk truck that comes every two days. (On a mechanized farm, the milk is drawn directly from the cow into a pipeline that carries it to a truck, which then takes it away to be pasteurized, processed, and packaged for sale.)

Dairy farms must provide a sanitary environment to make sure that their milk is of a high quality. This includes the careful cleaning and handling of utensils. Before the milk leaves a farm, it must be tested to ensure that it's clean and has a certain percentage of butter fat. [Ask students at this point if they have any idea how many people they depend on to get the milk they drink. Then present the steps accompanied by pictures/drawings of the workers. These include:

1. <u>Farmers</u> raise the cows. Usually machines do the actual milking.
2. <u>Truck drivers</u> take the milk from the farm to the dairy.
3. <u>Dairy workers</u> run the machines to pasteurize the milk by boiling it. This process kills any germs that may be in it.
4. <u>Inspectors</u> check the milk cartons and bottles that are filled by machines, to make sure they are filled and sealed properly.
5. <u>Workers at the loading dock</u> put the milk on trucks.
6. <u>Truck drivers</u> (using refrigerated trucks) drive the milk to grocery stores.

7. <u>Workers at the grocery stores</u> affix bar-coded prices to the milk cartons and then put them on shelves.
8. <u>Checkout workers</u> sell the milk.

Show a picture of the dairy farm just before you "depart."]

On this dairy farm, milk is the only food that the family produces to sell; however, the family produces other foods for its own use. This family raises chickens and has a large vegetable garden. The family goes to the store for some of the food that it needs, but it produces its own milk, vegetables, chickens, and eggs.

Poultry   We will leave the dairy farm now and journey to a large poultry farm in Michigan. [Point out on a U.S. map.] Poultry includes chickens, geese, turkeys, ducks, guinea fowl, and pigeons. Farmers keep poultry for their meat and their eggs. Chickens lay most of their eggs in the first year, so they are usually sold for meat during their second year. [Most eggs are not fertilized and will not turn into chicks. To produce baby chicks, a hen must be mated with a rooster.]

Chickens usually eat worms and seeds found on the ground, plus grain provided by the farmer. Some chickens are free-range and eat what's available. Free-range chickens usually need a portable shelter that can be transferred with them from field to field [show photos of chicken farms]. This protects them from wild animals such as foxes, who would eat them otherwise.

Sometimes large numbers of chickens are raised in separate cages stacked in large buildings [show photo illustrating a controlled environment]. They live in the cages under artificial light, which encourages them to lay more eggs. Their food and water is fed to them automatically.

Chickens and other types of poultry can be raised in many parts of the world, especially if they are raised indoors under controlled conditions. Many people prefer to eat chickens (and eggs) that were raised out of doors under natural conditions. The diets of these chickens are not always controlled, however, so there are trade-offs.

Vegetables and Fruit   Next, we will visit a truck (fruit and/or vegetable) farm. In Michigan [revisit on U.S. map], for example, truck farmers grow large quantities of apples, peaches, grapes, and cherries, and lots of fresh vegetables, including corn, beets, cabbage, onions, carrots, and potatoes during the spring and summer. These crops are picked and sold as they ripen over the summer and early fall. Truck farms usually produce large quantities of fruits and vegetables that the farmers grow mostly for profit (i.e., not just to feed their own families).

Truck farms are an important source of fresh food. They sell their crops to the canning and frozen food industries. Thanks to modern conveniences such as refrigerated trucks or rail cars, and airplane cargo holds, fresh vegetables and fruits can be delivered all around the world. Of course, they are more expensive when they are transported to places far away from where they were produced.

Because of their relatively small size, truck farms usually are only partly mechanized. Some of the work is done by hand and some by machine. For example, pea growers use machines called *pea viners* that cut down pea vines, remove the pods, and pop out the peas.

Some truck farms also have (temperature-controlled) greenhouses that allow them to produce crops inside even when it is cold outside. These crops need lots of care, so they often are expensive—and sometimes less tasty as well (e.g., hothouse tomatoes). Some truck farms do not use synthetic fertilizers or chemicals to fight diseases and pests, preferring to use only organic or natural means of producing crops. Organically grown foods are preferred by health-conscious individuals, but they are more expensive.

Fruit is farmed worldwide, and fruit growing is a scientific business. [Show the students examples of a range of fruits and ask them to identify the fruits grown in the local area. Remind them that many years ago, some of these varieties grew wild and were gathered.] Only certain fruits can do well in our local climate. For example, raspberries, strawberries, cherries, pears, peaches, and apples grow in Michigan during the growing season. Some of these fruits are grown only in areas that have a wetter, cooler climate year round. They usually cost more when they are less plentiful and have to be shipped in from other places.

Citrus fruits (oranges, lemons, grapefruit, and limes) are grown in warm places—tropical and subtropical areas such as California, Florida, and Texas. [Point out on a U.S. map.] A fully grown orange tree can produce one thousand to two thousand oranges in a year. Citrus trees need just the right climate to produce good fruit—lots of sun to make them sweet. The citrus fruit's greatest enemy is frost, which will kill the plant. Modern citrus farms known as *orchards* often have wind machines and special orchard heaters to use in case of frost. Of course, these modern technical advances cost money, and the cost is passed on to the consumer. Grapefruit, for example, will cost more when the supply is less than the demand because unusually cold weather has killed plants or forced the growers to take costly measures to protect them. [To tell the story of orange juice, see *My First Book of How Things Are Made*, by George Jones.]

Optional   Another stop on our trip could take us to a rice farm in Texas [show on a map] near the Gulf of Mexico. The weather in this location is hot and wet. The summer is long. Farmers grow rice here because it grows well in hot and wet places. They produce a lot of rice, but they don't need many people working on their farms because they have a lot of machinery to help them.

Some farmers plant rice in a very interesting way. First, they soak the rice seeds in water for about two days. Then an airplane flies over the field and drops the rice seeds. Next, the farmer turns on water pipes to flood the fields. The rice will begin to grow underwater. The farmer will continue to soak the rice fields all summer. At the end of the summer, a cluster of rice will hang from each stalk. Gradually, the stalks will dry out and the rice will turn golden brown. That's the clue that it's time to harvest the rice. Combines will be used to separate the rice from the stalks. The stalks will usually be left in the field, but the grain (rice) will be emptied into wagons/trucks and hauled away to be sold.

There are other places in the world where rice is raised in much the same way as it is in Texas, but there also are places where it is grown without modern equipment. In those places, it's usually grown by people who raise only enough for their families. Their work is accomplished by hand or with the use of simple tools such as plows. Machinery would be too expensive and too big for the tiny fields in which these farmers grow their crops.

One example of such a farm is found in Indonesia. [Point out on a world map or on the globe. Show pictures.] Here everyone in the family works on the rice farm, and families often work together as they plant their rice on mountainsides. They build ditches or steps on the slopes of mountains. These ditches collect rain and keep the places where the rice is growing flooded. This process wouldn't work well if the farmers had to farm big plots of land to grow a large crop to sell, but it works nicely for their small family farms.

The farmers first plant the rice seeds in a seed bed and cover them with soft mud. They do this by hand. Next they use water buffalo to pull wooden plows that prepare the soil for planting. Then the seedlings (in their seed beds) are moved to the paddy fields, where they are planted in straight lines and given plenty of space to grow [show pp. 10–11 in *Food and Farming*].

The rice is ready for harvesting in three to six months. The fields are drained and the plants cut down, tied in bundles, and left to dry. Finally, the rice is winnowed by crushing, sieving, and tossing to remove the husks.

Rice is the staple—the main source of food—in many parts of the world, especially in places where most of the rice is grown for local consumption. In places where large amounts of rice are grown to be sold—and heavy equipment is used to care for and harvest it—rice is shipped throughout the world either in its natural state (rice grains) or after it has been made into cereals, crackers, and other foods. [Other types of farms that could be included are pig, sheep, and fish.]

Activity

Have each table represent one type of farm that was addressed in the last several lessons and discuss the big ideas that they acquired. Have students give "thumbs up" when they have at least one idea. Record these on the board or a flip chart. Post the results and encourage students to refer to the responses for their journal writing.

Have each student listen as you read a riddle describing a farm type. Students at each table confer and signal when they have a response.

RIDDLES

1. My family lives on flat land that has very rich soil. We need lots of rain for our crop at the beginning of the growing season. We need dry, hot weather just before harvesting. We produce grain for cereals and flour for pastries and pastas. What kind of a farm do I live on? _____

2. My family lives in a plains area. Our soil is rich. Our ancestors learned from the Native Americans how to grow this crop. It grows only during warm weather. It needs lots of sunshine and plenty of rainfall. It is a grain used for cereals, tacos, and oils. What is it?

   _____

3. My family could live in many parts of the world. Our farm is described as rolling hills covered with grass. We raise animals and sell the products to people in the cities and towns. In the past, my family did all of its work by hand, but nowadays, we have machines to help us. What type of farm do I live on?

   _____

4. My family lives on a farm with little land with lots of plants. Our plants need lots of warm weather and sunshine. Sometimes we have to spray our crops. Sometimes we have to start heaters to protect them from a cold spell. Our farm is often called a *grove*. What do you think we raise? _____

5. My family lives on a small farm that could be located in the United States or in several other parts of the world where there is little farming space. My family lives on a small farm. Our animals could live off the land by eating scraps, worms, and whatever they could find. However, we have chosen to raise them in a controlled environment, and therefore our animals live in cages. Sometimes I think they make an awful lot of noise. We feed them grain. We sell some of them for their meat. The rest we keep for a while and sell their eggs to the supermarket. What kind of farm does my family have? _____

6. My family lives in California, where we can grow our crops year-round. It also could be found in Florida, Texas, or other parts of the world where there is lots of sunlight all year round. Lots of people around the world raise the same plants we do during summers, but when it gets cold, they have to buy crops transported from places that grow them all year. Often our farms are called *truck farms*. How do you think we got that name, and what do you think we raise? _____

Have the class compile a group journal entry focusing on farm types. Refer to charts compiled during the lessons and the review responses listed on the flip chart. Ask students to read this journal entry to at least one family member as a part of the home assignment. An option would be to have the class complete a diagram focusing on farm types.

Summarize

Summarize the key points from the mini-tour of the various farm types:

- Farmers decide what to grow or raise based on the type of climate, soil, physical features of the land, and space available.
- American farms tend to be large, mechanized, and focused on producing large crops for sale to food stores and companies. However, in many parts of the world, families operate small farms using simple tools to raise crops grown mostly to feed themselves.
- Farmers can't just plant crops and wait for them to grow; they have to nurture growth by providing sufficient water, protecting against insects, and so on.
- We are able to enjoy foods from all over the world. Transportation costs, seasonality of the product, packaging, and shelf life of the product are all factors that affect cost. Processed foods usually cost more than those in their natural state. Foods produced locally usually cost less than those that are shipped in from other parts of the country or world.

Assessment

Display a market basket containing farm products representing the range of farm types discussed during the lessons. As you hold up an item (e.g., cheese from Wisconsin or The Netherlands, chicken breasts, kiwi fruit, banana, milk) ask students to give a "thumbs up" when they are ready to tell what it is, what type of farm it represents, what type of conditions are needed to grow or raise it, and where it might have been grown or produced. If time permits, the class could develop a data retrieval chart. The major understandings to be underscored include:

- Food comes from many different kinds of farms.
- Farmers usually grow crops and raise animals that do well in their climate and the kinds of land (plains, grasslands) where they live.
- The natural resources of good soil, clean air, rain, and warm sunshine help farmers all over the world to raise food for people in our communities.
- People can live far away from where the food is produced.
- In many parts of the world, modern technology enables farmers to raise more than they need for their own families so they can sell their crops and use the income (money) to buy things they cannot grow, produce, or make themselves.

Optional Have each student decide which type of farm he or she would most like to live on, draw it, draw crops that would be raised, and draw or list the natural resources needed to raise the food and the places to which the food would be sent. Alternatively, have the students visit the computer room and use the paint-and-draw program. The writing aspects could be carried out at home with an adult or at school with a primary-grade partner.

Home Assignment
Encourage family members to serve as an audience as their child reads and discusses the class journal entry focusing on farm types. Then, as a family, they should discuss farm types: which one they would most like to live on and why, what the family would most likely raise, how the food would be processed, and where the excess might be sent. Students should be prepared to share with class members. Encourage the family to write a couple of paragraphs that describe its farm selections (see Figure 13).

Dear Parents,

We encourage you to serve as an audience as your child reads and discuss the class journal entry that focuses on farm types. Then as a family, spend more time discussing this topic, including types not included in the entry. Discuss which type of farm you would most like to live on, what you would most likely raise, how the food would be processed, and where the excess might be sent. It would be helpful if you would write a couple of paragraphs sharing your thoughts. Please send them with your child for our next class discussion.

Sincerely,

FIGURE 13 Model Letter to Parents

Lesson 7

The Story of Bananas

Resources
- Globe and world map
- Pictures depicting the story of bananas
- Time line with cutout pictures that illustrate the significance of events of the banana story
- Blank calendar for plotting the story of bananas (i.e., picked today, two weeks later they will be ready for purchase at supermarket)
- Role cards for reenacting the story of bananas
- Bananas—green to very ripe (show sequence in ripening)
- Armento, B., Nash, G., Salter, C., and Wixson, K. 1991. *Some People I Know*. Boston: Houghton Mifflin Social Studies Series, pp. 20–27 (or an alternative source that illustrates the land-to-land relationship of bananas).

Children's Literature
Moore, E. (1983). *The Great Banana Cookbook for Boys and Girls*. New York: Clarion.

General Comments
The story of the banana is especially interesting because, while it requires many workers to bring it to us, it is delivered in the same natural form as when it was harvested (although ripening has changed its color and flavor).

General Purposes or Goals
To help students understand and appreciate that: (1) climatic conditions determine what kinds of food can be grown; (2) although many foods cannot be grown locally, we can enjoy them because of modern means of transportation; and (3) we depend on many kinds of workers who perform many different tasks in order to have bananas on our tables or in our lunch boxes.

Main Ideas to Develop
- Bananas are an example of a food that is grown only in certain parts of the world due to climatic conditions but can be transported to other parts of the world. Bananas must be carefully preserved from the time they are picked until they reach the supermarket.
- We depend on many workers to bring this food to us.

Teaching Tips from Barbara

Sequencing and map skills are both bonuses in this lesson. Most kids love bananas and are interested to see where they come from and how they grow. Discuss cost, preparation time, transportation, effort (work involved), and availability. Bananas are low cost, require no prep time, are imported, involve low effort, and are available worldwide now. We had many responses to this home assignment, too.

Starting the Lesson

Begin the lesson by reviewing the home assignment. Using a globe, locate where the students live and then show where bananas are grown (Central America). Explain that bananas need a warm, moist climate, lots of sunshine, and lots of rain. Places such as Central America and parts of South America and Africa have the right year-round temperature and rainfall for bananas. Since Central America (countries such as Honduras) is so much closer to us than Africa, we get our bananas from that part of the world.

To add interest, spend a bit of time creating the setting for the banana plantation. Explain the jungle-like environment. As you carry out the interactive discussion about bananas, have a group of preselected students designated as the various workers. For example, the students will be the workers who spray for bugs and weeds. Have them show pictures of doing the work. (By the end of the discussion, make sure every student has played the role of at least one worker.)

Suggested Lesson Discussion

Bananas are grown on large farms called *plantations*. The banana workers live and work on these banana farms. The workers care for the banana plants. For example, they spray the plants for bugs and keep the weeds under control. Each banana plant has one stem. On the stem, bananas grow in bunches called *hands*. A hand may have up to four times as many bananas as the bunches we buy in stores. Each banana in a hand is called a *finger*.

It takes about three months for a banana bunch to form from the small flowers. Once formed, the bunches begin to grow. One day, the workers observe that the banana bunches are ready to harvest. They work in pairs to harvest the green bananas. One worker cuts the stems. The other carries away the heavy bananas. Workers need to be careful not to bruise the fruit. They carefully hook the bunches to a moving cable that takes them to the packing plant that is located on the plantation. Inside a packing plant, some workers do the cutting; others do the washing and weighing; yet others do the packing. They pack the bananas into cartons, which are then put into large metal containers that are refrigerated to keep the green bananas cool. [Show two bananas, one very green and the other very ripe. Discuss the idea that bananas have a sequence in their ripening.] As you probably have observed, when bananas get hot, they ripen and spoil. These coolers (metal containers) keep the bananas from becoming too ripe before they reach the market.

[Using the globe and map of Central America and Honduras, speculate how bananas from Honduras would most likely reach a market near you. Then, using pictures and the map/globe, explain that usually the containers travel by truck or train to a seaport in Honduras.] The seaport has docks that large ships can come to from the sea. Dock workers use cranes to lift the containers off the trucks or trains and into the waiting ship.

[Show globe or world map.] In less than a week, the ship will arrive at a U.S. seaport such as Gulfport, Mississippi. (Other seaports include Long Beach, California; Freeport, Texas; Jacksonville, Florida; Wilmington, Delaware; and New York City.) The banana containers are unloaded from the ship by dock workers and placed onto truck trailers. Truck drivers then take the banana containers to cities throughout the United States. Often the drivers need several days to reach their destination (a food warehouse or large building where many kinds of food are stored). [Locate one near you. If possible, take your students on a field trip to one of these facilities.]

When the bananas reach the warehouse, they are put in moist, wet rooms, where they ripen. The conditions in the ripening rooms are much like the climate in which the bananas were grown, so they can ripen almost naturally.

Market managers come to the food warehouse to buy the bananas and other foods for their stores. The bananas are loaded again onto trucks and moved to the stores, where they are unpacked and placed on tables, ready to be purchased. Your family goes to the store and buys some of these bananas, paying for them by weight. At last they reach your table or lunch box.

Group Activity

The time between the day when the bananas were picked in Honduras and the day they reached your table is about two weeks. Now, let's review what happens during that two weeks. [Use the time line, cutout pictures, and a blank calendar to retell the banana story, noting the many workers whom we depend on to bring bananas to us.]

Activity

If time permits, have each student draw a picture of the worker he/she enacted and share the responses with the class. Students will come to realize that many jobs and people are necessary in order for bananas to be available to us. All of the workers need to be paid. The money we pay for

bananas helps pay the workers and for the processes needed to get the
bananas to our supermarkets.

Summarize

Ask students to share the most interesting ideas they learned from the
lesson. They can each signal when of they have has a banana fact ready to
share. Write the ideas on the board (e.g., bananas are grown only in certain parts of the world; they need a hot, moist climate in order to grow;
they are transported to our part of the world by boat, train, and truck; we
depend on many workers to bring this food to us). Post the list. For self-
monitoring, encourage each student to keep track as to whether he or she
shared a response. When the teacher calls on him or her, the student
responds with "yes" or "no."

Assessment

As a group, list what was learned about bananas. Post the list and use it as
a reference for individual or group journal entries. If students have not
acquired writing skills, prepare a total-group journal entry. Encourage
them to read this story of bananas to a family member as a part of their
home assignment.

Optional Ask students to write individual responses or draw pictures
in their journals to the following open-ended questions:

- Where do bananas grow?
- Why do they grow there?
- How do bananas get to us?
- Which workers do we depend on to bring us bananas?

Home Assignment

Encourage students to share with their families what they have learned
regarding the story of bananas (land-to-hand relationship). Their (individual or group) reflective journal (picture and word story) could serve as
the stimulus.

Have the students list with their families the ways that bananas are
used in their diets (e.g., as dessert for lunch, sliced on cereal for breakfast,
blended in a fruit drink, used in muffins as the sweetener). Have students
bring their lists to class for group sharing.

Dear Parents,

We have been learning about the land-to-hand relationship of bananas. Encourage your child to share what he/she has learned about the story of bananas. Then discuss ways your family uses bananas in its diet. Please send the list to school for our class discussion.

Sincerely,

FIGURE 14 Model Letter to Parents

Lesson 8

The Story of Peanut Butter

Resources
- Globe
- World map
- Brandon, the puppet (optional)
- Pictures depicting the "story" of peanuts
- Flow chart with cutout pictures and words that illustrate the steps in bringing peanut butter to our table
- Peanuts
- Poster—peanut products
- Pictures/cutouts depicting Brandon and his family
- Ingredients and equipment for making peanut butter (optional)
- Sampling sticks for tasting (optional)

Children's Literature
Erlbach, A. (1994). *Peanut Butter*. Minneapolis: Lerner Publications.

Jones, G. (1995). *My First Book of How Things Are Made*. New York: Scholastic.

General Comments
The land-to-hand story of peanut butter is fascinating because it is a product that looks very different from the original crop because of the many processes it goes through, yet few substances are added to peanuts in order to produce peanut butter.

General Purposes or Goals
To help students understand and appreciate that: (1) climatic and soil conditions determine what kinds of food can be grown; (2) although many foods cannot be grown locally, we can enjoy them because of modern means of transportation; (3) we depend on many kinds of workers who perform many different tasks in order to have peanut butter; (4) there are many more people who buy peanut butter than there are farmers who grow peanuts; and (5) many products are made from peanuts.

Main Ideas to Develop
- The land-to-hand story of peanut butter begins with the planting of peanuts and is completed when jars of peanut butter are placed on the shelf in the store.

- Peanuts are an example of a food that is grown only in certain parts of the world due to climatic conditions, but they can be transported to other parts of the world.
- About half of all the peanuts grown in the United States are eaten in the form of peanut butter. Peanuts or peanut products are ingredients in many food recipes, cooking and salad oils, and in some products that we don't eat (soap, shampoo, paint, etc.).
- We depend on many people to bring peanuts and peanut products to us.
- There are many more people who buy peanuts and peanut butter than there are farmers who grow peanuts.

Teaching Tips from Barbara

One of the keys to these four lessons is to be constantly comparing and contrasting. Again, discuss cost, preparation time, transportation, effort (work involved), and availability. Peanut butter is medium cost, has no prep time, is domestic, takes a medium effort to make, and is available worldwide now. You also might want to add that it can be made at home. We combined the home assignments from Lessons 7, 8, and 9 together into one where students listed their favorite ways to eat bananas, peanut butter, and pasta.

Starting the Lesson

Review the home assignment from the lesson focusing on bananas. Explain that today we are going to learn about a food product that looks much different from its original form even though few ingredients have been added.

Using the globe and maps, locate where the students live and then show where peanuts are grown.

Suggested Lesson Discussion

Peanuts are grown in places that have rich, sandy soil and long hot summers. Alabama, Florida, Georgia, North Carolina, Oklahoma, Virginia, and Texas are states in our country that have the right conditions to grow peanuts. Peanuts are also grown in parts of Africa and China.

Let's take an imaginary trip to Georgia to visit Brandon, an eight-year-old who lives with his family on a peanut farm. [Trace the route on a U.S. map. Also, show a simple map of the farm with a corresponding map key for locating the peanut fields. Optional: Use the puppet to represent Brandon. Introduce him and explain that he will give a guided tour of the farm and explain the story of peanuts.] The peanut plants grow from seeds (peanuts). When the farmers plant the peanuts in the ground, they grow into leafy bushes about two feet tall. The bushes send up stalks that bend over and push back into the ground [show picture from p. 12 of *How Things Are Made*]. New peanuts, covered with shells, grow under the soil at the end of the stalk.

In the fall, peanut farmers like Brandon's father drive tractors hooked to machines called *diggers* that dig the peanut plants out of the ground. The plants are left out to dry in long piles. When the plants and peanuts are dry, Brandon's dad uses a machine called a *combine* to separate the plants from the peanuts. Then he dumps the nuts into a trailer. Either Brandon's father or a truck driver he hires takes the peanuts to a shelling plant, where machines remove the peanuts from their shells. [Explain that for Brandon's family, peanuts are a cash crop. This family would not eat many of the peanuts it raises. Instead, the parents use the money from the crop sales to buy the things the family needs.]

Let's imagine that we ride to the factory so we can observe the rest of the process. The shelled peanuts are sent to a peanut butter factory. First, a dumper unloads the peanuts into a separator that filters out any large stones and clumps of soil that may be mixed with the peanuts. Then the peanuts are sent through a de-stoner, which takes out the last tiny stones and gravel. From there, the peanuts are moved by belt to special ovens, where they are roasted in their skins. After they are roasted, they go through blanchers (machines that remove the peanut skins). From there, the blanched peanuts pass through another machine that checks their color. It gets rid of peanuts that are too dark because they were roasted too long or because their skins are still on.

Finally, the peanuts that pass this inspection are ready to be ground into peanut butter. Besides peanuts, three other ingredients must go into the mixers: sugar (or a sweetener called *dextrose*), salt, and a vegetable oil to keep the peanut butter from separating. A computer makes sure that the four ingredients come out of the feeder in the right amounts. Then the mixture is ground into a smooth and creamy peanut butter. In the lab, it is sampled often to make sure that the peanut butter has the right flavor and texture.

Clean, empty jars ride along a moving belt to a machine that squirts the right amount of peanut butter into each jar. The peanut butter is still warm and very soft. As it cools, it thickens. For crunchy-style peanut butter, chopped peanuts are blended in as the peanut butter is put into jars.

An automatic capper pops plastic caps onto the full jars of peanut butter. The next machine places a label on the jar. Also, an ink-jet printer marks each jar with a code that tells the jar's production line number as well as the date and hour that the jar was filled.

The packing machine prepares the jars for shipping. Plastic wrap is automatically placed around twelve jars at a time to hold them securely. The twelve-packs are placed in cases and shipped to large warehouses or to individual stores.

Only about half of the peanuts harvested are used to make peanut butter. The others are used as whole peanuts to be eaten as a protein snack, used in desserts, used for cooking oils, or used in non-food products. [Show a poster illustrating peanut products or generate a list on the white board.] You might also want to incorporate the biography of George Washington Carver into your literacy program.]

George Washington Carver (1864–1943) was a talented botanist who began his research into peanuts at Tuskegee Institute. This research led him to discover improvements in peanut farming, and he developed more than three hundred uses for peanuts. Carver recognized the value of the peanut as a cash crop that could be rotated in the Southeastern cotton-growing areas. Farmers listened, and farming in the region changed forever. For his work in promoting its cultivation and consumption, Carver is considered the father of the peanut industry.

Activity

Have students dictate sentences that tell about the various steps and the people involved in the story of peanut butter. The list should resemble the following:

1. Plant peanuts
2. Peanuts grow into leafy bushes
3. Harvest peanuts
4. Shell peanuts
5. Take peanuts to peanut butter factory
6. Unload the peanuts
7. Sort and separate peanuts
8. Roast peanuts
9. Blanch peanuts
10. Sort peanuts again
11. Grind peanuts
12. Add other ingredients
13. Mix ingredients
14. Test peanut butter
15. Bottle and cap peanut butter
16. Pack and ship peanut butter

Write the sentences on strips and then ask students to place them in order to show what happens first, second, and so on. An option is to have the strips prepared in advance (one set for each table) and ask the group at each table to sequence them.

Large-Group Activity

Upon completion of the lesson, the class could make its own version of peanut butter. See the recipe in Figure 15, on page 114. Review the steps with the students and send a copy home with them.

Summarize

- Peanuts are grown only in certain parts of the world.
- Peanuts need rich sandy soil and warm summers in order to grow.
- Peanut butter is made by squishing peanuts into paste, usually adding a sweetener, salt, and vegetable (or peanut) oil.
- Peanuts and peanut butter are transported to our part of the country by truck and/or train.

- We depend on many workers to bring this food to us. Part of the money we pay for the peanut butter is used to pay the workers.
- Many more people eat peanut butter—and other peanut products—than are needed on the farms for growing the peanut crop.
- Peanut butter looks quite different than the original peanuts. The product goes through many changes (processes), which add to its cost. (Note: Bananas look much the same at the supermarket as they did on the plantation. The only change is color. A pound of bananas would cost less than a pound of peanut butter because bananas don't require the manufacturing processes needed to transform peanuts into peanut butter.)

Assessment

Have the students quietly brainstorm at their tables about the story of peanuts and peanut butter: Where are peanuts grown? Why are they grown in the Southern United States? What are the steps in making peanut butter? Who are some of the workers we depend on to get the peanut butter for our lunch? When students have a response for each question, they should signal with "thumbs up."

The class will write a group story responding to the questions. Ask two groups (tables) to make illustrations explaining the steps in making peanut butter. Ask the other tables to draw pictures of the workers we depend on to bring peanut butter to our table. Share and discuss the visual responses in a large-group setting.

Provide each student with a sheet of paper numbered 1–10. Explain that as you read a statement, the student must decide whether it is correct (Y) or incorrect (N).

1. Peanuts are grown in every part of the world. (N)
2. Peanuts are grown in our state. (Y or N)
3. Peanuts are all made into peanut butter. (N)
4. Climate and soil determine what kinds of crops can be grown. (Y)
5. We depend on only a couple of people to bring peanuts and peanut products to us. (N)
6. George Washington developed over more than three hundred uses for peanuts. (N)
7. There are many more people who buy peanuts and peanut butter than there are farmers who grow peanuts. (Y)
8. A jar of peanut butter costs less than a bunch of bananas. (N)
9. Although many foods cannot be grown locally, we can enjoy them because of modern means of transportation. (Y)
10. Peanut butter is made by squishing peanuts into paste and adding sweetener, salt, and vegetable oil. (Y)

After correcting the papers, as a class discuss each and make the incorrect statements true.

Home Assignment

Encourage students to share the group story about peanuts and peanut butter with their families. Send home a copy of the recipe and the steps for making peanut butter. Following the sharing, have the student, with the help of a family member, brainstorm a list of possible nutritious snacks using peanut butter. The student should be prepared to share the list—and if possible, the recipes for the peanut butter snacks—during the next class session.

Optional Students could place the peanut butter snacks on the food pyramid to figure out how many food groups are represented.

Dear Parents,

We have been learning about the land-to-hand relationship of peanut butter. Encourage your child to read the group story that our class wrote.

We have enclosed a recipe for making peanut butter in case your family would like to do this.

Ingredients:	Equipment:
1 cup shelled peanuts	Blender or food processor
1 ½ T. vegetable or peanut oil	Measuring spoons
½ tsp. salt	Measuring cup
1 tsp. sugar (optional)	Rubber spatula
	Small jar or plastic container with a lid

Put the peanuts in the blender or food processor. Blend for about 1 minute. Peanuts need to be finely crushed into a pastelike consistency. Stir in oil and salt. If you would like chunky peanut butter, add some chopped peanuts to mixture. Put the peanut butter in the jar for storage.

With the help of a family member, have your child brainstorm a list of possible nutritious snacks using peanut butter. Send the list to school so your child can share it with his/her classmates. Recipes for peanut butter snacks would also be appreciated.

Sincerely,

FIGURE 15 Model Letter to Parents

Lesson 9

The Story of Pasta

Resources
- Sample of wheat
- Ingredients for making pasta: flour, water or milk, eggs, vegetable juices (for different colors)
- Picture of a pasta-making machine
- Variety of pasta samples
- Map of world illustrating places where wheat thrives
- Paper hats for the imaginary tour of Tutta Pasta Factory
- Puppet to serve as tour guide (optional)
- Fresh tortellini, multiple colors
- Fresh pasta sauce
- Pictures or drawings that tell the story of pasta (use for sequencing activity)
- Paper strips—steps in making pasta

Children's Literature
Enting, B. (1994). *Processed Food*. Bothell, WA: The Wright Group.

Halley, N. (1996). *Farm*. New York: Alfred A. Knopf.

Matchotka, H. (1992). *Pasta Factory*. Boston: Houghton Mifflin.

Meadowcroft, J. (1994). *Flour*. Bothell, WA: The Wright Group.

General Comments
The story of pasta will stimulate curiosity because it is a common food that children are familiar with but know little about (the pasta we purchase and cook looks very different from the grain from which it originated).

General Purposes or Goals
To develop an understanding and appreciation of: (1) the story of pasta; and (2) the range of workers needed and the processes involved in changing wheat into pasta.

Main Ideas to Develop
- The land-to-hand story of pasta begins with the planting of grain (wheat) and is completed when the pasta is packaged and ready for purchase (some people today make their own pasta).
- The pasta looks very different from the grain from which it originated, due to processing that transforms its appearance.

Teaching Tips from Barbara

It was much harder for students to make the connection from wheat to pasta. Use as many pictures as you can to show the steps. Making pasta in the classroom is a good idea before teaching this lesson. It helps students to identify the steps in the lesson. Be sure to keep referring back to the food pyramid and the purpose of food as you do these lessons. Pasta is a low-cost item, requires some prep time, is domestic, and is available worldwide now. It can also be homemade (but this requires more effort.)

Starting the Lesson

Begin the session by discussing the home assignment from Lesson 8. Underscore the idea that peanut butter has only a few things besides peanuts added.

Suggested Lesson Discussion

It's easy to figure out that peanut butter is made from peanuts. It's more difficult to realize that pasta [show examples] is made from wheat [show sprig of grain]. The wheat is ground into flour and mixed with other ingredients like eggs from chickens, water, and sometimes vegetable juices if we want to make different colors.

Wheat is grown in parts of the world that are moderate in temperature during the growing season, have plenty of rainfall early in the development of the wheat plants, then have hot/dry weather prior to harvesting. [Show a world map depicting the wheat-growing areas.]

Because of modern transportation methods, wheat can be shipped anywhere in the world either as raw grain or as a processed item (ground into flour). In the past, pasta tended to be found mostly in areas where wheat was grown. (People tend to rely first on resources that are nearby—and usually less expensive.) However, nowadays pasta can be enjoyed by people everywhere—if they have the funds available to purchase it.

In the past, stones were used to mill (grind) the grain into flour [show picture]. First, the milling was done by hand, later by animal power or by the use of a water wheel or a windmill. Today, wheat is ground into flour by machines run by electricity.

[Show the ingredients for making pasta. Make pasta by hand or by using a pasta machine. Compare homemade pasta and pasta making to that made in a factory. Underscore the ideas that homemade pasta is fresh, takes more time to make, and costs more if time and fresh ingredients are considered. Homemade pasta would probably not be feasible when volume is a factor. Mechanization and factories provide the equipment and the people for making a lot of a product in a short period of time. Indicate that during this lesson the students will take an imaginary field trip to Fortunato Di Natela's Tutta Pasta factory. You and the students might want to wear paper hats and briefly discuss safety/health conditions for a food factory. You may also wish to use a puppet as a tour guide to add interest and variety.

Tell students that after the tour, they will be asked to sequence the steps in making pasta, recall the range of workers in the pasta industry, and explain what they do. Use the pictures in *Pasta Factory* or *Image* series, Vol. 1, No. 6, to add interest and meaningfulness to the pasta story.

Students begin the tour by visiting the large silo that holds the flour until it's needed.] When flour is needed, a button is pushed on the panel and flour shoots from the silo through pipes along the ceiling to the mixing machine. [Show eggs and water and indicate that other pipes bring these ingredients from their containers to the mixing machine.] The ingredients are mixed to form a lumpy mass. The dough is pressed into sheets by a machine that functions like a rolling pin [show hand process of making pasta mixture].

The machine whirls and hums, and soon a sheet of dough is formed. It winds up onto a spindle to form a large roll [see p. 10, *Story of Pasta*]. Now the roll of dough is pressed into an even thinner sheet that travels through a steamer. The steam heats the dough to a very high temperature in order to kill any bacteria.

As the dough comes out, it's cut into strings, ribbons, and other shapes [show range]. A worker folds each batch into plastic containers. As the containers move along a conveyor belt, a plastic sheet covers each one [show plastic container of pasta], which is then sealed with a hot press. Another worker attaches a label that includes the type of pasta, the factory where it was made, the ingredients, cooking instructions, and the deadline for using the pasta. [Show label.]

[Next, show tortellini (actual product and pictures on pp. 14–15 of *Pasta Factory*.) Illustrate how the machine cuts small circles from the dough, inserts cheese filling, and presses the noodle just right so the tortellini will stay intact.] Workers are needed to keep the buckets of cheese available and to refill rolls of pasta so they can be cut into the designated shapes. Tortellini can be green (spinach), red (tomato), or white (eggs, flour, and water only).

The pressed tortellini are ready to be boxed. From the conveyor belt they are dropped into clear plastic boxes, labeled, and stored in large cardboard boxes. A forklift transfers them to a refrigerator, where they will remain until they are shipped to supermarkets and restaurants. Dies are used to provide a range of pasta shapes, such as fusilli, conchlietti (shells), vermicelli, and rigatoni (elbows).

Not all people buy fresh pasta. Some buy it dry. Dried pasta keeps longer and doesn't require refrigeration until after it has been cooked. The dry pasta is processed in a drying tank. It's loaded through little doors at one end, and hot air blows over it for about twenty-four hours until it's dry and hard. It's placed in storage bins until it's ready to be packaged into paper or cardboard boxes.

Activity

Give each pair of students a set of pictures or drawings that include the major steps in making pasta. Have the pairs put the strips in the proper sequence:

1. Harvest wheat
2. Grind flour
3. Store flour until needed
4. Push buttons so ingredients will flow through pipes and into mixing vats
5. Mix flour, eggs, water until lumpy
6. Roll mixture into sheets
7. Press sheets into desired pasta shape
8. Steam dough at a very high temperature to pasteurize it (kill bacteria)
9. Put pasta into plastic containers and seal
10. Label
11. Refrigerate
12. Ship to market

Review the appropriate pasta story sequence. Next, have the class list the many workers involved. Then ask for twelve "helpers," who will each get a card with one of the twelve steps for making pasta. As you hand out each card, read it aloud. You may wish to have the helpers pantomime the processes. Next, have the students arrange themselves in the appropriate chronological order to tell the pasta story.

Summarize

The story of pasta begins with wheat that is changed into flour. [Review the climatic conditions needed for growing wheat (i.e., dry, hot summers with moisture needed early in the growing season). Use a world map to show places around the world where lots of wheat is grown.] The wheat is ground into flour. Long, long ago, wheat kernels were ground up by hand, later with the help of animals, and today by machines powered by electricity. Several ingredients are added to make pasta dough. Pasta dough can be cut and pressed into many shapes. Pasta can be made by hand, by simple machines, or by high-tech machines. The original grain looks very different from the eventual pasta. [Explain why a pound of fresh pasta would probably cost more than a pound of bananas.]

Assessment

Give each student twelve strips of paper with the steps for making pasta. Have each individual place the steps in order. Then have the students check their responses with a partner. As a class, prepare a group journal entry that focuses on the main ideas about the story of pasta. Send home a copy of the group journal entry.

Home Assignment

Encourage each student to read the class story about pasta to one or more family members. After reading the story, families should list the many ways (including their favorite, which should be underlined) that pasta is used in their meals. The list should be returned to school to be shared with peers.

Dear Parents,

Encourage your child to read the class story about pasta. After reading the story, we would like your family to list the many ways (including your favorite) pasta is used in your meals. Please send the list to school with your child so it can be shared with the class during our next discussion.

Sincerely,

FIGURE 16 Model Letter to Parents

Lesson 10

The Story of Apple Pie

Resources
- World map
- Globe
- Tray with ingredients for apple pie (i.e., wheat flour, eggs, cinnamon, salt (optional), milk, shortening, sugar cane, apples)
- Apple pie

Children's Literature
Priceman, M. (1994). *How to Make an Apple Pie and See the World*. New York: Alfred A. Knopf.

General Comments
This lesson uses the story *How to Make an Apple Pie and See the World*. While it is a bit fanciful, students tend to enjoy it, and it emphasizes the geographic connections that lie behind an apple pie.

Optional The students could have a special treat at the conclusion of the lesson—a slice of apple pie.

General Purposes or Goals
To develop understanding and appreciation of: (1) the story of apple pie; (2) the geographic connections that bring us many of the foods we eat; and (3) division of labor and interdependence—and their trade-offs.

Main Ideas to Develop
- Apple pie begins with the planting of wheat for the flour for the pie crust, and the planting of the apple seed for the filling. The pie requires many ingredients—some of which come from other places (e.g., cinnamon, sugar).
- Ingredients for an apple pie, not unlike many foods that we eat, reflect our global connections.
- Division of labor and interdependence are reflected in the places and processes needed to produce a complex food such as an apple pie.
- Labor-intensive products tend to cost more.

Teaching Tips from Barbara
As I did this lesson, I also included some discussion of the difficulties I'd had in making apple pies in the past. I tied the discussions to the lessons

involving changes over time. This is also where we continued discussions about importing and exporting food that were begun in Lesson 7. Apple pies are higher-cost items, require lots of prep time, can be imported or domestic, involve a high effort, and are available worldwide now. They can be fresh, frozen, or homemade.

Starting the Lesson

Review the homework assignment from Lesson 9, emphasizing that many foods are consumed in forms very different from their original state (e.g., wheat to flour to bread, wheat to flour to piecrust). Others, such as apples, are quite recognizable.

Introduce the lesson by showing an apple pie. Encourage the students to speculate about the ingredients needed to make an apple pie. Then, pass a tray that exhibits the ingredients: flour, salt (optional), eggs, cinnamon, milk, sugar from cane or sugar beets, apples.

Suggested Lesson Discussion

We are interdependent with other people and places in our country and the world. [Show the globe or a world map. Indicate to the students that during this lesson they are going to learn about the global connections they can experience by learning about—and sampling—apple pie.] Some of the ingredients for apple pie are grown locally and are available part of the year, but we depend on crops grown in other places for other ingredients. They are processed, packaged, and shipped to supermarkets like the ones we have in our community. With the exception of the spices for the apple pie, all of the ingredients are produced in the United States.

Read the story and listen for the places the baker traveled to get the ingredients for the pie. In this story, the little baker travels the world, from the sugar cane fields of Jamaica to the apple orchards of Vermont, to find the finest ingredients for her apple pie. [At the end of the story, the class will retrace the baker's journey by drawing a line on a map from each ingredient to the place where it was gathered. Explain that the baker depended on many people and places to get the ingredients for the pie. This is known as interdependence.]

Optional   Discuss how your students' families secure ingredients from other parts of the world to make their favorite dishes.

Activity

Recreate the scenario of a family that decides to make an apple pie (e.g., perhaps it's a rainy Sunday afternoon and the family thought this would make a good group project).

As the teacher (parent), you can play the lead role. Get out the recipe. Together, you read the ingredients and discuss what each is, where it comes from, and what it looks like. Then, actually make an apple pie.

Explain the steps (processes) and the fact that many people were involved in preparing the ingredients for the pie. Select one ingredient (e.g., wheat to flour), then explain the concept of division of labor. After making the pie, have each student write a story about the experience.

Optional Post cue cards for spelling assistance.

Summarize

The story is fanciful and, of course, people (such as your parents) do not travel around the world to get the ingredients for an apple pie. Spices come from other parts of the world. Other ingredients may or may not (sugar). Some ingredients may come from other parts of the United States. If the ingredients are available locally, we try to use them because they tend to cost less.

Apple pie obviously looks very different than wheat and apples—two of its main ingredients. It is a lot more complicated to make a pie than to pick and ship a bunch of bananas or a bag of apples, so we can expect the pie to cost more.

Assessment

Elicit the big ideas of the lesson from the students. Students will close their eyes. When they have an idea they will signal by a "thumbs up." Record the ideas as a class journal entry. Send a copy home and encourage students to read the entry to their families.

Optional At the end of the lesson, provide students with a sample of apple pie.

Home Assignment

Encourage each student to read the class journal entry focusing on "our globalness/interdependence" with other parts of the United States and the world as it relates to apple pie. Then have family members explore with their children other favorite dishes that depend on ingredients from other parts of the world. Families should survey the cupboards and develop a composite list of ingredients from places around the world (Figure 17).

Discuss with a family member some of your favorite dishes. Do some of the ingredients come from other parts of the world? List them. Do you like other foods, such as bananas, that come from other parts of the world? List those too.

FAVORITE DISHES OUR FAMILY EATS THAT INCLUDE INGREDIENTS FROM OTHER PARTS OF THE WORLD	SPECIAL INGREDIENTS	COUNTRY OF ORIGIN
1. Coffee ice cream	Coffee	Brazil
2. Gouda cheese and tomato paste	Gouda cheese, Olive oil	Netherlands Greece
3.		
4.		
5.		
6.		
7.		

FIGURE 17 Origins of Favorite Dishes

Dear Parents,

We encourage your child to read the class journal entry focusing on our geographic connections/interdependence with other parts of the United States and world as it relates to apple pie. Then discuss your family's favorite dishes that depend on ingredients from other parts of the United States and world.

Sincerely,

FIGURE 18 Model Letter to Parents

Lesson 11

. . . .

A Trip to the Supermarket

Resources

- The 5-Day Adventure CD-ROM (compatible for both Mac and Windows) is available free to schools in any quantity needed. Teachers can order the program by mailing or faxing their request on school letterhead and indicating the number of disks needed to:

  Dole 5-Day Adventures
  155 Bovet, Suite 476
  San Mateo, CA 94402
  FAX: (415) 570-5250

- Permission slips for field trip to supermarket
- Volunteers and transportation if a supermarket isn't nearby
- Photos of supermarket (interior and exterior)

General Comments

The intent of this lesson is to take the class on an actual field trip to a nearby supermarket and make some planned observations regarding store layout, types of foods available, where they come from, how they are preserved, how they are displayed, and so on. The trip will give students an opportunity to observe some of the kinds of workers connected with the food industry, and to begin thinking about some of the indirect as well as direct costs for our foods. For this lesson, recruit parent volunteers to act as group leaders. Meet with them in advance to go over the orientation for group leaders (Figure 19). In addition, you (and perhaps parent volunteers as well) should previsit the store to work out the logistics of the trip, consult with the manager, and "walk through" the student activity sheet.

General Purposes or Goals

To develop an understanding and appreciation of: (1) the variety of ways food is prepared and preserved; (2) the choices we have as a result; and (3) the costs involved in the food industry—and what we pay for directly and indirectly.

Main Ideas to Develop

- Foods are prepared in a variety of ways and can be bought in a variety of preserved forms (e.g., beef: fresh, dried, canned).

General Goals

To develop an understanding and appreciation of: (1) the variety of ways food is prepared and preserved; (2) the choices we have as a result; (3) the costs involved in the food industry—what we pay for directly and indirectly.

Main Ideas to Develop

- Foods are prepared in a variety of ways and can be bought in a variety of preserved forms (e.g., beef: fresh, dried, canned)
- The layout of the market is planned to make the foods look appealing, to place food in the appropriate environmental conditions, and to make it accessible.
- We pay for foods directly as well as indirectly. Indirectly we pay workers' wages and other costs involved in the harvesting, shipping, advertising, storing, and so on. We even pay indirectly for the electricity that keeps foods at the appropriate temperature while they are stored at the supermarket.
- There is a range of jobs that need to be done in a supermarket.

Your role as a group leader is to facilitate the activity and record your students' responses as they "zero in" on one section of the supermarket. The section will be preassigned (e.g., frozen foods, ethnic foods, meat department, etc.).

FIGURE 19 Orientation for Group Leaders

- The layout of the market is planned to make the foods look appealing, to place food in the appropriate environmental conditions, and to make it accessible.
- We pay for foods directly as well as indirectly. Indirectly we pay workers' wages and other costs involved in the harvesting, shipping, advertising, and storing—even the electricity that keeps foods at the appropriate temperature while they are stored at the supermarket.
- There is a range of jobs that need to be done in a supermarket.

Teaching Tips from Barbara

My class was unable to do this field trip due to a last-minute transportation problem, but it would be very valuable. All of my students have had the experience of shopping in a grocery store regularly, so we were able to discuss some of the information without going to the actual store. If you can't get your students to the store, photographs of a familiar store will also work. If you do go, give your parent volunteers a clipboard and list of things for students to find. Be sure that you have them focus on the variety of foods, the jobs, and the simple economics of stores.

Starting the Lesson

Begin by discussing the home assignment. Introduce the lesson with an outline map showing the route to the supermarket, a photo of its exterior, and several photos of its various sections (e.g., produce, meat, deli, frozen foods, spices, ethnic foods, dairy, and so on.) Point out signs overhead in the market to orient the shopper.

Talk about the roles, norms, and expectations of a shopper and of a student on tour. Role-play guidelines to follow when on field trips.

If possible, organize each table as a group and assign each a parent volunteer to conduct an overall "broad brush" tour of the supermarket to observe the layout and types of work being done by the workers. Provide each small group of students and volunteer with a pencil and an activity sheet (see Figure 20, p. 128) attached to a clipboard. Then, each working group should "zero in" on a section (e.g., frozen foods, spices, ethnic foods, etc.). Coordinate this before you leave. After studying and discussing one section carefully, the groups will walk around the store to determine direct and indirect costs. Each volunteer will compile the list of indirect costs.

Arrange for a supermarket worker to spend a few minutes with each group responding to its questions or demonstrating some aspect of the operation of the store section that is the focus of the group's query.

At the conclusion of the field trip, hold a class debriefing and compile responses on a large piece of chart paper. Use the ideas from this "data retrieval chart" in the group reflective journal that the class will write. Emphasize the supermarket layout; supermarket workers; the variety of ways that foods are prepared, preserved, packaged, and displayed; and the diversity of places represented on the food labels. Encourage students to read the group story to a family member.

Activity

Have each group give a mini-report focusing on its preassigned section.

Optional   One of the segments of the CD-ROM developed by Dole visits a supermarket. It provides animated stories about how mini-peeled carrots are grown, cut, and packaged, and how fresh-cut salads in a bag get from the field to the supermarket. In another segment, students can explore the Food Guide Pyramid and learn how to read food labels.

1. How is this supermarket different from a convenience store?

    _____

    _____

2. What types of work do you see being done at this supermarket?

    _____

    _____

3. List the ways that food is preserved in this supermarket.

    _____

    _____

4. List all the places that the foods have come from

    Item   Place

    _____

    _____

5. Your emphasis area was _____

6. What kind of foods were located in your emphasis area?

    _____

    _____

7. What was the most interesting thing about your emphasis area?

    _____

8. How can you figure out the cost of the food items?

    _____

9. What did you learn by reading the food labels?

    _____

10. What indirect costs are "tacked on" to the price of our foods? Why?

    List indirect costs

    _____

    _____

FIGURE 20 Sample Activity Sheet

Summarize

Foods in the supermarket come from all over the world. Foods are pre-served, packaged, and displayed in a variety of ways. There are both direct and indirect costs associated with the foods we buy.

Assessment

Ask each student to draw the most important thing she or he learned about food during the trip to the supermarket and to write a caption establishing the big idea.

Home Assignment

Encourage the family members to serve as an audience for the student's reading of the group's journal entry. Also, ask family members to budget a few minutes on the next trip to the supermarket to allow the student to point out some of the features of the supermarket and to show the variety of ways food is prepared, preserved, and packaged. Send home a copy of the "activity sheet" provided during the field trip for use as a guide. If time permits during the family shopping trip, parents should encourage a visit to another interest area—one that the student wasn't able to explore on the class field trip.

Dear Parents,

We encourage at least one family member to serve as an audience for your child's reading related to our class trip to the supermarket.

We would also encourage you to budget a few minutes on your next trip to the supermarket to point out to your child other features of the market. Point out a variety of ways food is prepared, preserved, and packaged. A copy of the class activity sheet we used for our class trip is enclosed.

Your child will undoubtedly have lots of questions as well as information he/she acquired while on our class trip.

Sincerely,

FIGURE 21 Model Letter to Parents

Lesson 12

Careers in the Food Industry

Resources

- Paper cutouts of workers related to the story of peanut butter
- Flow chart depicting the land-to-hand story of peanut butter, focusing on career choices within the peanut butter industry
- Photos and pictures to illustrate the story of peanut butter
- Jar of peanut butter with label
- Advertising material focusing on peanut butter
- Role-playing cards focusing on careers associated with the story of peanut butter
- Armento, B., Nash, G., Salter, C., and Wixson, K., (1991). *Some Places I Know*. Boston: Houghton Mifflin, (pp. 8–15).

Children's Literature

Erlach, A. (1994). *Peanut Butter*. Minneapolis: Lerner.

Jones, G. (1995). *My First Book of How Things Work*. New York: Scholastic.

Tomchek, A. H. (1985). *I Can Be a Chef*. Chicago: Children's Press.

General Comments

For this lesson, students will revisit the story of peanut butter. However, this time the focus will be on the careers associated with peanut butter, rather than on its production. The class might engage in additional dialogue about other careers in the food industry. If parents' careers involve the food industry, this would be a good time to invite them to the class to describe their work.

General Purposes and Goals

To develop: (1) understanding and appreciation for the diversity of career opportunities involved in the food industry; (2) understanding of the roles of food service people and the costs associated with their work; and (3) a sense of efficacy regarding the possibilities for pursuing existing careers in the food industry or even inventing new ones.

Main Ideas to Develop

- We depend on many people for the food we eat (e.g., farmer, truck driver, government inspector, graphic artist for advertising, researchers for new products, etc.).
- We pay for the services that these people provide to us.

Teaching Tips from Barbara

One of the keys to this lesson is to make ties to past lessons. You can use more discussion methods (and less lecture) if you use the steps already laid out from the peanut butter lesson. The home assignment works well because almost everyone will be able to find a food worker to interview.

Starting the Lesson

Begin by reviewing the prior lesson focusing on the supermarket and the data provided by family members. Note all the types of workers and the work they do. Then show a jar of peanut butter and indicate that this lesson will review the "peanut butter story." However, this time the emphasis will be on the workers, rather than the process.

Suggested Lesson Discussion

This lesson lends itself to an interactive session encouraging the students to speculate about the workers' jobs—and whether or not they might enjoy such jobs in the future. Use the flow chart to depict the "story of peanut butter" and the paper cutouts to represent the workers. Use additional photos and pictures to illustrate the story. Have students assist in building the flow chart with illustrations. Attach the cutouts to the flow chart as the lesson unfolds.

The following highlights should be included in the story:

1. Farmers buy seeds from a peanut seed company. The farmers might employ several "temporary" workers/helpers to prepare the soil, plant the seeds, and maintain the machinery.
2. Then, in the fall, the farmers return to the fields to harvest the crop. They use a machine called a *combine* to separate the peanuts and dump the nuts into a trailer.
3. Truck drivers bring the peanuts to a shelling plant, where machines remove the peanuts from their shells. [Note by the picture that nowadays few workers handle the product. Instead, most workers are computer operators/maintenance workers—people needed to make sure that the machines function correctly.]
4. Inside the shelling plant there also is a manager who oversees the workers and office staff who take care of telephone calls, faxes (messages sent by machine), schedules, and so on.
5. The shelled peanuts go to the peanut butter factory—which may be on site (in another building) or quite far away. If on site, peanuts are moved by a conveyor belt. If far away, truck drivers are needed to move the peanuts.
6. Once the peanuts reach the factory, several other machines are needed (e.g., box dumper, sorter, mixer where ingredients of peanut butter are mixed together). A computer is programmed to

make sure that proper amounts of ingredients come out of a feeder and get mixed properly.

7. Then the mixture goes to another machine that adds salt and vegetable oil. Quality control technicians test the peanut butter to make sure it has the right flavor and texture.

8. Automation (using equipment that is designed, built, and maintained by still other workers) is responsible for filling the jars, sealing them, and labeling them. The labels have been designed by graphic artists, and the ingredients have been figured out by researchers who take into account the fat grams, carbohydrates, and calories.

9. When the jars reach the shipping area, they are loaded onto trucks. Then, some are delivered to local supermarkets and restaurants, but most are sent by truck, rail, and boat throughout the world. Once again, lots of people are needed to move the product.

10. At the warehouses, people are needed to put the product in the proper storage area until it is purchased by a supermarket or restaurant.

11. At the supermarket, there are managers, supervisors, stockers, baggers, and cashiers.

12. People in advertising agencies prepare ads for the supermarket each week.

13. Sometimes products go on sale or are featured in a newspaper or on TV to encourage customers to purchase a certain brand. Many workers are needed to create commercials to stimulate interest in the products.

Activity

Using paper figures and/or role-play cards describing career opportunities in the peanut butter industry, have each student select a figure or card, describe the type of job the worker has, indicate whether or not it would be a job or career he or she might like to try someday, and explain why or why not.

Have students share their ideas about other food-related jobs they are familiar with—drawing from those revealed during prior lessons as well as those they might have come in contact with during out-of-school activities.

Summarize

We depend on many people for the foods we eat. All of these people get paid through the companies and businesses associated with these products. Indirectly, we pay them when we buy the product (e.g., the price of a jar of peanut butter reflects money paid to farmers for peanuts, to truck drivers for transportation, etc.).

Optional   Invite a family member to the class as a resource person to talk about his or her work associated with the food industry, underscoring the ideas that we depend on many people for the food we eat and that we pay for the services that these people provide us with.

Assessment

Invite upper-grade peer mentors to assist your students in selecting one thing they'd like to do that relates to the food industry and then writing about their choices.

Home Assignment

Encourage the students to read what they have written about career choices in food to family members. Then ask families to talk about the work they have experienced in the food industry and encourage their children to talk with friends/neighbors in the food industry. Send home copies of Figures 22A and 22B to help families stimulate discussions and record highlights.

Careers in the Food Industry:
Examples Drawn from the Peanut Industry

The following is a partial list of workers who are a part of the peanut industry. Use the list to identify and stimulate discussion about individuals you know who are connected to the food industry. If possible, have your child talk to one or more individuals about what tasks she or he does and why these are important jobs in the food industry. Encourage your child to complete the attached form for sharing during the next social studies lesson.

PREPRODUCTION	PRODUCTION		POSTPRODUCTION	
Researchers (new seeds)	Owner of shelling plant	Owner of peanut butter factory	Truck drivers (transport cases of peanut butter from factory to warehouses, stores)	Warehouse workers	Store owner, manager, dept. supervisors, coders, cashiers, stockers, baggers
Farmers	Manager of plant	Manager of factory workers		Truck drivers (transport cases from warehouses to stores, restaurants)	Restaurant owner, manager, wait staff, chef
Farm helpers	Shelling machine operators	Workers (make sure machines are maintained)	Other transportation workers		
Equipment manufacturers	Government inspectors	Graphic artist (design labels)	Quality control technicians	Advertising/ designers	Home (enjoy peanut butter)
Truck drivers (transport crops to plants for processing)					

©2001 by Janet Alleman and Jere Brophy from *Social Studies Excursions, K–3*. Portsmouth, NH: Heinemann

FIGURE 22A Careers in the Food Industry: Overview

I talked with _____ about his/her work in the food industry.

His/her jobs include

_____

_____

_____

_____

_____

Special skills needed to do a good job include

_____

_____

_____

This work is important because

_____

_____

_____

I would/would not like to do this job someday because

_____

_____

_____

FIGURE 22B Careers in the Food Industry: Overview

Lesson 13

....

Special Foods

Resources
- World map and/or globe
- Display of breads from around the world
- Photos of breads from around the world
- Mortar and pestle for grinding
- Dried corn
- Flour, water, yeast

Children's Literature

Dooley, N. (1997). *Everybody Bakes Bread*. Minneapolis, MN: Lerner.

King, V. (1994). *What's for Dinner*. Bothell, WA: Wright Group.

Morris, A. (1989). *Bread, Bread, Bread*. New York: Lothrop, Lee, & Shepard.

General Comments

Bread will be used to illustrate a food that is often described as a cultural universal. Throughout the world, it has been a very important food, often known as a *staple*. It is made from a variety of plants (e.g., wheat, corn, taro, manioc, millet, etc.), which depend on the climatic conditions. The beliefs, customs, and preferences of the people determine how it is prepared and served.

General Purposes and Goals

To develop understanding and appreciation of: (1) the role that culture plays in determining the way food is prepared (e.g., bread); (2) the role that climate and land formations play in deciding what grains to grow; and (3) the fact that bread or any other food from around the world that we desire is available to us—for a price.

Main Ideas to Develop
- Some foods (e.g., bread) are found throughout the world; however, they take different forms (and are made from a range of grains) due to climate, weather, land formations (plains, valleys, mountains, etc.), culture, and economics.
- Almost every food can be shipped to any place in the world; however, transportation costs can be very expensive.
- Often people eat special foods for special occasions. This reflects their culture and personal preference.

- Some people eat (or refrain from eating) certain foods due to religious beliefs.

Teaching Tips from Barbara

The book *Bread, Bread, Bread* is a wonderful support for this lesson. I chose to read it aloud first and then used it as a springboard for discussions about bread around the world and the history of bread. I also added another day to teach about food in other countries. I asked all of the parents to send in any foods special to their family for taste-testing. I was surprised by some things that were sent in that I wouldn't have thought of! This is when we put together the recipe book. Once again, look for a parent to help with this big job.

Starting the Lesson

Review the home assignment. Begin the lesson by asking a student to draw a picture of bread. Then, as a class, discuss its color, shape, and smell. Elicit student responses regarding agreement or disagreement on a common description of bread.

Show the students soft white bread in a long loaf, cut in perfect slices. Indicate that because it's so familiar, it's hard to imagine that if you traveled outside the United States, you probably wouldn't find people eating this kind of bread. However, almost anywhere in the world, you would find people eating some kind of bread. Ask students to picture in their heads the various kinds of breads they have seen and perhaps eaten. Show a display of breads from around the world. The kinds made locally depend on the plants that are available for making flour (e.g., wheat, corn, millet, taro, manioc, etc.) and the beliefs and values of the people. Show pictures.

Suggested Lesson Discussion

The first bread was made in the Nile Valley about ten thousand years ago. There, hunter-gatherers discovered how to extract the seeds from cereal grasses and use them for food. They used stones to crush the grain into coarse flour and make forms of bread. News of this new food spread, and people in the Middle East began to collect seed, cultivate it, plant it, harvest it, and turn it into flour (by first crushing the seeds with stones and then grinding the crushed seeds between flat stones). At first, people must have eaten the ground grain raw, like a bowl of cereal. Then they learned to mix it with water. Possibly it was an accident when they left some flour and water in the sun and they found that it was tasty.

Both wheat and barley grew in ancient Egypt; however, for many, many years, flat barley cakes were their main food. Later, the Egyptians discovered that when dough stood a long time, it turned sour and would rise. They would save a small piece of sour dough from the last batch and use it as a starter with the fresh dough. (Some starter was often put into tombs of dead people so the soul would have enough food for the long journey to heaven.) Eventually, the Egyptians ate more wheat bread. Poor people ate almost nothing else. Bread was sometimes used as money or for bartering.

In the New World, the Native Americans grew corn and made corn bread. [Demonstrate pounding/grinding of corn to make the corn flour for making the bread.] When settlers arrived from Europe, they brought their ideas about bread, and they learned about grains (grasses) that would grow in America and could be ground into flour and made into bread. Johnny cake (corn bread), hoecakes (bread cooked over a fire), and corn-meal slappers (fried bread) were all favorites.

[Introduce the book *Bread, Bread, Bread*. Explain that people all over the world eat some form of bread. Show pictures and breads and use a world map or globe during your explanation. It depends largely on the grains available. The following content is included in the book. Using pictures from the book and selected breads, expand on a few of the bread types.]

Enchiladas and tortillas are still favorites of Mexican people today. In some Mexican villages, women spend much of their day grinding corn and preparing it with water to form a paste called *masa*. The lumps of masa are patted back and forth to form a pancake, which is then baked on a stone slab over an open fire. In the cities in Mexico or in the United States or in other parts of the world, it is possible to buy masa already ground—or to buy tortillas canned or frozen.

Flat breads are still eaten in many parts of the world. Sometimes it is because the wheat necessary for making raised bread will not grow where it is too cold or too hot or too wet. And sometimes it is because the people have always eaten flat bread and see no reason to change.

India is a wheat-growing country, and the favorite bread there is the *chapati*. Chapatis are made of whole-wheat flour, cooked like pancakes, and eaten with lots of butter. Indians use chapatis the way Mexicans use tortillas.

In some places, people make bread out of things that seem very strange to us. For example, no grain grows in the South Pacific islands, so people pound the roots of the taro plant to make poi. In the tropical rain forests of Brazil, the natives bake flat hard cakes from manioc plant that has been pounded into cassava flour. In the Middle East, lots of millet is grown, so it is used to make their flat bread.

You might not even need to leave your hometown in order to find many of the kinds of bread eaten in other parts of the world. In many cities and towns, people from around the world have established small bakeries that make their favorite breads and pastries. [Show examples and photos. Use a world map or globe.] These breads include:

- Long crusty white loaves (France)
- Dark heavy loaves of rye (Russia, Germany)
- Round, hard flat sheets (Scandinavia)
- Bread sticks (Italy)
- Grissini bagels (Israel)
- Pocket bread (Middle East)

The shapes and ingredients are different from country to country and even from one part of the country to the next. People are different, and so are their preferences and traditions. Some like sweeter breads; some like them more spicy; some use more eggs, and so on.

Each culture also has its own ways of celebrating, and many celebrations include bread. Breads that originated with our ancestors are often made in America for religious holidays and other special occasions:

- Lefsa from Scandinavia
- Challah (a yellow braided bread served on special Jewish occasions such as the end of Yom Kippur)
- Bread and salt (served by Russians as a symbol of welcome)
- Stollen (sweet bread with fruits and nuts served in Germany for festivals)
- Matzoh or thin crackers (unleavened bread for Passover)

Optional   Create a map of local ethnic bakeries and restaurants. Plot on local map. Connect to country of origin. Use yarn to connect on world map. Ethnic foods that could be used as examples include baklava, spinach pie, lefsa, and stollen.

Invite parent volunteers to prepare, serve, and "share stories" about breads and other foods, customs, and traditions that they enjoy based on their cultural backgrounds. The festival might be expanded to include other foods. Describe these special foods in writing and provide the students with samples.

Summarize

Bread is enjoyed around the world. The types are based on climate/weather conditions, grain crops available, and special contents provided by the people. People throughout the world have made "bread treats" for special occasions, some of which have been brought to America.

Many of us enjoy other customs and traditions, which include breads and other ethnic foods that have been passed on to us by our cultural heritage. Many of these special foods take extra time in preparation, so they are usually enjoyed only on special occasions. In some towns and cities, special restaurants and bakeries prepare and sell these foods on a regular basis. They usually have an adequate market if large numbers of the ethnic group live in the area or if the specialty becomes popular with several other ethnic groups.

Assessment

Have each student draw the most important thing he or she has learned about breads from around the world (and other foods if included in the ethnic festival). Then, discuss their ideas as a class and prepare a group journal entry focusing on bread and other special foods.

Optional   Have individual students complete an open-ended journal entry: People around the world eat many different kinds of bread because

_____ .

Home Assignment

Encourage students to read the class journal entry to a family member, and then talk with the family member about breads and other foods they enjoy for special occasions as the result of their cultural heritage. Students should bring these favorite food recipes to class so a booklet can be assembled by a parent volunteer and given as a holiday gift.

Dear Parents,

We want to encourage at least one family member to serve as the audience as your child reads the class journal entry about breads and other special foods enjoyed around the world.

Discuss the foods your family enjoys for special occasions. Please send your family's favorite food recipe enjoyed on special occasions. Our class will compile a recipe book.

Sincerely,

FIGURE 23 Model Letter to Parents

Lesson 14
....
Making Choices

Resources
- Display of potatoes prepared in various ways
- Decision-making diagram
- Photos or pictures of families depicted in the role-plays
- Newspaper fliers, coupons, menus, and other decision-making tools
- Word cards: location, climatic conditions, seasons, weather, availability of food items, family size, personal preferences, religious beliefs

General Comments
This lesson is intended to be very interactive, with discourse centered around the variables and trade-offs that need to be considered in making decisions about eating.

General Purposes or Goals
To develop understanding and appreciation of: (1) the fact that people have the opportunity to make many decisions about food in order to satisfy this basic need; (2) the trade-offs involved in the choices they make regarding food; and (3) the variables that influence our choices about foods (location, climatic conditions, seasons, weather, availability of food items, cost, family size, personal preferences, and religious beliefs).

Main Ideas to Develop
- People make decisions about the foods they eat: what they eat, where they eat, how the food is prepared, and so on.
- Location, climatic conditions, seasons, weather, availability of food items, cost, family size, personal preferences, and religious beliefs influence our choices.

Teaching Tips from Barbara
I found that the most interesting discussion came after the home assignment. Students were very interested in talking about the actual meals that their families chose to write about. Before that assignment, it was difficult for them to discuss hypothetical situations. Afterward, more children were able to add comments and share thoughts and ideas. Many parents commented about the interesting discussions that came up while doing the homework—and more than a year later, while grocery shopping!

Starting the Lesson

Begin by sharing results from the home assignment. Underscore the idea that many of our favorite cultural foods are prepared and eaten only on special occasions. Often these food dishes take lots of time to prepare, and frequently the ingredients—or special equipment needed—are relatively expensive.

Remind students that families not only need to plan ahead in order to enjoy these favorite dishes, but they also have to plan for and make many decisions about eating every day. Pose the question "What are some of the decisions your family has to make about food and about eating every day?" List the responses on the board. Responses will include some of the following ideas: what to eat, what to buy, how much to buy, where to get the food, whether to eat at home or at a restaurant, whether to cook the food or prepare ready-made food, how much to spend, whether to eat a balanced meal or have junk food.

Use the potato as an example for illustrating the range of possibilities with this very common food.

Suggested Lesson Discussion

During the fall, in a place where potatoes have grown well over the summer, a family could eat potatoes out of its garden very inexpensively. Weather, climate, and location are all factors that make potatoes a "good" buy in such places, especially in the fall. Even if they must be shipped to our supermarket, they are inexpensive because they store well and they haven't been changed from their original forms. For a family of four, boiled, baked, or mashed potatoes for dinner would cost about $_____. If a family member decides to mash the potato, more preparation is needed, so time becomes a consideration.

Potatoes also can be scalloped (homemade, out of a box, frozen, or purchased at a deli). Note the ingredients and cost. Processing costs money, and additives aren't always healthy. Another choice is french-fried potatoes (homemade, frozen, purchased at a fast-food chain and brought home to eat, or purchased and eaten at a sit-down restaurant). Again, potatoes that have been changed, packaged, shipped, advertised, or served to the customer cost more because we pay for direct and indirect services. [Recall the supermarket lesson.]

In our part of the world where we have access to supermarkets and a range of restaurant types, all of the choices are available for a price. While we have access to almost any food any time of the year due to modern transportation and communication, foods that are grown here during the growing season and are plentiful tend to cost less. Location, seasons, and climatic conditions dictate what can be grown in a given area. Foods prepared at home tend to cost less money (e.g., they are not served by waiters or waitresses), but they cost us more in terms of time. Family members may have jobs that require long hours away from the house, or other responsibilities that make meal preparation at home difficult.

Family size determines in part how much money is available for meals. Personal preferences are another factor. [Show a range of scenarios illustrating the cost for a family of four.] For example, even if baked potatoes prepared at home are the most economical choice, preparing and serving them would be a bad choice if no family member likes them or will eat them.

Still another factor is religious beliefs. For example, some groups believe that they should eat only certain foods, only foods prepared in certain ways, or only at certain times during religious holidays. For example, baked potatoes for lunch during Ramadan would not be acceptable for Moslems because they fast during the day during this extended holiday. Mashed potatoes with beef gravy would not be acceptable for a Hindu family that does not eat beef.

Review the range of variables that need to be considered in making choices about eating. Then conduct a series of role-plays with you serving as the key player/facilitator to assist students in examining and discussing the range of considerations that contribute to choice making about food. Use menus, coupons, newspaper advertisements, and other decision-making tools to add interest. Provide a list of prices for eating at home as well as at expensive, moderate, and inexpensive restaurants (Table 10). Here are some scenarios to include:

1. Robert and his mother have to watch their pennies because they have limited funds to spend on food. They rarely eat out; they never eat at expensive restaurants; they need to buy foods on sale and buy large quantities in bulk where appropriate. What could they eat for dinners this week that will be nutritious but not too expensive? If they decide to eat out, where could they go? Why? What could they order? Why?

2. Carlos, his five brothers and sisters, and his parents live near vegetable and fruit farms. Their father explains to the family that the food budget is $_____ per week. How should the family plan for the week? Can it afford to eat out at an expensive, moderate, or inexpensive restaurant? How can it take advantage of the local fruit and vegetable market?

3. Mary and Josh and their parents live in a high-rise apartment in a large city. Their parents tell them that they have about $_____ to spend on food for the week. What types of food planning should

TABLE 10 Home/Restaurant Comparison

AT HOME	AT A RESTAURANT		
LEAST EXPENSIVE	EXPENSIVE	MODERATE	INEXPENSIVE
$2.75 PER PERSON	$16.95 PER PERSON	$7.95 PER PERSON	$3.95 PER PERSON
Roast	Steak	Pot roast	Hamburger
Potatoes	French fries	Mashed potatoes	French fries
Carrots	Salad	Broccoli	Milk shake
Onions	Roll	Salad	
Lettuce salad	Apple pie	Roll	
Fresh fruit	Ice cream	Cherry cobbler	
Oatmeal cookie	Milk	Milk	
Milk			

they do? Should they make one trip to the supermarket? If so, what kinds of foods should they buy? Should they plan to eat out? If so, where—expensive, moderate, or inexpensive restaurants? How often? Explain your response.

The focus of the discussion should be choice making and the range of factors that enter into our decisions about eating. Factors to consider include cost (money available for buying food), personal taste, nutrition, time available for preparation, religious and cultural beliefs, and traditions. Review the factors using word cards. Post each card as it is addressed.

Activity

Have students (with their upper-grade partners) complete the first section of a choice-making activity sheet focusing on decisions they think would be appropriate for their individual family about the what, where, and why of eating dinner tonight. Provide a price list of foods available at the supermarket and restaurant menus/prices. After the second half of the activity sheet has been completed, urge students to share them with their families as a part of the home assignment. Then discuss it. Was it a realistic choice? Why was it selected? If another decision was made, why?

Summarize

People make many food choices. Decisions about foods include what to eat, when to eat, where to eat, how much to spend, and how the food should be prepared.

Assessment

Have students as a class write a group journal entry focusing on what it learned about food choices—the what, how, where, and why. Encourage them to read the group story to a family member as part of the home assignment.

Home Assignment

Have each student share the group story about choice making with a
family member and then engage in a discussion about the family's favorite restaurants. Send home copies of Figures 24 and 25 and encourage
the students to return it completed for a follow-up class discussion.

We have _____ family members.

1. <u>My ideas about my family's food choices</u>:

Tonight I think we should eat at _____ because _____

_____.

I think we should spend about $ _____ per person because _____

_____.

Food on our menu should include _____

because _____

_____

_____.

2. <u>My family's actual food choices</u>

Tonight we ate at _____ because _____

_____.

We spent about $ _____ per person because _____

_____

_____.

Foods on our menu tonight included

_____

_____

because _____

_____

_____.

FIGURE 24 My Family's Eating Choices

Why does eating at a restaurant usually cost our family more than eating at home?

_____

_____

List our family's favorite restaurants

1.

2.

3.

4.

5.

Why are these our favorites?

_____

_____

Which is most expensive? _____

Why?

_____

_____

_____

Which is least expensive? _____

Why?

_____

_____

_____

FIGURE 25 Family Discussion Guide

Lesson 15

....

Hunger

Resources

- Map of local area, highlighting locations of food sources for the needy (e.g., soup kitchens)
- Photos of local soup kitchens
- Student mentors

Children's Literature

DiSalvo-Ryan, D. (1991). *Uncle Willie and the Soup Kitchen*. New York: Morrow.

General Comments

This lesson is designed to expose students to a social issue—and to the importance of becoming socially conscious and active citizens. While young students are not capable of independently working to improve the human condition, they can, under adult guidance, get a sense of what it means to contribute to society. (Ideally, upper-grade student mentors are present for the entire lesson.)

General Purposes or Goals

To: (1) develop an understanding that in extreme cases, people are unable to pay for the food that they need; and (2) help students acquire a sensitivity for people in need and a desire to practice citizenship as it relates to assisting other people.

Main Ideas to Develop

- Sometimes people cannot pay for the foods they need, and the result is that they seek assistance from organizations in the community (e.g., food stamps from social services, a food bank, a soup kitchen).
- As members of the community, we can contribute to organizations that assist people in need of food by donating time, food, and money.

Teaching Tips from Barbara

Keep this lesson simple. Let the story do the talking. That way you can avoid any upsetting conversations if children in your class receive help for their family in this way. We also chose to connect this with a service-to-community project involving collecting food for the Red Cross.

Starting the Lesson

Discuss the home assignment and underscore the idea that we are very fortunate to be able to make choices about the foods we eat and where we eat them (e.g., in a fast-food restaurant, at home, at an expensive restaurant, etc.). However, there are people in the world who have few choices of where to eat or what to eat because they are poor, unemployed, or homeless.

Suggested Lesson Discussion

Each day in cities all across the country, volunteers and paid workers prepare meals to feed men, women, and children who come to eat at local soup kitchens. [Share a local map and plot the locations of soup kitchens where food is provided free or at a reduced price for those in need. Also show photos of these local places.] Religious organizations, neighborhood stores, food banks, individual donations, and money from the government support these efforts to provide hot meals to people in need.

Nationally, one out of every eight people is poor. Many of these individuals are children. Not all people who come to the soup kitchens to eat are unemployed or homeless. Sometimes working people do not make enough money to take care of their basic needs for food, shelter, and clothing. Sometimes elderly people live on small fixed incomes. In these situations, these people often come to soup kitchens for their main meal. The Salvation Army and the Rescue Mission are examples of local organizations that assist people in need of food. Some people in our community give money to these organizations to buy food for the hungry; others donate food; still others volunteer time to help those in need.

In this lesson you are going to hear about a boy about your age who is very curious about his uncle's volunteer work at a soup kitchen. One day the boy has a day off from school and goes with Uncle Willie to the soup kitchen. As you listen to the story, think about these questions:

Why would anybody want to work in a soup kitchen?
How would you describe the soup kitchen?
How did you feel when you observed all of these people in need?
How did Willie feel about his work at the soup kitchen—and about the people he helped feed?
Based on the boy's experience going to the soup kitchen with his Uncle Willie, would you be willing to go with an adult family member? Why? Why not?

Repeat these questions as part of the debriefing discussion after the reading. Then ask them what they—and their families—might do locally to help others in need.

Optional   Invite a local resource person to talk about a local organization that supports people in need and how, as members of the local community, we can contribute to assist people by donating time, food, and money.

Activity

Have students, as a class, write an editorial for the local newspaper explaining their ideas for helping people in the local community who are in need of food. Encourage the students to read a copy of the editorial to family members as part of the home assignment.

Summarize

Sometimes people have crises and are unable to pay for the food they need. There are places in our community that stand ready to assist. We, as members of the community, can help to support these organizations and those in need by donating time, food, and money.

Assessment

Have students meet with their upper-grade mentors to complete the following open-ended statements. Spelling could be displayed on the board.

1. A soup kitchen is described as _____ .
2. People go to soup kitchens because _____ .
3. Uncle Willie is a good citizen because _____ .
4. People in need can _____ .
5. Being a volunteer is _____ .
6. Places in our community where people can go to get food free or at a lower price include _____, _____, and _____ .

Dear Parents,

We would like at least one family member to serve as the audience as your child reads the editorial our class prepared explaining our ideas for helping people in our local community who are in need of food.

Discuss other ways we as members of the community and you as a family can contribute to this cause.

Sincerely,

FIGURE 26 Model Letter to Parents

Lesson 16

Review

Resources

- Tape recorder (optional)
- Time line bulletin board focusing on changes in food and food processes over time
- Posters of food pyramid, story of bananas, story of peanut butter, story of making grape jelly, can of food, class journal entries, etc.
- "In a Minute" game: key questions printed on strips of paper, timer, bag for the questions
- Adult volunteers for the carousel activity
- Markers (various colors) and question sheets for carousel activity

General Comments

For this lesson, students will have the opportunity to revisit the entire food unit and review the major understandings developed. The class will review the big ideas associated with the changes in food and food processes over time by using the bulletin board time line. Posters, props, and student work used previously during the lessons will be looked at again to stimulate discussion and reemphasize the key points.

The "In a Minute" game and a large-group carousel activity will also be used for pulling the unit together.

General Purposes and Goals

To: (1) draw on prior knowledge, understanding, appreciation, and applications conducted at home and at school that collectively will enhance meaningfulness and continued curiosity in learning about food; (2) revisit and reflect on the big ideas developed about food; and (3) provide students with an opportunity to experience authentic assessment by having parents in the food industry serve as their reviewers.

Main Ideas to Develop

- Food is a basic need.
- Food provides us with the nutrients needed to build strong and healthy bodies and give us energy.
- Some foods are especially healthful and nutritious (pyramid).
- People around the world tend to eat foods from these basic food groups. However, the foods may look quite different due to culture and geography. They may also taste different due to seasonings that people from different parts of the world prefer.

- People all over the world make choices about the foods they eat due to availability (geography and climate), personal preferences, and cultural values.
- Snacks are "small meals" or food eaten between meals. Since our bodies are growing, we may need the extra nutrients and calories (fuel) provided by snacks. Snacks can be a part of a healthy diet if we choose them carefully.
- People very long ago hunted and fished for food. Then they began to domesticate animals. (They became herders.) Later, people began to raise their own crops.
- Farming has changed over time. Early farmers often were only able to raise enough food for their own families.
- In the early days, people's diets reflected the availability of local foods. This pattern still exists to some extent, but modern transportation has allowed choices to be expanded.
- New methods for producing (seeds), growing (irrigation and rotation), caring for (spraying with pesticides), and harvesting (combines, pickers, dryers) foods have been developed.
- Modern technology enables farmers to raise more than they need for their own families, so they can sell their crops and use the money (income) to buy things that they can't make themselves.
- Food comes from many different kinds of farms. Farmers usually grow crops and raise animals that do well in their climate and the kinds of land (plains, grasslands) found where they live.
- The natural resources of good soil, clean air, rain, and warm sunshine help farmers all over the world to raise food for people in our communities.
- Some people live far away from where food is produced.
- Bananas are an example of a food that is grown only in certain parts of the world due to climatic conditions but can be transported to other parts of the world. Bananas must be carefully preserved from the time they are picked until they reach the supermarket.
- Peanuts are an example of a food that is grown only in certain parts of the world due to climatic conditions, but they can be transported to other parts of the world.
- The land-to-hand story of peanut butter begins with the planting of peanuts and is complete when jars of peanut butter are placed on the shelf in the store.
- About half of all the peanuts grown in the United States are eaten in the form of peanut butter. Peanuts or peanut products are ingredients for many recipes, for making cooking and salad

oils, and for making some products that we don't eat (soap, shampoo, paint, etc.).

- There are many more people who buy peanuts and peanut butter than there are farmers who grow peanuts.

- The land-to-hand story of pasta begins with the planting of grain (wheat) and is completed when the pasta is packaged and ready for purchase (some people today make their own pasta).

- The pasta looks very different from the grain from which it originated. Several steps occur that transform its appearances.

- Apple pie begins with the planting of wheat for the flour for the pie crust, and the planting of the apple seed for the filling. The pie requires ingredients from various places around the world.

- Ingredients for an apple pie, as for many foods that we eat, reflect our global connections.

- Division of labor and interdependence are reflected in the places and processes needed to produce a complex food such as an apple pie.

- Foods are prepared in a variety of ways and can be bought in a variety of preserved forms (e.g., beef—fresh, dried, canned).

- The layout of the supermarket is planned to make the foods look appealing, to place food in the appropriate environmental conditions, and to make it accessible.

- We pay for foods directly as well as indirectly. Indirectly we pay for the harvesting, shipping, advertising, storing, and workers' wages. We even pay indirectly for the electricity that keeps foods at the appropriate temperature while they are stored at the supermarket.

- Some foods (e.g., bread) are found throughout the world; however, they take different forms because different grains are grown in different places due to climate, weather, and types of land formations, and due to differences in culture and economics.

- Almost every food can be shipped to any place in the world; however, transportation costs can be very expensive.

- People eat special foods for special occasions. Often this is due to their culture and personal preference.

- Some people eat (or refrain from eating) certain foods due to their religious beliefs, health reasons, or personal preferences (e.g., vegetarian).

- People make choices about the foods they eat: what they eat, where they eat, and how the food is prepared.

- Location, climatic conditions, seasons, weather, availability of food items, cost, family size, personal preferences, and religious beliefs influence our choices.

- Sometimes people cannot pay for the foods they need, and so they seek assistance from organizations in the community (e.g., food stamps from social services, food bank, soup kitchen).
- As members of the community, we can contribute to organizations that assist people in need of food by donating time, food, and money.

Teaching Tips from Barbara

Playing the "In a Minute" game works very well to review. I would suggest that you tape-record the answers. You can publish the answers later and send them home. Continue to focus on the fact that the functions of food are the same worldwide, but those needs are met differently by different people. If your students have never done a carousel activity before, you might want to practice doing one with very simple poster headings first, such as: colors, foods, pets, games, and TV shows. That way, they can concentrate on the information instead of the structure of the activity.

Starting the Lesson

Begin the lesson by reviewing the home assignment from Lesson 15. (If time permits, make a graph depicting favorite restaurants. Briefly discuss reasons.) Then indicate that this lesson will conclude the formal unit on food, although books about food will be available in the room library and students may want to do additional reading about food. Remind students, too, that many of them will be experiencing special foods during the holidays—and that they'll have a chance to apply much of what they learned (e.g., the need for practicing the guidelines of the food pyramid—especially during holiday time when so many tempting but not particularly healthy foods are available).

First, hold an interactive review discussion focusing on the changes in food and food processes over time, using the bulletin board time line as the stimulus for discussion. Then ask the students to revisit the posters, props, and student work from the unit and review the big ideas formulated during the lessons. Encourage them to raise questions and engage in comprehensive review.

The third segment of the lesson is a game called "In a Minute." One student, who has been designated as "it," will pull a strip of paper from a bag. On each strip is a theme/big idea discussed during the unit. The student has one minute (specified by a timer) to share what he or she has learned about the topic.

Model the rules of the activity and select the first student participant. The student selects a strip (e.g., rice farm, wheat farm, truck farm, food pyramid, snack foods, story of bananas, story of peanuts, the supermarket, people in need of food, etc.) and shares key points about it. After one minute, you and the other students clear up any misconceptions related during the response. Then the student who was "it" selects a new participant.

The final section of the review is a "carousel" activity that involves the entire class. Write five to seven questions at the tops of large pieces of paper. Suggested questions are:

1. What did you learn about food groups?
2. What are the functions of food?
3. What have you learned about snacks?
4. What are some of the changes that have occurred in foods/food processes over time?
5. What foods do we eat that were not available to cave dwellers and pioneers?
6. What are some of the decisions families have to make about food?
7. Why do some foods cost more than others?
8. How can we help people in need of food?

Engage adult volunteers or older students with writing and reading competencies to act as facilitators. Place about five students and one facilitator in each group and give each group a different colored marker. Students will rotate around the room, huddling in groups around the posted question sheets. For five minutes, the facilitator writes the group's responses to the question. Then the groups rotate clockwise. The facilitator should review all groups' responses and make any needed clarifications.

Unit 2: Clothing

Introduction

. . . .

As a way to help you think about clothing as a cultural universal and begin to plan your teaching on the topic, we have provided a list of questions that address some of the big ideas developed in our unit plans (Figure 1). The questions focus on what we believe are the most important ideas for children to learn about clothing. These include its basic nature (garments are woven from thread, which is spun from cotton, wool, or some other raw material) and purposes (protection, modesty, decoration, and communication of personal identity or values). Other important ideas include knowledge about the ways in which clothing has evolved over time, clothing worn in different places and cultures, clothing worn in different settings (business, work, play), and issues to consider in making decisions about clothing.

To find out what primary-grade students know (or think they know) about these questions, we interviewed more than fifty students in each of grades K–3. You may want to use some or all of these questions yourself during preunit or prelesson assessments of your students' prior knowledge (see Figure 1). For now, though, we recommend that you jot down your own answers to the questions, before going on to read about the answers that we elicited in our interviews. This will sharpen your awareness of ways in which adults' knowledge about clothing differs from children's knowledge, as well as reduce the likelihood that you will assume that your students already know certain things that seem obvious to you but may need to be spelled out for them.

If you want to use some of the questions to assess your students' prior knowledge before beginning the unit, you can do this either by interviewing selected students individually or by asking the class as a

1. All over the world, people wear clothes. Do they wear clothes because they need to, or just because they want to? . . . Why? [If child's response only mentions keeping warm] Do they wear clothes in warm places like Hawaii? . . . Why?

2. Bankers and lawyers and certain other business people wear business clothes. Can you describe these business clothes that bankers or lawyers wear? . . . Why do they wear these clothes?

3. People who work on farms or in factories wear work clothes. Can you describe these work clothes? . . . Why do workers wear work clothes?

4. When we are just relaxing at home, we wear casual clothes, or play clothes. Can you describe these play clothes? . . . Why do we wear play clothes when we want to relax or play?

5. Some workers wear uniforms, like the police or the people who work at McDonald's. Why do some workers wear uniforms?

6. What are our clothes made from? . . . What do we call this material that clothes are made out of?

7. [If child has not said so already, say, "Our clothes are made out of cloth."] What is cloth made from? . . . How is _____ made into cloth?

8. [Show spool of thread] Most cloth is made by weaving it from threads. Where do threads come from? [If necessary, probe by asking, "How is thread made from _____?"]

9. Let's talk about clothing in the past. Way back when people lived in caves—what kind of clothes did they wear? . . . What were their clothes made of? . . . How did they make the _____ into clothes?

10. Back in the days of the Pilgrims and the pioneers, what kind of clothes did people wear? What were these clothes made of? . . . Where did the pioneers get their clothes?

11. Back when your great-grandparents were children, what were people's clothes like? . . . How were clothes back then different from today's clothes?

12. How have today's clothes been improved over clothes in the past? . . . Do you know about any inventions that have made clothes better than they used to be?

13. How do you think your shirt [dress] was made? . . . What was the first step in making it? . . . Then what? [Probe for specifics of process, not just statements about what it was made from.]

14. Where do you think your shirt [dress] was made? [If child says, "In a factory," ask, "Where do you think the factory is?"]

15. Are there people in other parts of the world who dress differently than we do? . . . Tell me about that. . . . Why do they dress like that?

16. Are clothes today easier or harder to take care of than they used to be? . . . Why?

17. Let's talk about shopping for clothes. If you were going to buy a shirt, where would you go to buy it? . . . Why? . . . How would you decide what shirt to buy? . . . Would you think about anything besides _____ when deciding what shirt to buy?

18. Along with our clothes, we wear shoes. What are our shoes made from? [If child says "Leather," ask, "What is leather?"] . . . Are there other shoes that are made out of different materials?

19. [Show picture of shoe.] How do you think this shoe was made? . . . What was the first step? . . . Then what?

FIGURE 1 (Continued)

whole to respond to the questions and recording their answers for future reference. If you take the latter approach, an option would be to embed it within the KWL technique by initially questioning students to determine what they <u>k</u>now and what they <u>w</u>ant to find out, then later revisiting their answers and recording what they <u>l</u>earned. An alternative to preassessing your students' knowledge about topics developed in the unit as a whole would be to conduct separate preassessments prior to each lesson, using only the questions that apply to that lesson (and perhaps adding others of your own choosing).

Children's Responses to Our Interviews

Students' responses to these questions generally improve as they progress through the K–3 range, especially between first grade and second grade. However, the most interesting findings involved variation in knowledge displayed by the group as a whole in their answers to different questions. Even most kindergartners were able to supply acceptable answers to some questions, but even most third graders were unable to supply acceptable responses to other questions.

More than 90 percent of the students understood that clothing is a basic need, although a few said that this depends on the climate (i.e., people who live in warm places don't need clothes). In describing the functions of clothing, 72 percent mentioned protection against cold and 42 percent mentioned modesty, whereas only 16 percent mentioned protection against dirt, sun, insects, or other hazards; only 5 percent mentioned clothing's decorative functions; and only a few mentioned that clothing can be a way to express one's identity or values.

About three-fourths of the students accurately described business clothes as semiformal attire (although some of them referred to tuxedos instead of suits or sport jackets). About three-fourths also accurately described work clothes as old, worn clothes that you do not mind getting dirty or as heavy clothes that provide protection to workers. Almost all of the students accurately described play clothes as jeans, T-shirts, sweatshirts, shorts, or other casual clothes (including pajamas). In general, responses to these initial questions tended to be accurate and free of misconceptions.

This was not true of responses to the next questions about the nature of cloth and thread. Most students said that clothing is made from cloth, but only 25 percent understood that cloth is woven fabric. Many thought that cloth is a solid (like leather or plastic), or that it is made by pressing raw material (e.g., fluffy cotton) flat. Even fewer students (13 percent) understood that thread is spun from raw material. The rest could not explain, said that thread is made by unraveling existing cloth, or guessed that it is a natural material (hair, animal fur, etc.). Thus, although most students understood the basic functions of clothing and were familiar with different types of clothes, most did not understand the basic nature and manufacturing of cloth. In attempting to describe how cloth is made, students often depicted pieces of wool or cotton being glued or sewn to a (presumably solid) cloth substrate. Among the minority of students who did understand that clothing is woven, some were confined to a "knitting" model, in which the entire garment is woven/knitted in one continuous operation from beginning to end. The others articulated a "parts assembly" model, in which patterns are used to cut pieces of woven cloth into shaped garment components, which are then stitched together to form the complete garment.

Responses to questions about evolution of clothing over time indicated that half or more of the students were able to describe the clothing of prehistoric cave dwellers, the pilgrims or pioneers, or their great-great grandparents, or to describe ways in which today's clothes are improved over clothes from the past. Most of the responses concerning cave dwellers' clothing reflected the stereotypes shown in the Flintstones and Alley Oop cartoons, and most descriptions of Pilgrim clothing clearly were based on illustrations shown in history texts, children's literature, or movies and television programs about the Pilgrims. Descriptions of pioneers' clothing were more varied, although clearly influenced by the buckskin outfits shown in history texts, children's literature, and movies and television programs about Daniel Boone, Davy Crockett, and other pioneer heroes. The students did not have a clear stereotype to work from in talking about clothing when their great-great grandparents were children. Most said that clothes at that time were similar to today's clothes but perhaps heavier or less colorful.

Explanations about how today's clothes are improved over clothes from earlier times tended to focus on aesthetics (our clothes are more colorful, decorated with pictures or designs, etc.). Few students talked about today's clothes as being more comfortable, better at keeping us warm, lighter or softer, or available in better variety and quantity. Furthermore, only 25 percent were able to name one or more inventions that have made clothes better (typically, the sewing machine). Several students were under the impression that earlier clothes were sewn poorly and fell apart easily.

Questions about whether clothes are easier or harder to take care of today produced interesting differences of opinion relating to how the students interpreted the phrase "to take care of." A majority stated that clothes are easier to take care of today because of modern machines (washers and dryers), better fabrics (more durable, easy care), and modern storage (closets, hampers). However, a minority suggested that clothes are harder to take care of today because we have more clothes to keep track of and higher cleanliness expectations in modern business environments.

Responses to questions about modern clothing manufacture reflected the students' lack of knowledge about the nature of cloth. When asked how their shirt or dress was made, most students spoke of sewing (already existing) pieces of cloth together to form the basic garment and then adding color, trim, or decorative design. Only 5 percent spoke of spinning thread or yarn and only 29 percent spoke of weaving cloth. Students who made reference to machines sometimes described large pressing machines that would "smish" raw cotton or wool into cloth as part of the manufacturing process. Older students usually understood that manufacturing clothing in factories is not the same as making garments at home using patterns and a simple sewing machine, but they had not yet developed clear images of the processes involved in mass production. Consequently, they tended to give "black box" explanations of automated clothing manufacture (e.g., "Then they put the cloth into a machine that makes it into a shirt"). Many of these students did not realize that machines in factories perform essentially the same steps that are performed by individuals making clothes at home (cutting cloth to form major parts of the garment following pattern specifications, then stitching these together to form the basic garment, etc.). A few students thought that one machine produced garments that were all the same size, and these then were moved on to other machines for shrinking or stretching to create other sizes.

When asked where their shirt or dress was probably made, 29 percent of the students guessed that it was made in or near the store where it was purchased, and only 27 percent said that it was probably made at a location where raw materials are plentiful. When asked why they would select a particular shirt, the majority mentioned appearance, color, or design/print (along with fit). Much smaller numbers mentioned price, fabric, or other issues (matches current wardrobe, suited to gender, well made, matches current style/fashion, etc.). Answers to these questions were generally sensible and free of misconceptions, although they reflected greater preoccupation with the shirt's appearance and less concern about its cost or quality than most adults would express.

When asked whether people in other parts of the world dress differently than we do, more than 90 percent of the students said yes, but fewer than 25 percent could give specific examples (Mexican sombreros, Chinese robes, Indian saris, etc.). Others could only offer explanations based on climate (fewer/lighter clothes in hot climates) or economic development (a few students noted that some people lack access to our variety of clothing and have to make their own clothes). Along with the misconception that clothes are made in or near the stores that sell them, the students' ideas about clothing in other parts of the world indicated limited understanding of ways that geography and climate interact with economics and culture.

The students' responses concerning shoes paralleled their responses concerning clothing. That is, although most were able to respond accurately to initial questions about the nature of shoes (made of leather, fabric, rubber, etc.), only a minority could respond accurately when probed for deeper understanding. Only about half of the students mentioned leather, and only half of those understood that leather is animal hide. The others could not explain what it is or thought that it is a type of cloth or that it is made from glue and fabric, from rubber and tar, from wax, from string, and so on.

Responses concerning steps in the manufacture of shoes were often vague but accurate as far as they went. However, a few interesting misconceptions emerged: a shoe is a single piece of leather rather than a product assembled by combining separate parts; shoes are made by reprocessing the leather and buckles of old belts; and first one type of machine is used to make a standard-sized shoe and then other machines are used to make these shoes larger or smaller to create additional sizes.

Overall, the students displayed more knowledge and fewer misconceptions about clothing than about shelter, probably because clothing is much less complex and does not incorporate as many key understandings. Even so, the students once again were focused more on easily observable forms and functions of the cultural universal than on less obvious cause-effect relationships and explanations. Levels of understanding increased across the K–3 range, but even at third grade, fewer than half of the students understood the fundamental nature of cloth or thread.

Replicating a major finding from the shelter study, these findings on clothing provide more evidence that K–3 students have little awareness of the geographic and economic reasons why particular types of human artifacts are favored in particular climates and locations. A few students displayed glimmerings of understandings that geographical locations differ in their natural resources and that societies differ in their degrees of economic development, but no student could generate specific explanations for why clothing is manufactured in particular places or why certain people have more clothing options available to them than others.

Some of the responses to questions about how people dress in other parts of the world were troubling because they reflected stereotypes. Several suggested that students already possessed negative stereotypes of Mexicans, Africans, and even African Americans. These troublesome themes were more prominent in responses to the clothing interview than in responses to the shelter interview, perhaps because the students tended to attribute housing differences mostly to differences in access to resources, but to attribute clothing differences more to differences in cultural style or preference. Only a few students explicitly communicated a sense of moral superiority to people whom they identified as dressing differently, but most implied a preference for the familiar and had difficulty understanding how people might prefer something different. Thus, just as K–3 students show a tendency toward presentism in their attitudes toward people and technology from the past (tending to disparage what is primitive by modern standards), they show a tendency toward chauvinism in their attitudes toward unfamiliar contemporary cultures and technology. These findings again emphasize the need to "make strange familiar" for students by helping them to empathize with people they are studying, view them in the context of their time and place, and appreciate their culture and technology as adaptive rather than exotic, inexplicable, or indicative of intellectual or moral deficiencies. For a detailed technical report of findings from our interviews on clothing, see Brophy and Alleman (1999).

Overview of the Clothing Unit
—Barbara Knighton

Clothing is a great cultural universal to start with. All children wear clothing and see clothes every day, but most have never really given it much thought. Once you start them down the "I wonder" path, they will begin generating many questions about their formerly taken-for-granted clothing—questions about the origins and content of fabric, clothing from the past and other countries, and clothing manufacturing.

This is a great unit for lots of hands-on artifacts. Before you begin teaching, start to collect articles of clothing that students can touch, examine, and perhaps even try on. Get parents involved by asking for culturally specific clothes or pictures of family members in special clothing. Another terrific source for artifacts is garage sales and secondhand stores. Be on the lookout for things that your students might not have seen before. Also, check with your local fabric stores to find one that might be willing to donate small scraps of fabric. You won't need much of each fabric, but be sure to label each piece with its name and fiber content.

Parent involvement during the clothing unit is important but relatively simple. Parents will be asked to explore closets, read clothing labels, discuss decision-making processes, and share their history with clothes, to name a few. I have found that I receive many of these assignments back because they don't require "right or wrong" answers, just information.

Throughout this unit, there are many opportunities for students to write. It often works well to save these assignments for your class writing time. Another suggestion is to pair your students with older mentors to help with the writing. One way to manage the writing is to put together a journal of all of the response sheets so that at the end you will have a compilation of all the writing from the unit. It's a nice way to assess student learning and share information with parents. Try to use a combination of close-ended prompts (e.g., "Clothing protects people by _____") and open-ended questions (e.g., "Why do people wear clothes?").

Send a letter home briefly outlining the learning for this unit. Include the things that you'd like parents to send to school to help with the lessons. Also, suggest that parents start discussing clothing with their children to get them interested and excited about the new unit.

Finally, be sure to keep the big ideas in mind as you teach. The more often you come back to those ideas in different discussions and in different ways, the more students will begin to internalize them. Don't allow yourself to get overinvolved with specific details of the lessons and miss out on the important ideas.

Lesson 1

Functions of Clothing

Resources

- Large sheets of paper
- Pictures and books in the interest center focusing on clothing
- Bulletin board or larger poster that has been started and depicts the functions of clothing: protection, communication, decoration, and modesty
- Props to represent the four functions of clothing (hat for protection from sun and wool jacket for protection from cold weather; football jerseys for communication; shawl or glitzy jacket for decoration; and blouse for modesty)
- A "clothing corner" or learning center with a trunk of clothing articles for the students to try on or use in dramatics and role-plays
- Uniform worn by a parent, such as a firefighter outfit, which children can take turns putting on (optional)
- *World Book Encyclopedia*. (1994). Chicago: World Book, Inc., A Scott Fetzer Co. Vol. 4, pp. 686–692. (Electronic version also available)

Children's Literature

Borden, Louise. (1989). *Caps, Hats, Socks, and Mittens*. New York: Scholastic, Inc.

Morris, Ann. (1989). *Hats. Hats. Hats*. New York: Scholastic, Inc.

Rowland-Warne, L. (1992). *Costume*. New York: Alfred A. Knopf.

General Comments

To launch the unit, collect the instructional resources and display visual prompts to generate interest in the topic. Post questions (written on wide strips of paper) around the room and on the bulletin board. These might include: Why do people wear clothing? Why do they wear different kinds of clothing at different times? How do climate and geography influence the types of clothing people wear?

General Purposes or Goals

To help students: (1) understand why people wear clothing (protection, communication, decoration, and modesty); and (2) acquire an appreciation for cultural diversity that exists in the nature and functions of clothing.

Main Ideas to Develop

- Clothing is a basic human need.
- Throughout history, people have used clothing for protection from the elements (sun in hot weather, cold in cold weather, precipitation); communication (self-expression, group identity); decoration (status, ceremonies); and to conform to codes of modesty.
- People in various cultures dress differently for many reasons. They may need protection from different kinds of weather, use different methods and materials for making cloth, or have different customs or habits of dress.

Teaching Tips from Barbara

Actual clothing examples and pictures are the keys to this lesson. *People* magazine is a great resource for color picture examples of clothing. Another good and authentic assessment is to have students orally analyze a piece of clothing they are wearing. The closet inventory exercise is a fun one, and the information can be shared easily in the whole group or in small groups.

Starting the Lesson

Pose questions regarding the functions of clothing. Sample questions might include: Why do people wear clothing? Why do they wear different kinds of clothing at different times? How do climate and geography influence the types of clothing people wear? What kinds of protective clothing are available for hot weather? Cold weather? How do people communicate by what they wear? Why do people like to wear decorative clothing?

After preliminary discussion of these questions, show the class a bulletin board that you have begun as a way to show the functions of clothing. It should contain four headings: protection, communication, decoration, and modesty.

Use the following information as introductory material for each category. You can personalize the learning by starting with your interests. For example, if you are a sports fan, you could start with a team jacket or hat and ask the students why they think you wear it. Throughout the lesson, add props and pictures into the conversation. Encourage students to bring pictures to add to the appropriate categories over the next several days. As more data become available, encourage students to share their knowledge and insights in both visual and written/oral forms. Guided discussions should focus on how and why the cultural universal—clothing—functions as it does. Spend time on higher-order thinking: Why do you think the UPS drivers dress as they do? Why do some people wear very fancy clothes for a wedding and others do not?

Suggested Lesson Discussion

Protection   Humans lack the natural protection that most animals have. Our skin is easily pierced or bruised. Also, we don't have thick skin or fur, so we have to depend on protective coverings to enable us to survive in extreme climates.

In arctic climates, early humans realized that the fur coat that kept animals from freezing to death might also help them survive. Later, people began to wear many layers of clothing to keep warm. Air spaces between the layers served as insulation against the cold.

In warm climates, people wear clothes of lightweight materials such as cotton or linen, which have fairly open weaves. These fabrics absorb perspiration and allow air to flow around the body. Other warm-climate clothes include light-colored clothes that reflect the sun's rays, open sandals that keep the feet cool, and large hats, often made of straw, that protect the face and neck from the sun. In the Arabian desert, for example, people often wear loose, flowing garments as protection from the hot sun.

In our part of the world where we have four seasons, we have a fall/winter wardrobe to keep us warm (e.g., sweater, sweatshirt, long trousers, coats, mittens, etc.) and a spring/summer wardrobe to keep us cool (e.g., shorts, short-sleeved shirts, etc.). [*Caps, Hats, Socks, and Mittens* could be shown. It is about the four seasons and includes good pictures.]

Besides clothing to protect them from the elements, humans learned to design special clothing to protect them when they were hunting animals or fighting against human enemies. Hide or wicker shields and helmets came into use long before the age of metals. Later came quilted cotton armor, metal shields and helmets, leather breastplates, and so on. Much later came camouflage clothing that was designed to blend into the landscape and was made of materials appropriate to the climate.

More recently, we have developed specialized clothing for people in certain occupations, such as surgeons' gowns or auto mechanics' coveralls. Astronauts and deep-sea divers wear special suits and helmets for protection against changes in air pressure and temperature. The hazards of industry and the challenges of space travel have increased the need for special types of protective clothing that are safe, comfortable, and durable. We will talk more about this in our next lesson, which is about special clothing.

Communication   Another function of clothing is to communicate. Clothing can communicate how people feel. In our society, clothing with bright colors and bold designs may indicate happiness, whereas people in mourning may wear black. Such color designations vary across cultures, however. Many brides in the United States wear white, while in India white is worn for mourning.

Sometimes people wear clothes to indicate what they want to be. Children use clothes to play "grown up" and imitate adults in certain roles, and teenagers choose clothes that signify favored values or lifestyles.

Clothing is used to communicate what people do (police uniforms), what team or club they belong to (hockey uniforms or Brownie uniforms), what team they like (logo on shirt), or what country or army they represent (costume or military uniform). Some professional people wear uniforms and others do not. Sometimes this is because the organizations where they work have rules about what people should wear. For example, some banks require their workers to wear suits, and ties, while other banks allow more casual clothes. In many places, norms and expectations are becoming more casual and relaxed; however, workers are expected to dress neatly.

Decoration People wear clothing for decoration. They may wear shirts with a logo they like or because they identify with characters on TV programs. People often think decorative clothing makes them look attractive. People often wear ceremonial costumes with decorative features. These include feathers, paint, jewels, and so on.

Decoration is also related to style, which keeps changing. A person may stop wearing a suit or dress not because it is worn out, but because it is out of style. Style can be fun because it adds novelty and variety to our lives, and certain styles of clothing can make us look more attractive. However, styles also can be arbitrary, restricting, or oppressive.

Modesty Standards of modesty vary with cultures as well as with changing social conditions. The concept of modesty held by native women of the Congo, where nothing may be worn above the waist, differs greatly from the concept of modesty held by Moslem women, who cover their entire bodies and veil their faces. In our part of the world, there is a generally accepted concept of modesty, although what is acceptable at home may differ from what is required in public. Most people need to wear clothes once they are old enough to go to school.

In many public settings, we are expected not only to meet modesty standards, but to wear certain types of clothing. Clothing expectations vary from the informality of beaches and ball parks, to the "No Shirt/ No Shoes/No Service" rules in many restaurants, to the more formal dress codes that are enforced, or at least expected, at certain restaurants, in certain work places, and at church services, weddings, and funerals.

Hats. Hats. Hats by Ann Morris provides illustrations of the functions of clothing. It includes modesty if you take into account the religious dimension.

Activity

After you've described the functional uses of clothing, ask students to share (in triads) the most interesting ideas they learned. Then elicit ideas from the groups and write these ideas on the board. Ask the students to indicate other questions they would like to have answered about the functions of clothing. Post the new questions and encourage individuals to find information to share with the class. Make sure numerous library books are available.

Alternately, have students place a set of pictures into categories and explain their reasoning. They may wish to work in small groups. Note that students will see that some pictures can fit into more than one category. For example, a sports-related jacket might be worn for protection against cold weather and also to communicate that the individual likes a particular team.

Summarize

- Clothing serves many functions.
- Some of these functions are universal across time and cultures.
- During one's life, clothing will probably serve all of the functions described in the lesson.
- Protection and modesty are probably the most important functions of clothing among children.

Assessment

Have students quietly brainstorm at their tables the things they learned about clothing related to protection, communication, decoration, and modesty. Then ask them to read the statements shown in Figure 2 and then list examples that represent each category. If time permits, they can draw pictures to illustrate their responses. Begin the next lesson with your responses to these statements.

Home Assignment

Encourage students to share with their families what they have learned about the functions of clothing and to bring a clothing example to school that serves one or more of the functions. A display will be created, so unique items are desired. The display will serve as the stimulus for an expanded and enriched discussion regarding the purposes and uses of clothing.

Send home copies of Figure 3. As students complete the closet inventory exercise, they can revisit the functions of clothing and realize that many articles of clothing serve more than one function.

Name _____

Journal Entry—Lesson 1

People wear clothing because

1. They need protection. Examples: _____

_____

_____

_____

2. They want to communicate who they are. Examples: _____

_____

_____

3. They want to decorate themselves. Examples: _____

_____

_____

4. They want to be modest and cover their private parts. Examples: _____

_____

_____

FIGURE 2 Journal Entry: Lesson 1

Name _____

With a parent or older brother or sister, look through one or more of your closets. List articles of clothing that represent each of the clothing functions. (One article of clothing might serve more than one function. For example, a shawl might serve as protection from the cool air and it might also be decorative.)

PROTECTION	COMMUNICATION	DECORATION	MODESTY
1.	1.	1.	1
2.	2.	2.	2.
3.	3.	3.	3.
4.	4.	4.	4.
5.	5.	5.	5

As a family, discuss functions of clothing. If possible, bring articles of clothing to school for a display on the functions of clothing.

FIGURE 3 Home Assignment: A Look in Closets

Lesson 2

. . . .

Special Clothing

Resources

- Articles of clothing to represent specialness (e.g., fire fighter's hat, Easter bonnet, overalls, etc.)
- Cutout pictures of clothing appropriate for festivals and carnivals; birthdays, mourning, weddings; recreational activities (clothes for sports, etc.); jobs (uniforms and work clothes)
- Word cards (factors that contribute to specialness): culture, gender, climate, economics, careers
- Graphic to depict special clothing and contributing factors
- *Jeopardy*-like instructional activity as review (optional)

Children's Literature

Carle, E. (1994). *My Apron*. New York: Scholastic, Inc.

Childcraft (Vol. 8, pp. 62–63; Vol. 9, pp. 144–145). Chicago: World Book, Inc.

Geringer, L. (1987). *A Three Hat Day*. Mexico: Harper Trophy.

Kindersley, B., & Kindersley, A. (1995). *Children Just Like Me*. New York: Dorling Kindersley, in association with United Nations Children's Fund.

Neitzel, S. (1992). *The Dress I'll Wear to the Party*. New York: Scholastic, Inc.

Waters, K., & Slovenz-Low, M. (1990). *Lion Dancer*. New York: Scholastic, Inc.

Winthrop, E. (1986). *Shoes*. Mexico: Harper Trophy.

General Comments

Show students pictures that depict a range of special types of clothing. Refer to the articles of clothing that the students brought to depict protection, communication, decoration, and modesty. Encourage them to share stories about the special garments.

Other factors that are related to special clothing include culture, gender, climate, careers, and economics. People wear special clothing to perform certain jobs, to take part in recreational activities, to celebrate holidays, to participate in festivals, and to express certain emotions (e.g., weddings, funerals, etc.).

General Purposes or Goals

- To develop knowledge, understanding, appreciation, and life application regarding clothing considerations for special situations: festivals and carnivals, birthdays, mourning, weddings, recreational activities, and jobs.
- To develop knowledge, understanding, appreciation, and life application regarding factors that contribute to "specialness": culture, gender, climate, careers, and economics.

Main Ideas to Develop

- People wear special clothing to participate in festivals, celebrate holidays and special occasions, take part in recreational activities, and perform certain jobs.
- Cultures, gender, climate, careers, and economics are all factors related to special types of clothing.

Teaching Tips from Barbara

For simplicity, you can use the pictures and articles of clothing from Lesson 1. It is important to tie the information from Lesson 1 to this lesson. For example, a firefighter chooses her clothing because of her work. The clothing she chooses protects her from the fire and communicates what her job is. The homework assignment is a longer survey. You might want to adjust the length or the questions to fit your students.

Starting the Lesson

Share the results of the home assignment from Lesson 1. Then explain that there are other ways of thinking about clothing. One way is specialness.

Use the display of clothing and pictures to explain special clothing. You might begin by talking about your own special clothing that relates to holidays you celebrate, as well as special clothing that your family members wear for their jobs, for recreation, and for celebrations. Factors to consider include culture, gender, climate, careers, and economics. Show and describe various items from your closet that you have worn during the past year for special occasions (e.g., Halloween costume, special dress or suit for a wedding, Easter hat, etc.). Then show several clothing items that you have borrowed from a friend. Note that individuals interpret specialness differently. (For example, your friend has a special hat that's worn for religious occasions, a jacket that is special because a relative brought it from Spain, etc.). The following information provides a sampling of what you might include. The information can be as expansive as you desire.

Suggested Lesson Discussion

Holidays, Festivals, and Carnivals   Holidays, festivals, and carnivals are occasions when special clothing is often worn. Easter and Halloween are days when children tend to dress up. A carnival that is somewhat popular in the United States is the Mardi Gras celebration in New Orleans. On that occasion, people wear costumes and dance in the streets.

The Chinese celebrate their new year with costumes and dances. The lion is one of the animals made for performing the dances during the celebration. [Show the book *Lion Dancer* or a similar trade book that illustrates how different cultures celebrate.]

Birthdays, Mourning, Weddings   Some families wear special clothing for celebrating their birthdays (for example, party hats and special "dress up" clothes). It merely adds to the festivity.

Some cultures have special clothing for certain occasions. In North America and Europe, people often wear black clothing or black arm bands when a member of their family dies. In India, China, and other countries, however, people often wear white clothing when someone they love has died.

Weddings are occasions where certain traditions are expressed through clothing. At most Shinto weddings in Japan, brides wear beautiful traditional kimonos and cover their faces with white powder. In America, men often wear tuxedos and women wear special bride and bridesmaid dresses for traditional, formal weddings.

Recreation   Football players wear special helmets and lots of padding for protection. Their uniforms are made of very sturdy cloth that stretches (spandex), and they wear special shoes with metal cleats to prevent slipping. Team members wear the same uniforms, which helps players to locate their teammates and helps fans to identify the players (because the players have individual numbers). Other team sports, such as hockey, baseball, and basketball, also use special uniforms to designate who is on their team and help fans identify team members.

Skiers, snowmobilers, mountain climbers, and joggers use special clothing for their individual sports. Choices are based on factors such as the amount of protection needed, climatic conditions, and the amount of money the individual decides to spend on specialized clothing. Pajamas are worn for sleeping, and often they are worn as casual attire when at home.

When we are relaxing at home, we usually wear casual or play clothes so we will be more comfortable and so we won't soil our dress clothes. Some people buy nylon warm-up suits or jeans to wear as play clothes, while others wear their old dress clothes. Again, pajamas are worn for sleeping and often are worn as casual attire when at home.

Work   Farmers and factory workers usually wear overalls or blue jeans that are made of sturdy materials that won't easily tear, often with pockets for tools. Many factory workers have special protective clothing such as hats, goggles, gloves, or masks.

Some occupations require special clothing for protection and/or identity. Examples include astronauts, military personnel, fire fighters, police officers, postal workers, hospital employees, and fast-food employees such as people who work at McDonald's or Burger King. They wear what are known as *uniforms*. Some jobs require aprons or hats (e.g., baker). [Share *My Apron* and connect back to Lesson 1.]

Some businesses don't require uniforms but do require people to dress up (e.g., bankers, lawyers). Some offices even have dress codes, although more and more organizations are going casual.

Choices People Have   People have a lot of choices of what to wear in most situations. Many types of work allow lots of choices in wearing apparel. For example, in many workplaces men can decide whether or not they will wear ties and jackets, and women can decide if they will wear suits, skirts and blouses, or slacks. For holidays, you can decide whether or not you want to "dress up" for the occasion. If you decide to participate in a certain sport, you may be required to wear special hats or shoes. You decide how much to spend and whether to buy new or used equipment. Also, there are cases where special articles of clothing are needed for protection or identity.

Some people choose to wear certain articles of clothing because they believe that these clothes make them look more attractive. Some people are more concerned with style than others. Some people choose to spend less money on clothing than others. This can be because they have a limited budget or it might be because they aren't that interested in clothes. All of us probably have favorite outfits. For some of us, our favorites are play or casual clothes; for others, dress-up clothes; for still others, special work outfits.

Activity

Using a class-discussion format, have students complete a chart to illustrate the key points of the lesson with words and pictures gleaned from magazines and catalogs.

List the functions. Have students describe and illustrate them with pictures and words. Categories to be included are as follows:

Clothing Choices

Protection	Communication	Decoration	Modesty

Clothing Choices Based On

Climate	Gender	Culture	Economics	Work	Recreation

Optional   Create a series of scenarios about the choices people make about specialness. Use props to add interest.

Examples might include:

1. Planning a birthday party that involves going to a swimming pool
2. Celebrating Halloween
3. Acquiring the special clothing in order to be on a hockey team
4. Participating in a special ceremony (e.g., graduation)
5. Getting married
6. Going to a prom
7. Attending a school where uniforms are worn
8. Attending a family holiday dinner

Summarize

- People wear special clothing for a variety of reasons, such as for protection, communication of identity, or participation in special events, such as holiday celebrations, weddings, or funerals.
- Sometimes people wear special clothing by choice, but they may be required to do so if they join a team or an organization that requires special uniforms or dress codes.
- Culture, climate, gender, and cost considerations are among the factors that determine what people wear.

Assessment

Have students complete a page in their journals that summarizes one or more of the features of special clothing (Table 1). Encourage students to draw from the chart or picture story created by the class. Pictures or drawings to accompany the written responses are optional and to be done at home or during "free" time. Prompts you might consider include:
Examples of special clothing include _____.
Special clothing is worn because _____. My favorite outfit is _____. I wear it when _____.

Home Assignment

Provide the students copies of Figure 4. Encourage them to discuss with their parents some of the choices they make about clothing. Together, they should examine some of the outfits their family members wear for specified occasions.

TABLE 1 Special Clothing Choices

CULTURE	GENDER	CLIMATE	ECONOMICS	WORK	RECREATION
We wear folk dancing outfits that came from Norway (our heritage). We wear dark clothes at funerals.	Males wear outfits with trousers and females wear long skirts.		We paid $100 for each outfit. (It was a want, not a need.)		

Please complete the survey with at least one member of your family. Be ready to share the results with the class.

Members of my family wear special clothing for _____

_____

The special clothing includes _____

_____

They wear it because _____

_____

Our family's decisions for special clothing are based on _____

_____

_____

My favorite special clothing is _____ because _____

_____

_____

I wear it when I _____

_____

My favorite outfit is _____ because _____

_____

_____

FIGURE 4 Special Clothing

Lesson 3

Changes in Clothing Over Time

Resources

- Time line for bulletin board accompanied by focus questions: What did they use for clothes? How did they make the clothing? Why was it a lot of work to make clothes by hand? Were their clothes comfortable? How has clothing changed?
- Pictures showing the evolution of clothing (e.g., tunics, loin-cloth, footwear changes over time)
- Props: fleece; flax plant; linen material; tanned hide; zipper; Velcro; water-repellant garment; Lycra garment; anti-inflammable garment; Gortex garment; articles of clothing made from a range of materials; articles of clothing that illustrate style changes; handmade articles of clothing
- Time line information (teacher reference)
- Pictures showing the story of wool (steps)

Children's Literature

Cobb, Vicki. (1989). *Snap, Button, Zip: Inventions to Keep Our Clothes On.* Mexico: Harper Trophy.

Horenstein, Henry. (1993). *How Are Sneakers Made?* New York: Simon & Schuster.

Kalman, B. (1993). *Historic Communities: 18th Century Clothing.* New York: Crabtree Publishing Company.

Kalman, B. (1993). *Historic Communities: 19th Century Clothing.* New York: Crabtree Publishing Company.

Kindersley, B., & Kindersley, A. (1995) *Children Just Like Me.* New York: Dorling Kindersley in association with United Nations Children's Fund.

Morley, J. (1992). *Clothes.* New York: Franklin Watts.

Rowland-Warne, L. (1992). *Costumes.* New York: Alfred A. Knopf.

Tierney, T. (1987). *Famous American Women: Paper Dolls in Full Color.* New York: Dover Publications.

General Comments

This lesson describes how clothing has changed over time. Styles have evolved from very simple, practical, and primarily for protection to quite complicated and unusual (for communication and decoration) and back to more practical and comfortable. The shifts in clothing design have been more dramatic and frequent than shifts in housing/shelter, probably because clothing is far less costly.

Clothing has improved over time in quality, flexibility, and ease of use. It has become more practical and easier to care for and maintain. Most of our clothing is mass-produced in a range of standardized sizes and fits.

General Purposes or Goals

To: (1) help students understand and appreciate the changes that have occurred in clothing manufacture across time; (2) engender a positive attitude about history; (3) stimulate students' curiosity regarding clothing, styles, customs, and tastes; and (4) develop an awareness about and appreciation for the idea that any member of the class might become a person who invents or designs something very special that we could all benefit from and wear in the future.

Main Ideas to Develop

- Clothing has undergone a variety of changes over time. These changes have produced clothes that are more durable, water-repellant, lightweight, and convenient to use.
- Long ago, clothing was used for protection, decoration, communication, and later modesty, as well.
- Thread/yarn is spun from wool (or cotton, etc.).
- Cloth is woven from thread/yarn. It is a fabric, not a solid.

Teaching Tips from Barbara

This time line lesson will probably take you two sessions. I suggest doing the "Long, Long Ago" and the "Long Ago" parts on the first day. Then do "Today," with all the innovations, on the second day. One thing that I find to be singularly effective with the history lessons is to choose a few main changes to continually tie into. The ones I chose were clothing's comfort, origin, and cost. As I would introduce new eras and pictures, I kept coming back to those ideas. Also, anything you can do to dramatize this information helps bring it to life for your students. Be sure to take some time to discuss possible future changes.

Starting the Lesson

Discuss the results of the home assignment. Begin the lesson by showing pictures of clothing long, long ago, long ago, and today. Place these pictures on the time line and indicate that during this lesson the class will fill in the spaces.

As the lesson unfolds, revisit the functions of clothing: protection, communication, decoration, and modesty. Also, where appropriate, mention that our clothing is influenced by climate, culture, money available, and work. Allow the children to help decide the chronology of the pictures that have been selected to tell the story of clothing over time.

Suggested Lesson Discussion

Long, Long Ago   Clothing is covering for the human body. Since prehistoric times, clothing has been worn for protection, communication, decoration, and modesty. (The concern for modesty was less important in the past than it is today.)

Early humans lived in warm climates, so they did not need clothing for protection from cold. However, these cave people often used clothing to communicate and decorate. On their bodies they wore their prized trophies of battle and hunting. Strings of teeth, bones, and polished stones were often worn around the neck. Around the waist, they hung skins of animals, pieces of antelope horn, feathers, and scalps. These "flapping trophies," as they are often referred to, also protected individuals from annoying insects. Later a tunic or shirt replaced the necklace. Still later, skirts were added to the waistbands.

The next step in the development of clothing was actual covering for the body. The earliest people were used to tropical weather, but as they moved to cold places they needed clothing as protection from the elements. Often the cave people would seek out wild animals to kill (e.g., bears). They would cut the fur skins into several pieces and sizes and sew them together using very thin pieces of skin as thread and sharp pieces of ivory and bone as needles. Better tools and techniques for cutting, sewing, and tailoring were developed gradually.

Long, long ago, loose-flowing garments were made in warm countries to keep out the heat. [Show pictures to illustrate the range of fashions.] Egyptian dress is the earliest fashion we know much about. In this society, the clothing that people wore communicated their level of importance. Men of rank wore long, thin pleated tunics over knee-length loincloths. Belts held them in place. Laborers and slaves wore only a loin cloth or a short skirt. Women wore long, straight skirts, often with a tunic worn over it. Both men and women wore sandals. The rulers and the wealthy could afford finer clothes and jewels, so dress became a mark of rank and wealth. Even long, long ago, culture and economics were factors in how people dressed, and they wore clothes for protection, communication, decoration, and modesty.

Long Ago   Europeans sailed to the New World during the sixteenth and seventeenth centuries and settled on the east coast of North America. They brought their clothes with them. Most of them were able to pack and ship only a few things, so they brought what was practical (plain, made of sturdy material that could withstand everyday wear). When their clothes wore out, they had to make new ones. They made their own clothes of wool from sheep, flax from plants, and leather from animals.

For leather, the colonists tanned animal hides, [Show a tanned hide, which can be borrowed from a local taxidermist.] They placed the hide in water and added oak or hemlock bark. [Show pictures.] The bark released acid into the water. This acidic solution prevented the hide from rotting. The hide was left to soak for several months. When the leather was finally dried, it was stiff. To make it soft enough to wear, the colonists rubbed it with oil or animal fat.

For wool, farmers raised sheep [show a fleece]. Each spring they sheared the thick, heavy coats of the animals [show pictures of the steps]. They cleaned the wool, removing the dirt, sticks, and burrs, and then greased the wool in order to add the oils lost during cleaning. After the oils were added, the wool was ready for carding (combing), spinning (drawing out and twisting fibers into thread), dyeing (from plants and berries), and weaving into cloth (a process of crossing two sets of threads over and under each other).

[If possible, arrange for students to observe or participate in the process of spinning and/or weaving. In any case, make sure that they understand that: (1) thread/yarn is spun from raw wool or cotton; and (2) cloth is woven from thread/yarn—it is *not* solid like leather or plastic.]

The colonists grew flax plants, and the fibers of the plants were used to make linen. [Show a picture of a flax plant and a piece of linen cloth.] Since linen was lighter than wool, it was ideal for summer-weight clothing. The fine, combed strands of flax were spun into threads, and these threads then were woven into linen cloth.

Pilgrims and pioneers used the materials that were available to them for making their clothing. They wore woolen clothing in the winter and lighter-weight fabrics in the summer. They spent many hours spinning threads and making cloth (by weaving it from threads), then sewing clothes for the whole family. Because clothes making was done by hand and took so much time, most people had few outfits and the clothes were made of sturdy fabric. Often the clothing was heavy, as well, because their homes were cold and drafty in the winter. Clothes had to be washed by hand and hung up to dry, which took a long time because the clothes were so heavy. The farmers themselves wore clothing that wouldn't tear easily and usually dark colors that wouldn't show dirt.

Of course, not all of the people who settled in America were farmers. Some owned businesses or became town and government officials. These people tended to have more stylish clothing, mostly brought from Europe at first. As more and more people came to America and began doing many types of work, the styles of clothing, shoes, and headgear became more varied. People wore clothing appropriate for their work, and some dressed to show what they could afford (communication and decoration). [Show samples of silk and fur.] Silks and fine furs were worn only by the wealthy.

The velvet suit was typical among professional gentlemen long ago (1700s). The coat usually had rows of buttons, a long vest, and loose breeches (see *Costume*, p. 31). This suit communicated importance. The wealthy men wore powdered wigs (decoration, communication). Farmers didn't wear wigs because they were expensive and would be very uncomfortable if worn while working in the fields.

The women wore heavy brocaded dresses with lots of overskirts—again, quite uncomfortable. They were difficult to put on, and lots of time was needed for dressing. The wealthy women also wore powdered wigs for decoration. The working-class women wore simple cotton and linen dresses—again, most of them were made by hand.

Gradually, businesses were started to take care of people's clothing needs, especially those of people who didn't have the time or desire to make their own clothes. [Show pictures of early footwear and the styles as they evolved over time.] For example, shoemakers would travel from town to town, staying at the homes of customers while making boots and shoes for the families. Early shoes could be worn on either foot. A few had fasteners with laces, but most had buckles. Most shoes for children were made several sizes too big—because of the time involved in making a single pair by hand.

As time passed, more fabrics became available, and inventions such as the cotton gin (a machine that separates seeds from the cotton fiber) and the sewing machine came into being. They added speed to the clothes-making process. For many years, however, styles remained quite formal—women wearing long dresses, bustles, bonnets, shawls, and aprons. [Show pictures of formal wear.] Tight corsets and bustles gave women a thin look. Men, with the exception of farmers, wore trousers, waistcoats, and coats. Hats were popular for both men and women (top hat for men, bonnet for women).

By the end of the nineteenth century, clothing started to become more practical—and many more choices started to become available. Inventions in the industry continued. For example, there is a story that a man by the name of Mr. Whitcomb Judson of Chicago had a friend who suffered a bad back. His friend couldn't bend over and use two hands to button his shoes. Mr. Judson wanted to invent a fastener that his friend could use with one hand. [See *Snap, Button, Zip*, pp. 22–24.] The trouble with his fastener was that it came open unexpectedly. Several years later, another inventor made a zipper with teeth on two tapes [show *Zipper*]. A more recent advance was sticky tape (Velcro®)

invented by George deMestral, a Swiss engineer who got his idea by noticing how burrs stick to our clothing. [Show naps, zipper, Velcro. Show how these items function on actual articles of clothing. Demonstrate use of Velcro.]

Gradually, clothing factories were built; equipment became more sophisticated (including sewing machines), and articles of clothing could be mass-produced. For example, sneakers began being mass-produced (for everyone, not just athletes) when your grandparents were about your age. [Share *How Are Sneakers Made?*]

Today [Illustrate with pictures on time line]   There continues to be a range of styles and qualities of clothing. (Social pressures are often created and some people think they must have the latest thing. The latest usually costs more; often there is no functional gain or even a loss in comfort or warmth.) Wealthy shop owners travel to Paris and other parts of the world to get the very latest in fashion. However, the average American purchases clothing that is copied from high-fashion designer houses, produced in factories around the world, and sold in stores like K-Mart, Penney's, or Sears.

[Show articles of your clothing that illustrate style changes, and explain that styles continue to change. Demonstrate with pictures on time line.] Sometimes pants are wide, other times they are skinny; sometimes skirts are long, but some years they are short; and clothes continue to be made out of a range of materials. Today, we have clothing made out of not only natural fibers but also plastic, metals, paper, rubber, and synthetics made by chemists. [Show examples of clothing items made from a range of materials.]

Today the trend seems to be to wear the style you prefer—that best meets your individual needs and tastes. Therefore, we see a great variety in what people wear. The trend also seems to be toward comfort and much more casual clothing. Male bankers and lawyers still often dress in suits and ties, and women in suits and blouses, but workers in many other businesses have adopted a more sporty look.

Today, few people wear the uncomfortable undergarments of the past. Shoes tend to be selected more for comfort than for style, and fabrics tend to be chosen for ease or convenience of care (e.g., washing instead of dry cleaning). Today's clothes are easier to manipulate (e.g., buttons and buckles have been replaced with zippers and Velcro®) and made of materials that are light in weight (Gor-tex®) and do not require ironing.

Just as technology and inventions have made our homes more comfortable and allow us to enjoy a range of modern conveniences, so too have they made our clothing more comfortable and more easily cared for.

Also, mass production methods have made our clothing quicker and cheaper to produce. Some people still make handmade items—some are extremely special and unique and are very expensive.

In general, however, based on technology, modern transportation, and reasonable prices due to mass production, people wear similar clothing—except for special occasions or unusual cultural circumstances.

The Future   The twenty-first century will bring even more changes. [Illustrate with pictures on timeline.] Clothes that change color with body heat have already been developed. Their value would be primarily for individuals who are too young or unable to talk and indicate their level of comfort with the temperature of their environment. They, of course, are rare yet today. Clothes that protect us from pollutants will become available—and who knows what else? Some of you might be a part of that development. What might you like to invent or design?

Activity

At the conclusion of the picture-story timeline presentation, ask children to study the picture timeline in pairs, discuss what they thought was the most interesting change in clothing and why, and then share their responses with the whole class.

Optional   Have students use old Sears catalogs for comparing prices of clothing items long ago with those of today. During the students' grandparents' times, the average wage might have been $1.00 per hour. Today, it might be $10.00 per hour. In the past, a shirt might have cost two hours of wages. Today it could also cost two hours ($2.00 for a shirt in the past, $20.00 today).

Summarize

- Clothing has changed in a variety of ways over time.
- However, two basics have remained constant: (1) thread/yarn is made by spinning it from raw material (wool, cotton, or synthetic substances); and (2) cloth is made by weaving it from threads or yarn.
- Styles have evolved from very simple and practical to quite complicated and unusual and back to more practical.
- Clothing has improved in quality, flexibility, ease of use, and ease of maintenance. For example, clothing today is lighter-weight and dries faster. We have water-repellant and fire-retardant clothing.
- People all over the country can wear similar clothing due to mass production techniques and modern transportation and retailing methods.

- People's work roles and the amounts of money they have or are willing to spend on clothes are factors in their selections of articles of clothing.

Assessment

Have students describe in writing the most interesting thing they have learned regarding changes in the clothing industry, and explain why. They should add pictures or line drawings to illustrate and to enhance meaningfulness.

Alternatively, provide a time line and a series of pictures that depict the changes in clothing over time. Have each group sort through the pictures and place them in sequence on the time line. Elicit responses from each group that explain what the group learned. Next, give each student an individual time line. Show articles or pictures of clothing and ask students to classify them as long, long ago; long ago; or today.

Home Assignment

Have children interview their parents to determine what changes in clothing have occurred in their lifetimes. Send home copies of Figure 5.

Name _____

Parent Interview Information Sheet

Questions to Parent:

Describe the styles when you were growing up. _____

_____

_____

What did your mother/father (my grandparents) wear to work? _____

_____

_____

How is that different from what you wear on your job? _____

_____

_____

What did your mother/father (my grandparents) wear when they dressed up?

_____

_____

How is what you wear to dress up different? _____

_____

_____

Why? _____

_____

_____

FIGURE 5 Changes in Clothing Over Time

How is your clothing more comfortable than that of your parents (my grandparents)?

_____

_____

What new types of materials (fabrics) have been created in your lifetime?

_____

_____

What is your favorite article of clothing? _____

_____

_____

Why? _____

_____

_____

Was it available to your parents (my grandparents)? _____

_____

_____

Note: If possible, encourage your child to talk to grandparents or other older adults about their clothing and the changes that have occurred over time. The same interview sheet could be used.

FIGURE 5 (Continued)

Dear Parents,

We have been learning about the changes in clothing over time. Please allow your child to interview you about changes in clothing that have occurred during your lifetime. We will use your responses in our next class discussion.

Sincerely,

FIGURE 6 Model Letter to Parents

Lesson 4

Changes in Children's Clothing Over Time

Resources

- Time line for bulletin board accompanied by focus questions: What did they use for clothes? How did they make the clothing? Did making the clothing require a lot of effort? How comfortable was the clothing?
- Pictures showing the evolution of children's clothing over time
- Props: period clothing (optional); zipper; Velcro; water-repellant garment; flame-retardant garment
- Dolls dressed in period clothing (optional)
- Time line
- Scenario cards describing clothing, clothing situations long, long ago (cave days); long ago (pioneer time); and today

Children's Literature

Cobb, Vicki. (1989). *Snap, Button, Zip: Inventions to Keep Your Clothes On*. Mexico: Harper Trophy.

Kalman, Bobbie. (1993). *Historic Communities: 18th Century Clothing*. New York: Crabtree Publishing Company.

Kalman, Bobbie. (1993). *Historic Communities: 19th Century Clothing*. New York: Crabtree Publishing Company.

Kindersley, B., & Kindersley, A. (1995). *Children Just Like Me*. New York: Dorling-Kindersley in association with United Nations Children's Fund.

Rowland-Warne, L. (1992). *Costume*. New York: Alfred A. Knopf.

Tierney, F. (1987). *Famous American Women: Paper Dolls in Full Color*. New York: Dover Publications.

General Comments

This lesson will focus on the changes in children's clothing over time. The students will come to realize that children wore the same styles of clothes as their parents until the late eighteenth century. At that time, children's clothes began to have a style of their own, and the wearers stopped looking like miniature adults.

General Purposes or Goals

To: (1) help children understand and appreciate the changes that have occurred in clothing for individuals their age; (2) stimulate children's curiosity regarding children's clothing styles, customs, and tastes over time; and (3) help children acquire a sense of efficacy—that they too might design or invent something related to the clothing industry that we could all benefit from in the future.

Main Ideas to Develop

- Children's clothing has undergone a variety of changes in the last two centuries.
- Children's clothing of the past was based primarily on needs, while today wants are also considered.
- Children's clothing today is more durable, water-repellant, and flame-retardant, yet also lighter and more comfortable.
- Children all over the world tend to dress quite similarly, although they may wear native costumes for special occasions.
- Climate, specific activity, and cost are among the factors that determine what children wear.

Teaching Tips from Barbara

The best part of this lesson is having students compare their own outfits with the outfits of colonial children. A bit of drama as you list the layers of clothing can make all the difference. Again, refer to the same points of comparison as in Lesson 3. The American Girl dolls are also great for this lesson if you can borrow one or more. The assessment piece of the lesson is having the children fill out a time line. I allowed my students to use either words or pictures to show what they learned. This works best if they can do so while interacting one at a time with an adult volunteer or paraprofessional.

Starting the Lesson*

Discuss the results of the home assignment. Begin the lesson by showing pictures of children's clothing very long ago and today. [If dolls dressed in period children's clothing are available, incorporate them into the lesson to enhance interest.] Ask, "How has children's clothing changed? What do you notice?" The students should notice that long ago children wore the same styles of clothing as their parents. The garments tended to be cumbersome, difficult to care for, and uncomfortable. It took quite a bit of time to get dressed and undressed. Today, children's styles are still similar to styles worn by their parents; however, in general, they tend to be more casual.

Place a picture that represents a very long time ago and one that represents today on the time line. Indicate that during the lesson the class will fill in the spaces. As the lesson unfolds, revisit the functions of clothing: protection, communication, decoration, and modesty. Also, where

*You may prefer to start with children's clothing today before moving to children's clothing in the past.

appropriate, mention that children's clothing is influenced by climate, culture, and cost.

Suggested Lesson Discussion

By the late eighteenth century or early nineteenth century (1800s), children's clothing began to have a style of its own [see *Costume*, p. 60]. The new styles however, were still quite formal, especially for dress up or Sunday wear [show pictures to illustrate]. Boys and girls dressed much alike. For example, in the 1860s, a silk tartan dress might be worn by either sex. Boys often wore dresses and had long curly hair. Girls often wore fancy hats and bustles. The bustle would be tied into shape with tapes inside. A type of girl's coat and bonnet of the early twentieth century would be made of a crisp, light-colored material—not suitable for playing in the dirt. Waterproof coats were introduced around 1915. By the mid-1920s and early 1930s, dresses and boys' clothes were more comfortable. The zipper was first used on clothes. Clothing was still more formal for everyday wear than it is today. Boys often wore double-breasted coats with matching hats made of fine woolen tweeds, and girls often had matching coats and leggings. The leggings would zip tightly over the shoes for extra warmth.

After World War II, children's clothing became more relaxed and casual. Around 1954, the T-shirt, originally a U.S. Navy undervest, was popularized. Since the mid-1950s, denim jeans have been universal casual wear. Brand-name clothes played a big part in the 1980s. Often people were willing to pay more money for lines of clothing that were endorsed by famous athletes (we pay for that advertising). The fitness craze brought lycra (stretch fabric), originally developed for cycling, to the fashion scene.

Today, the "in look" for children combines casual blue jeans and T-shirts [show the picture of the "in look" for second graders in *Costume*, p. 60]. The style originated in the United States and has been adopted all over the world. Children in other parts of the world, based on their cultural heritage, do wear native clothing for special occasions [see *Children Just Like Me*].

In summary, today's children's clothing and fashions are much different from those of 150 years ago. In the past, needs were the most important. Today, wants are also considered. One change is that children today have a much simpler process of getting ready for school. Boys and girls today, in general, put on the following items:

1. Underwear
2. Shirt or dress
3. Pants
4. Socks
5. Shoes

However, girls who lived 150 years ago had to wear:

1. A long frilly undershirt
2. A bodice—a tight girdle with buttons up the back
3. A garter belt to hold up stockings
4. Long cotton or wool stockings
5. Long underpants that buttoned to the bodice
6. High-buttoned shoes
7. A red-flannel petticoat
8. A starched petticoat
9. A long stiff dress
10. An apron, called a *pinafore*, to keep the dress clean
11. A hair ribbon, tied in a bow
12. A bonnet, tied under the chin

At the same time, boys had to wear:

1. An undershirt of wool or cotton
2. Long underpants (winter garments were made of wool; summer garments were made of linen and later cotton)
3. A shirt, often with ruffles and tie
4. Long black stockings held up by garters
5. High-buttoned shoes
6. Pants that buttoned on to the shirt
7. A buttoned-up waistcoat or vest
8. A wool jacket
9. A hat
10. A coat

[Dramatizing the act of dressing 150 years ago can add appeal and enhance meaningfulness. After you pantomime getting dressed for school, have a child of the opposite sex pantomime what she or he would wear to school. Discuss differences worn by gender then, and differences today. Articles of actual period clothing would also generate a great deal of interest and engender appreciation. These can often be secured from a community theater. Some antique shops also have articles of clothing that could be acquired for the lesson.]

Children of the past took half an hour to get dressed, whereas children today take only a few minutes. The reasons for the changes include the creation of such inventions as the zipper and Velcro [read *Snap, Button, Zip*]. We also have lightweight materials that serve as insulation, and today's homes are insulated, so children do not have to wear as many layers of clothing to keep warm.

Also, styles have changed, and clothing is not nearly as formal. Clothes look very much alike for boys and girls today, especially the garments worn for school and play. Even for very special occasions, people have a range of choices regarding what to wear and how much to spend.

Comfort and ease of care (cleaning and storage) are often the top considerations instead of communication and decoration. In general, clothing care is much easier today because we have washing machines and dry cleaners.

Activity

At the conclusion of the picture-story presentation, ask students to study the picture timeline in pairs, discuss what they thought was the most interesting change in children's clothing and why, and then share their responses with the whole class.

Using items, pictures, and photos of children long ago and today, have students decide which items fit the categories "long ago" (button shoes, socks) and "today" (Velcro, zippers, socks).

If enough time is available, give each table an envelop of pictures and words and a piece of paper divided into three columns—"long, long, ago"; "long ago"; and "today." Have students classify and explain where each item belongs and be prepared to explain why.

Summarize

- Children's clothing has changed in a variety of ways over time.
- Like adults' styles, children's styles have evolved from simple and practical to quite complicated and unusual and back to more practical.
- Children's clothing has undergone a variety of changes in the last two centuries.
- Children's clothing today is more durable, simpler, water-repellant, and comfortable than in the past. Several inventions (e.g., zipper, Velcro) have made it easier to dress and undress.
- Today, children all over the world tend to dress quite similarly, due to technology, mass production, transportation, and communication, although children often wear their native costumes for special occasions.
- Climate, culture, specific activity, and cost are among the factors that determine what children wear.
- The four functions of clothing (protection, communication, decoration, and modesty) were true for children of the past as well as the present.

Assessment

Have students describe in writing the most interesting thing they learned regarding the changes in the children's clothing industry and explain why. They should add pictures or line drawings to illustrate and enhance meaningfulness. Have students plot the interesting change on their own copy of a simple time line marked "long, long ago"; "long ago"; and "today."

Option Create a series of scenarios (on cards) for students. Each student will read the scenario and then move to the proper place on the time line. Each student should be able to explain the reasons for the choice. Examples:

> I am having difficulty buttoning my shoes.
>
> I just can't seem to hook my waist coat.
>
> I just tore my bustle.
>
> I think I need some new Velcro for my tennis shoes.
>
> My father gave me a pelt, which I wear for modesty.
>
> I try to keep the big silver buckles on my shoes polished.
>
> My clothes are mostly brown and blue.
>
> I really like my new Disney T-shirt.
>
> Most of the time I wear clothes like children in the United States,
>   but once in awhile, for special occasions, I wear a kimono.

Home Assignment

Have students interview their parents to determine what changes have occurred in children's clothing since their childhood. Send home two copies of Figure 7.

Interview a parent to find out about the clothing he or she wore as a child.

Describe the styles you wore as a school-age child. _____

_____

What did you wear for play? _____

_____

_____

What did you wear for special occasions? _____

_____

_____

_____

_____

How is my clothing as a child more comfortable than yours was? _____

_____

_____

How is my clothing as a child easier to care for than yours was? _____

_____

What new fabrics (materials) are my clothes made of that weren't available when you were a child? _____

_____

_____

What was your favorite article of clothing as a child? _____

_____

_____

Why? _____

_____

FIGURE 7 Children's Clothing

Dear Parents,

We have been studying about children's clothing and how it has changed over time. Enclosed is an interview guide for you to use as you and your child talk about what you wore when you were growing up.

Encourage your child to talk to grandparents or other older adults about clothing they wore as children. (A second copy of the interview guide is attached.)

If photographs are available, please share them!

Sincerely,

FIGURE 8 Model Letter to Parents

Lesson 5

Land to Hand: The Story of Wool

Resources

- Wool samples
- Articles of woolen clothing (factory and handmade)
- Flip-chart paper
- Pictures depicting steps in making cloth from wool (a local museum and/or weaver could serve as great resources)
- Hand loom
- Pictures of factory—steps in making cloth and clothes
- Skein of yarn
- Video clip describing the steps in the land-to-hand relationship (optional)
- Pictures and/or word cards for individual and paired sequencing activity focusing on the steps in making wool
- Materials for making individual or class booklets (optional)
- *World Book Encyclopedia*. (1994). Volume 21, pp. 173–175. Chicago: Scott Fetzer Co.

Children's Literature

Blood, C., and Parker, N. (1990). *The Goat in the Rug*. New York: Aladdin Books, Macmillan.

de Paolo, T. (1973). *Charlie Needs a Cloak*. New York: Simon & Schuster.

Harthern, A. T. (1988). *Families and Their Needs*. Atlanta: Silver Burdett & Ginn.

Keeler, P., & McCall, F. X., Jr. (1995). *Unraveling Fibers*. New York: Atheneum Books.

General Comments

These next two lessons will explore land-to-hand relationships that lead to the clothing that is worn by your students and their families (namely, the raw materials and manufacturing processes that lie behind articles of wool and cotton clothing). They will also help students to appreciate how families long ago had to be almost totally self-sufficient, whereas today most clothing is mass-produced. Animal and plant fibers will be used to examine these land-to-hand relationships.

General Purposes or Goals

To help students develop an understanding and appreciation of: (1) the "story" of their woolen clothing; (2) the interdependence of people involved in the clothing industry (each person has a special job to do, and all jobs must be done well in order to produce a quality product); and (3) the differences between mass-produced and handmade garments (mass production allows us to make many products quickly, whereas handmade garments are more individualized, usually take much more time to make, and cannot be made readily available for many people). People of the past spun and wove or knit often out of necessity, while today some do it as an art.

Main Ideas to Develop

- Wool is warm and thus used in cold climates.
- A variety of raw materials is used in making clothing. One of these is wool. It comes from animals.
- The land-to-hand story of wool begins with the animal (sheep, alpacas, or llamas) and is completed when a woolen garment is produced.
- Some cloth is made from wool. Wool threads are spun from the fleece shorn from sheep, and then woolen cloth is made by weaving it from the wool threads.
- Because of technology and job specialization, we depend on the combined efforts of many different people working in different places to produce today's woolen garments.

Teaching Tips from Barbara

This lesson is wonderful for teaching about sequencing. First, I talked through the steps of going from sheep to cloth. Then I had the students help me list the steps as I used the book *The Goat in the Rug*. It matches this lesson wonderfully. Next, I created a simple sheet with seven steps. I had the students cut them apart and glue them onto the pages of a book.

Starting the Lesson

Begin the lesson by having students share the results of the home assignment. This is a place where you might want to explore children's conceptions and misconceptions about how cloth is made. What do they think they know? Record it on the board or chart paper. Be sure to revisit the responses at the end of the lesson.

Suggested Lesson Discussion

Long ago, it took a long time to make clothes. Just as there was little equipment for making homes, there was little equipment for making clothes. Many clothes were made from wool. Wool was especially popular in cold climates, because wool fibers hold water away from your skin. This keeps your skin drier, so you feel warmer.

Pioneer families made their own woolen clothing. First, the father would clip the wool (fleece) from the sheep (give sheep a haircut). The mother would wash the wool, then comb it into eight- or ten-inch slivers by pulling it between two cards [show picture of carding wool]. This would make the wool straight. Then it was spun (twisted) into yarn (thick thread). To make the yarn, she used a spinning wheel [show picture of spinning wheel—demonstrate or use pictures for the explanation]. The fluffy slivers of carded wool were spun on a large single-grooved wheel, which the pioneer woman turned by hand. Normally, she stood at her work, stepping backward and forward as the yarn was wound on the spindle. The spun yarn was then wound onto a reel [show a skein of yarn] and tied into bundles—often called *hands* or *skeins*—or wound into balls.

Once the woolen yarn had been spun, it was woven into cloth. [Show pictures of looms, including a hand loom.] Weaving is a process of making cloth by crossing two sets of threads over and under each other. One set is called the *warp*. [Demonstrate by using a hand loom.] It stretches lengthwise on a loom or a frame. To make cloth, the weaver repeatedly pulls (draws) a set of crosswise threads, called the *weft*, over and under the *warp*. In pioneer times, most of the weaving was done at home on a loom. This is done by crossing one set of yarns over and under another set of yarns. This is done over and over. Finally the cloth is made. The cloth is cut into pieces, and the pieces are sewn together by hand. The pioneers used the resources available to them (e.g., wood for making their own spinning wheels and looms, sheep for wool, and berries for dye). During pioneer days, the mother spent much of her time making clothes for the family.

[Upon completion of the story of wool, give six students a picture illustrating part of the story and ask them to stand and sequence themselves in the order that reveals the story. Next, read a fanciful story entitled *Charlie Needs a Cloak*, which reviews the land-to-hand steps in the production of wool clothing. An interesting sidelight of the story is that the male is engaged in carrying out the processes—an entry to a class discussion regarding involvement of both genders in the clothing industry. Mention that goats, rabbits, llamas, and alpacas are among the other animals that provide us with animal fibers used to make woolen clothing. You may also wish to read aloud *The Goat in the Rug*, a true story of a Navajo weaver and her goat. It also illustrates land-to-hand relationships.]

While a few people still choose to spin, weave, and sew their own clothes, today we have lots of technology that allows people in clothing factories to make many garments quickly. The steps are basically the same [show steps in modern cloth making], although they can be accomplished much faster using modern technology and mass-production techniques. Of course, the *uniqueness* and *creativity* involved in producing a one-of-a-kind clothing item are not possible when clothes are mass-produced in a factory. [Show pictures of the inside of a factory.]

The fleeces are rolled up and tied together with twine, then packed in burlap bags and *shipped* to market. After the wool is sold, it is transported to the factory, where it is *cleaned* and *sorted*. Machines *comb* out the knotty wool. Then the wool is *spun* into thread, and the threads are *woven* together to make fabric (cloth). The cloth is manufactured in many different patterns or weaves, as well as dyed in many colors. Some of the material is shipped to fabric shops, where people who sew their own clothes can purchase bolts of cloth. Most of the material, however, is shipped to factories, where, using a variety of patterns and styles, it is transformed into articles of clothing.

The clothing that is manufactured is shipped to stores around the world. Because of modern technology and transportation and communication systems, people throughout the world have access to the same types of clothing—if they choose [see *World Book*, Vol. 21, pp. 173–175]. People in the past made clothing without modern technology and primarily in response to basic needs. Today, people buy clothing based on their wants as well. Culture, climate, personal choices, and amount of money available enter into the clothing choices that people make. [Stress the interdependence in the processes that connect "land to hand."]

Activity

Using a series of pictures and/or word cards depicting the processes involved in making wool, have students work in pairs to place them in the correct sequence and describe the process in detail. As a group, discuss the results and note how the people involved are interdependent as contributors to the final products. If time permits—and if students are interested—compare and contrast the wool-making industry of the past with today.

PAST	PRESENT
1. Raise a few sheep.	1. Raise many sheep (ranch).
2. Shear the sheep.	2. Shear the sheep.
3. Clean the fleeces.	3. Package the fleeces and send them to market by truck or train; sell the fleeces; send the fleeces to factories; clean the fleeces.
4. Card the wool.	4. Comb out the knotty wool by machine.
5. Spin the wool into yarn.	5. Spin the wool into yarn.
6. Weave the yarn into cloth.	6. Weave the yarn into cloth.
7. Dye the cloth.	7. Dye the cloth.

PAST	PRESENT
8. Using a simple pattern, cut out the cloth and sew the pieces together by hand.	8. Using a range of patterns designed by people who create a variety of styles and sizes, cut out the pieces for specified garments (making hundreds, thousands, or even millions of each type of garment produced). Use machines to sew the pieces of garments together.
9. Keep the garments for family use or sell them locally.	9. Label each garment; package the finished garments; send garments to stores all around the country, or even the world, according to specified orders; unpack garments; put them on racks for sale.

Here are some other points that might be included in the discussion:

- Wool acts as a natural insulator, protecting the body from extremes of temperature.
- Woolen clothing is found throughout the world.
- Sheep's wool comes from the thick, spongy fleece of a sheep in natural shades of black, white, or brown. Today, sheep are raised all over the world in places where the climate is cool.
- Specific costumes made from wool sometimes require unique designs that people create by hand (e.g., Laplander clothing).
- Some people choose to make clothing by hand or on their own sewing machine as an art form, a hobby, or a means of saving money.

If possible, arrange for students to observe or participate in spinning and weaving processes.

Summarize

- There are many steps (processes) and people involved in creating a woolen garment.
- Yarn is spun wool; woolen cloth is woven yarn.
- Technology has greatly changed the clothing industry.
- Technology and modern transportation and communication, as applied to woolen clothing, provide more choices to people.

- There are still people who elect to make their own clothing. Some create unique articles of clothing, for themselves or for sale, that are considered art.

Assessment

Have students make individual books that summarize "How the sheep's coat becomes my coat." An option would be for the class to make a book and each student complete one page of the story. The pictures or line illustrations that the children might like to include could be done as a home assignment.

Optional   Duplicate drawings that depict the land-to-hand story of wool. Prepare a complete set of cards for each student. As you proceed with steps, you will visually be able to see which students understand sequencing. Select students to post the steps in the story of wool, in each case explaining the step and the process associated with it. Discuss as a class how the process is different today than it was during pioneer times.

Home Assignment

Students will inventory one or more clothes closets with an adult to determine which articles are made of wool—and if time permits, where the articles were made and in what seasons they are worn. Send home copies of Figure 9 to help families retrieve data.

Name _____

I found the following articles made of wool in our closets.

Article of clothing made of wool	Is it made by machine or by hand?	The garment was made in	In what season(s) is it worn?	Where in the world might children wear this?
1. _____	_____	_____	_____	_____
2. _____	_____	_____	_____	_____
3. _____	_____	_____	_____	_____
4. _____	_____	_____	_____	_____
5. _____	_____	_____	_____	_____

FIGURE 9 Closet Inventory: Wool

Dear Parents,

We have been learning about the story of wool. Please spend a few minutes with your child to inventory one or more clothes closets to determine which articles are made of wool. If time permits, also try to figure out where the articles were made and in what seasons they are worn.

Sincerely,

FIGURE 10 Model Letter to Parents

Lesson 6

Land to Hand: The Story of Cotton

Resources

- Cotton samples, including canvas
- Articles of cotton clothing
- Bulletin board "The Story of My Jeans"
- Flip-chart paper
- Pictures depicting steps in making cloth from cotton
- Cards and pictures for paired sequencing activity
- Materials for making individual or class book
- Video: Levi Strauss (optional; for information, contact nearest Levi Strauss store)
- Jarolimek, J. S. (1987). *Families and Friends*. New York: Macmillan.

Children's Literature

Jones, G. (1995). *My First Book of How Things Are Made*. New York: Cartwheel Books, Scholastic, Inc.

Keeler, P. A. & McCall, F. X., Jr. (1995). *Unraveling Fibers*. New York: Atheneum.

Weidt, Maryann. (1990). *Mr. Blue Jeans*. Minneapolis, MN: Carolrhoda Books.

General Comments

This is the second of two lessons on land-to-hand relationships. It focuses on the story of cotton. It addresses the steps involved, starting with the picking of cotton and ending with the purchase of cotton (denim) jeans. Processes used in the past are compared with modern technology and mass-production techniques. Additionally, a human interest story is included, namely the story of Levi Strauss, a young peddler from Europe who started a company for the manufacture of jeans.

General Purposes and Goals

To help students develop an understanding and appreciation of: (1) the story of their cotton clothing; (2) the interdependence of people involved in the clothing industry (e.g., cotton); (3) factors that contribute to the choices of materials for garments (e.g., climate, culture, and economics); (4) the differences between mass-produced and handmade garments; and (5) the fact that individual inventors and workers are responsible for the things that we have. Some have become more famous than others. People with ideas should be encouraged.

Main Ideas to Develop

- What people wear depends on a variety of factors (e.g., climate, culture, jobs, and costs).
- A variety of raw materials is used in making clothing. One of these is cotton. It comes from the cotton plant.
- The story of cotton begins with a plant and ends when a garment is produced.
- Because of technology and job specialization, we depend on the combined efforts of many different people working in different places to produce today's cotton garments.
- People with ideas create new products and processes. Many of these individuals have made contributions to the clothing industry.

Teaching Tips from Barbara

We did a similar activity after the wool lesson. Again, I talked through the steps of going from the cotton boll to cotton cloth. Then I had the students help me list the steps. I created a simple sheet with the steps. I had the students cut them apart and glue them in the pages of a book. They illustrated each. Then they were able to use their own books to compare and contrast these two processes. Also, try to get some raw cotton and fleece for the students to touch and pull apart. They were fascinated, and the term *fiber* became much more meaningful to them.

Starting the Lesson

Begin the lesson by discussing the results of the home assignment.

Suggested Lesson Discussion

In the last lesson, we looked at wool and how wool cloth is made. Let's review the characteristics of wool and compare them to those of cotton.

WOOL	COTTON
Comes from animals	Comes from plants
Heavy	Lightweight
Usually worn in cold weather	Usually worn in warm weather
Stays wet for a long time	Dries quickly
Used for making heavy socks, jackets, coats, trousers, some dresses	Used for making light socks, jackets, trousers, and shirts

Wool comes from animals. Now we are going to look at clothing made from plants. While there are several, we will focus on cotton. [Spend a few minutes allowing students to become familiar with their own clothes—paying particular attention to those made of cotton.]

It would be difficult to go through a day without using cotton. You probably sleep between cotton sheets and wash your face with a cotton washcloth. Your shirts, skirts, jeans, and even your shoelaces are often made of cotton. Today we are going to examine the steps in making a pair of jeans. [Show the book *Mr. Blue Jeans* and dramatically tell the story. Survey the class to see how many are wearing blue jeans. Encourage the students to examine the weave of their jeans.] In 1853, Levi Strauss, a young peddler from Europe, had made his way to California after spending time working in the dry goods industry (selling cloth to individuals and stores) in New York. One sunny day, he was enjoying lunch on the banks of the Sacramento River when a miner came and asked Levi what he had for sale. He pulled out a bolt of canvas [show a piece of canvas] from his wagon and suggested that the prospector might want a new tent. The miner said he didn't need a tent but did need some good sturdy pants. Levi thought for a moment and then took the man's measurements. Later he asked a tailor to make a pair of canvas pants in the miner's size and to sew the rest of the fabric in various other sizes. When the pants were ready, the miner cheerfully paid Levi $6.00 in gold dust. The word soon spread, and very soon Levi had sold all the pants he'd ordered from the tailor. (People's needs create demand.)

Levi contacted his brothers in New York to order canvas for more pants. However, the fabric they shipped was not canvas but a heavy cotton material called *denim*. It was made in France and had been popular with sailors, who nicknamed the pants *jeans* (i.e., Jean's pants). Soon not only miners were wearing Levi's pants, but so were cowboys and farmers. They called them "Levis." The Levis were comfortable and long-lasting.

The story of jeans begins with the cotton plant. Cotton grows best where it stays warm and sunny for at least half of the year. Large amounts of cotton are grown in the Southern United States, in Russia, and in India [see pp. 8–10, *Unraveling Fibers*]. Farmers plant the seeds in the spring, and after a couple of months, the cotton plants bloom. After the flowering stage is finished, a *seed pod* or *cotton boll* is formed [show cotton boll]. Inside the boll, cotton fibers form around the cotton seeds. By early fall, the bolls turn brown. Soon they pop open and the cotton fibers begin to dry and fluff out. Then the cotton is picked by a machine. (In the past, cotton was picked by hand. People create inventions to make things easier or save time, so we can work less to have what we have.) The cotton is loaded into trailers and hauled to a separating plant, where it's loaded into cotton gins (huge, noisy machines that pull the cotton fibers from the seeds). [See page 10, *Unraveling Fibers*.] Other machines clean and dry the cotton.

The cleaned cotton is bundled and baled, then sent to factories (mills) to be made into cloth. [Revisit students' conceptions and misconceptions regarding how cloth is made. Label the sheet of chart paper "What We Think We Know." List the responses. Revisit them at the end of the lesson.] At the factory, the cotton is cleaned again, spun into yarn, and woven into cloth. It may be dyed either while it's still yarn or after it has been woven into cloth [show pictures from *Families and Friends*, pp. 90–93].

Patterns and sizes are determined. Jeans are made using cardboard or plywood patterns for each of the designs that will be made in large numbers. [Show students a tissue-paper pattern that would be used if only a few pair were being made. Indicate that heavy patterns need to be used when many pairs will be made. Compare patterns to blueprints for houses.] The pattern is sent to the cutting room, where material is laid out on tables. Sometimes as many as fifty layers of material are stacked on one table. The pattern is fitted on the top layer and chalk is used to draw around it. Huge cutting machines then cut through the many layers of material.

The cut patterns are sent to the sewing room, where workers use large sewing machines to assemble the pieces into garments. One machine operator may do straight seams. Another may do pockets. Another will sew in the zippers. Much of the work is still done by hand, but machines are gradually taking over because, when perfected, the machines can work faster and better. Each operator has a different job. The workers divide the jobs among them, making sure that all tasks get accomplished (interdependence). We depend on all of these workers to ensure that we get a quality pair of blue jeans.

Electric sewing machines can sew five thousand stitches a minute. They can sew forward and backward, make button holes, sew in zippers, and embroider. Some are fully automatic; others have hand-operated levers that change the direction of the cloth or the type of stitch.

Completed jeans are pressed with large steam irons. Then they are sent to shipping rooms, where they are packed and labeled to be sent out to stores. Today, most of our clothes are made in factories—often overseas, where labor is much cheaper.

Option Exploring:
1. How technological advances render certain jobs obsolete, causing upheavals in some families
2. Ethical and social policy issues relating to child labor, worker exploitation, and third-world economies

Other Interesting Aspects of Cotton

Cotton fibers suck up moisture easily and dry quickly. They are soft and lightweight. Each inch-long fiber has a couple hundred twists in it that make cotton stretchy. All of these qualities make cotton cloth feel light, cool, and comfortable. It is a popular type of cloth in warm climates—and during our spring and summer seasons.

Activity

Have students work in pairs using pictures and words to sequence the land-to-hand relationships that tell the story of cotton.

Optional Underscore the idea that children all over the world have access to jeans due to modern transportation, economic feasibility of the garment, and mass production. Explain that there are places in the world where it is too hot for them; where, due to cultural preferences, children may wear other garments; and that not all families can afford jeans.

Summarize

- Cotton comes from plants. The steps in producing an article of clothing are very similar to those used in making a woolen garment.
- Both wool and cotton clothing were made during pioneer times.
- Woolen clothing is usually worn to keep warm and cotton clothing is usually worn to keep cool.
- There are many steps (processes) and people involved in creating a cotton garment. Cotton clothes are made out of cotton cloth.
- Cotton cloth is made by weaving it from threads spun from raw cotton that has been picked and cleaned.
- Cotton thread is spun cotton; cotton cloth is woven from cotton thread.
- Technology has greatly changed the clothing industry.
- Technology and modern transportation and communication as applied to cotton clothing provide more choices to people.
- Climate, culture, economics, and human activities are among the many factors that determine the type of fiber used in garments.

Assessment

Have students make individual books that summarize "How Cotton Plants Became My Jeans." An option would be for the class to make a book and have each student complete a page/step of the story. The pictures or line illustrations could be done as a home assignment.

Alternately, have the class members create the bulletin board "The Story of My Jeans." Assign each table or group a step in the sequence. Each group should use pictures and words to explain the meaning. They may wish to teach the story of jeans to their upper-grade mentors.

Home Assignment

Encourage each student to inventory one or more clothes closets with an adult to determine which articles of clothing are cotton—and if time permits, what the articles are used for, where they were made, and the seasons during which they are worn. Send home copies of Figure 11.

Name _____

I found the following articles made of cotton in our closets.

Article of clothing made of cotton.	Where else in the world might people wear this garment?	The garment is used for (school, work, recreation, dress-up, other)	The garment was made in	During which season(s) is it worn?
1. _____	_____	_____	_____	_____
2. _____	_____	_____	_____	_____
3. _____	_____	_____	_____	_____
4. _____	_____	_____	_____	_____
5. _____	_____	_____	_____	_____

FIGURE 11 Closet Inventory: Cotton

Dear Parents,

We have been learning about the story of cotton. Please spend a few minutes with your child to inventory one or more clothes closets to determine which articles are made of cotton. If time permits, also try to determine where the articles were made and in what seasons they are worn.

Sincerely,

FIGURE 12 Model Letter to Parents

Lesson 7

Silk and Synthetics

Resources
- Silk and synthetic samples
- Articles of clothing made from silk and synthetics as well as articles made from wool and cotton
- World map
- Pictures depicting steps in making clothing from silk and synthetics
- "Mystery Bag" containing a range of fabrics (e.g., wool, cotton, silk, polyester, nylon, rayon, etc.)

Children's Literature
Keeler, P. A., & McCall, F. X., Jr. (1995). *Unraveling Fibers*. New York: Atheneum Books.

General Comments
This lesson will focus on fabric and clothing that are: (1) made as the result of animals and plants interacting to produce silk; and (2) produced chemically by humans using wood, coal, or chemicals.

General Purposes or Goals
To help students understand and appreciate: (1) how different natural fibers are made into cloth (silk fibers from silkworms, wool from sheep, or cotton from plants); (2) that cloth is also made from synthetic fibers created by scientists (chemists); (3) how technology has influenced the clothing industry; and (4) the importance of labels in clothing for identifying the types of cloth, where the article of clothing was made, and how to care for it.

Main Ideas to Develop
- Silk is made as the result of silkworms eating mulberry leaves, going through a series of stages, and then producing silk fibers in the process.
- Some fibers and cloth, such as nylon, rayon, and polyester, are made by chemists. These fibers originate with trees, petroleum, natural gas, and chemicals.
- The label in a garment identifies the type of material that is used, tells where it is made, and explains how it should be cared for.

Teaching Tips from Barbara

One of the bonuses of this lesson is the opportunity to sneak some economic ideas into the unit. My students really grasped the relationship between supply and demand as we talked about the scarcity of silk, the lengths people would go to get it, and the cost. The review activity involving swatches of clothing in a "mystery bag" is a must! You can even make it into a bingo game where the kids create their own cards using twenty-four different fabrics.

Starting the Lesson

Begin the lesson by discussing the home assignment.

Suggested Lesson Discussion

Silk   [As you explain the story of silk, use lots of visualization. Show silk thread and swatches of silk cloth. Explain that silk fibers are very fine and that several need to be twisted together to form thread.]

The story of silk is a very interesting one because in order to have a silk tie, scarf, or blouse, contributions by both plants and animals are needed. [See *Unraveling Fibers*, pp. 23–27. Secure a video that illustrates the silk story.] The finest silk fibers are made by a special type of caterpillar called a *silkworm*. Silkworms are raised on silkworm farms, mostly in China, Japan, India, and South Korea [point out these places on a world map or globe]. They are hatched from eggs as small as the head of a pin. They prefer to eat only one food—leaves from the mulberry tree. They eat and eat until they become too big for their skin. Each time they shed their skin, the new skin is bigger, giving the silkworm more room to grow. The whole time the silkworm is eating, it is making silk. The silk is created as a liquid inside two long curly glands on either side of the silkworm's body.

After about a month, the silkworms stop eating and become full-grown caterpillars. They are placed on frames to spin their silk. The caterpillars hunt around the frame, looking for places to build their cocoons. Soon each silkworm settles in to spin its silk. It does this by squeezing liquid silk out of an opening in its head, which is called a *spinneret*. The silk hardens when it touches the air and becomes a thin thread.

First, the silkworm throws a web with its silk. The web anchors the silkworm's cocoon safely to the frame. Then the silkworm builds a cocoon around itself. In about three days, the cocoon is complete and you can't see the silkworm at all. In each cocoon is a single fiber of silk nearly a mile long. [Compare to a familiar site one mile away.]

The silkworm changes from a caterpillar into a chrysalis inside the cocoon [see *Unraveling Fibers*, p. 26, for pictures of stages]. In about three weeks it develops into a moth. Then it pushes its way out of the cocoon. When this occurs, the long silk fiber is broken into many short ones that are not as useful for making clothes. To be sure there are many long silk fibers, most of the cocoons are placed in ovens where heat or steam kills the silkworm inside while it is still a chrysalis. This process is called *stifling*. The stifled cocoons then are placed in hot water to loosen the silk fibers. Some of the silkworms are kept alive, allowed to develop into moths, and then allowed to escape, however, because mature moths need to mate and lay eggs in order to create new silkworms [see *Unraveling Fibers*, pp. 26–27].

Silk is very strong and lightweight. It's also warm. Some silk cloth is finely woven [show a silk garment]. It feels good and looks translucent—light shines through it and looks lovely. Some silk is nubby and coarse [show samples to illustrate the different kinds of silk].

People often are willing to pay high prices for silk. One reason why silk is expensive is that to create silk threads, silkworms and mulberry bushes are needed—and they can be found only in a few places in the world. [Review the locations using a globe or world map.]

Synthetic Fibers   We have learned about cloth that has been created from silk threads spun by silkworms, from woolen threads spun from the fleece of sheep, and from cotton threads spun from the fibers of the cotton plant. All of these fibers gathered from naturally growing plants and animals are called *natural fibers* [show pictures and garments to illustrate natural fibers].

Other fibers are made by chemists. They are called *synthetic fibers*. Inventors studied how silkworms made silk and figured out how to do it with machines, using fibers that originate from trees, petroleum, natural gas, and chemicals. [Show examples of these materials to further students' sense of wonder.] One of the first synthetic fibers was rayon. [Show an item of clothing made from rayon.] It is produced by cooking wood chips, chemicals, and water to get an oozy pulp. The pulp is bleached, squashed, and dried into thick, white sheets [show photos or a video to illustrate]. The sheets make it easier to transport to a factory, where they are changed from a solid to a liquid.

First they are soaked in a strong chemical. Next, the soggy sheets are shredded into small white crumbs. More chemicals are mixed into the crumbs, turning them orange and changing them into a gooey, honey-like liquid [see *Unraveling Fibers*, pp. 28–29 for pictures]. The liquid is pushed through a metal plate with many small holes. The plate is called a *spinneret*, named after the silkworm's spinneret. The liquid shoots out of the spinneret into an acid bath, where it hardens into fibers. As the fibers leave the acid, they are twisted together into a single strand of yarn. Rayon fibers can be very fine or very thick. Shirts, skirts, and dresses are often made from rayon [show examples]. Other synthetic fibers include

TABLE 2 Fabric Chart

	UNIQUE PROPERTIES	HOW PRODUCED	TYPICAL GARMENTS	SEASON(S) WORN	CARE
Wool					
Cotton					
Silk					
Polyester					

nylon, polyester, and ramie [show samples of articles of clothing made from these synthetic fibers].

Activity

Have students participate in a "mystery bag," activity to distinguish among fabrics and to explain their basic characteristics. Give each student a turn to reach into a bag filled with fabric samples, pull out one sample, and then indicate whether it is natural or synthetic, how it was produced, and the season(s) during which the fabric would most likely be worn. Create a class chart focusing on fabrics as the students provide correct responses (see Table 2).

Summarize

- Silk is produced by silkworms, which eat mulberry leaves, go through a series of stages, and produce silk fibers in the process. Silkworms are raised on silkworm farms.
- Some fibers, such as nylon, rayon, and polyester, were created by humans in a laboratory, and now are made in factories.
- People choose types of fabric based on factors such as climate, cost, availability, suitability for a season, and use.
- Technology has dramatically changed the clothing industry. For example, chemists can now make synthetic fibers that are more easily cared for than natural fibers. Often synthetic fibers are less expensive than natural ones.
- People make choices regarding the types of cloth they select for their garments. If they buy clothing ready-made, the information found on the label is helpful for making decisions about what to buy.

Assessment

Have students write individual stories about the kind of cloth they find most interesting and why.

Post the words associated with the big ideas to encourage correct spellings and to support the use of a language that leads to major understandings. If time permits, encourage students to check out and discuss the labels in their clothing. Use the chart in Table 2 to frame the discussion.

The most interesting kind of cloth, to me, is _____ because _____

_____

_____

_____

_____

_____

It is made by _____

_____

_____

_____

_____

_____

_____

_____

_____

FIGURE 13 Most Interesting Cloth

Name _____

With a parent, inventory closets by looking for clothing made of silk and synthetics.

Articles of Clothing	Silk or Synthetic	Care
1. _____	_____	_____
2. _____	_____	_____
3. _____	_____	_____
4. _____	_____	_____
5. _____	_____	_____

Explain why the silk articles of clothing in your closet probably cost more than the synthetic ones.

FIGURE 14 Silk and Synthetics Inventory

Dear Parents,

We have been learning about silk and synthetics. Please spend a few minutes with your child to inventory one or more closets to determine which articles are made of silk, which of synthetics. If time permits, read labels to find out what kind of care each needs.

Sincerely,

FIGURE 15 Model Letter to Parents

Lesson 8

. . . .

Careers and Inventions

Resources
- Word cards: invention; interdependence; fashion house; designer; mass production
- Pictures or photos of a sewing machine, factory, fashion house, and designer
- Portable sewing machine
- Paper dolls (optional)
- Samples of a variety of footwear types
- Panel of local people who work in the clothing industry (optional)

Children's Literature

Geringer, L. (1985). *A Three Hat Day*. Mexico: Harper Trophy.

Hest, A. (1986). *The Purple Coat*. New York: Macmillan.

Horenstein, H. (1993). *How Are Sneakers Made?* New York: Simon & Schuster.

Morley, J. (1992). *Clothes—For Work, Play, and Display*. New York: Franklin Watts.

Parton, D. *Coat of Many Colors*. New York: HarperCollins.

Rowlands-Warne, L. (1992). *Costume*. London: Dorling-Kindersley.

Sandler, M. W. (1996). *Inventors*. New York: HarperCollins Children's Books.

Tierney, T. (1995). *Great Fashion Designs of the Seventies, Paper Dolls*. Minneola, New York: Dover Publications, Inc.

Winthrop, E. (1986). *Shoes*. New York: Harper Trophy, Division of HarperCollins Publishers.

General Comments

Show students pictures that include a variety of fashions and explain that clothing provides a range of opportunities for individuals to be creative and pursue careers. While today most clothing is mass-produced from basic patterns, often they are copies of designer originals. Several things have had a profound effect on clothing in the last two hundred years. One was the invention of the sewing machine and another was the development of the fashion house concept. This lesson will provide students with a glimpse of the career opportunities connected to clothing. It is intended to pique their interest in the range of career opportunities (choices) that exist in the clothing industry and to instill a realization that people are responsible for changes that have come about in how clothing is produced and what it looks like. Select designs popular when you were a child to share with the students. This will provide a special touch to the design story and generate a lot of interest. Designer books for every ten-year period are available in bookstores.

General Purposes or Goals

To develop: (1) knowledge, understanding, and appreciation regarding career opportunities that exist within the clothing industry; (2) understanding and appreciation for how inventions can change the way work is done and how people can change the way clothing looks; and (3) a sense of efficacy—any of your students might invent a machine or process or design an article of clothing that will benefit all of us in the future.

Main Ideas to Develop

- The clothing industry provides a range of opportunities for individuals to be creative and pursue careers.
- Today, most clothing is mass-produced from basic patterns, often copies of designer originals.
- Several changes have occurred in the clothing industry over the past two hundred years.

Teaching Tips from Barbara

I found that this lesson lent itself well to creating a concept web at the end. That way, we were able to add any other clothing careers that we learned or read about as we continued the unit. Many of the students had focused initially on clothing designers, and the web pushed them to think in other directions, such as manufacturing and marketing.

Starting the Lesson

Begin the lesson by discussing the home assignment.

Suggested Lesson Discussion

Early clothing was all made by hand. Each garment was different and unique. The more detailed it was, the longer it took to make. Today, most people buy their clothes ready-made, although some people still make their own clothing—usually with machines. Also, some people have small shops where they tailor clothes for others. In this town, we have [name local tailor shops].

Tailors use machines too, just not heavy equipment. Tailors can make a better fit, especially if a person doesn't wear a standard size. If you have a tailor sew for you, you can also select your own fabric. [You may want to read *The Purple Coat* by Amy Hest. Also, *Coat of Many*

Colors may be read for language arts. It provides an example of creativity, a one-of-a-kind creation.]

Several things have changed the clothing industry during the last 150 years. Among them are the invention of the sewing machine [show a picture] and opening of fashion houses [show a picture], where people who design clothes present them on models for the first time.

The first sewing machine [show picture] was invented in 1846 by Elias Howe. Five years later, Isaac Singer received a patent for a slightly different model. Some of the first sewing machines were destroyed by people who thought that their jobs were being threatened by automation. Some jobs were eliminated, but the sewing machine created a whole new industry that provided more work for more people. The machine was responsible for an entirely new concept of clothing—mass production. [Explain and show pictures to illustrate.]

Sewing machines do not spin or weave. They sew the pieces of fabric or cloth together. [Bring a portable sewing machine to class and demonstrate how it works.] Many other inventions (e.g., the cotton gin, power-driven weaving looms) have aided (mechanized) the clothing industry. Today, many people work on refining designs for machinery to produce clothing; others use the machines to make clothes; others transport the clothes; others sell them.

While there are many types of work within the clothing industry (designers, models, sales people, etc.), the remainder of this lesson will focus on fashion and design. About 150 years ago, Charles Worth set up the first fashion house in Paris. It was a completely new idea. Designers (people who draw patterns or blueprints for clothes, parallel to blueprints and designers of homes) invented new patterns, made unique articles of clothing based on the patterns, and presented them on models for potential customers.

Today there are designer houses in many large cities throughout the world. [If relevant, identify individuals in your area who create original patterns for clothes.] Similar to designers of homes, designers of clothing make sketches and drape materials on plastic figures. They give the draped figure to a seamstress or tailor, who makes a sample garment out of a flimsy material called *muslin*. The designer may make changes in the sample before completing the design phase and then selecting a material to be used to make the actual garment. Designer clothing is more expensive because only a few copies are made from specially created patterns, and designers must purchase exclusive rights to make them [show pictures of designer clothes]. Usually, the more individualized they are and the more detail they have, the more they cost [show *Costume*, p. 63]. These designs change often in an attempt to sell more clothes. Most clothes sold in most stores are mass-produced in factories that turn out hundreds, thousands, or even millions of identical garments based on the same patterns (e.g., a Sears-brand, size 7, white T-shirt). Today people have careers as models, designers, and boutique shop owners as well as in the mass production of clothes. Designers of the future may be developing anti-pollutant garments, temperature-controlled suits, and other unique items. [Show designs of the future from *Clothes*, p. 43.] [Use paper dolls (cutouts) found in the bookstore replicating designer clothing to illustrate the range of designs. Allow students to "dress the dolls" in their favorite outfits. Discuss why they are favorites, and why the designer clothing would be so expensive.]

Many designers focus only on what are known as *accessories*, such as hats and shoes. Hats have been worn by men and women throughout all the ages and in all parts of the world [show pictures, pp. 46–47, *Costume*]. Originally, they were worn mainly for protection from the weather. Later they were worn to communicate—who the people were, what they did, and how they felt. [See *The Three Hat Day* by Laura Geringer. This could be shared during language arts class.]

Boots, sandals, and shoes originally developed from the basic need to protect the feet, but as with hats, footwear became an important accessory. Shoes have come in many different styles over the years (see pp. 24–25, *Costume*)—long, pointed toes; plain square toes; lavishly decorated; chunky high platform shoes; and lots of others. Most shoes are made of leather or suede (animal hides). Other materials include rubber, canvas (cotton), silk, wood, and plastic. [Show a variety of footwear to illustrate the range of styles and materials used.]

Many changes in athletic/casual shoes have been made since the 1920s. The steps in making sneakers today are carried out by many people (interdependent) who work in the shoe industry. [Share *How Are Sneakers Made?* by Henry Horenstein. A book that might be shared during language arts is entitled *Shoes* by Elizabeth Winthrop.]

Optional   This would be a great spot for adding a panel of local people who work in various aspects of the clothing industry. The panel should focus on what they do, why they like their work, how inventions and creative discoveries have changed their work, and what types of career opportunities they envision in the future.

Activity

Have students share with a partner their ideas about one career opportunity that exists in the clothing industry. Use probing questions to stimulate thinking: What might you like to do in the clothing industry? What skills would you probably need to learn? What questions about the career do you have? Be sure to have these questions visible (e.g., on chart paper) to ensure that the paired sharing activity stays focused. Conclude with a large-group discussion using students' responses.

Optional   Have students design and dress paper dolls. First they will decide on the type of fabric, season for wearing, care of the fabric, and so on. Then they will write about their design and the model wearing it.

Summarize

- There are many career opportunities within the clothing industry.
- Inventions such as the sewing machine and cotton gin brought major changes to the clothing industry.
- People are responsible for the technology and designs that have resulted in major changes to the clothing industry.
- Most clothing is patterned after basic designs and is mass-produced. These basic patterns are often copied from designer originals. Clothing that has original designer labels is very expensive.

Assessment

Have each student write a paragraph explaining one type of work in the clothing industry that he or she would like to investigate and why. Students should also explain any training they'd need to attain the position.

Alternately, give students role cards that focus on careers and inventions related to the clothing industry. Ask them to explain what they do (or invented), how their invention or discovery has changed the clothing industry, why they are proud of what they do (or have done), and so forth.

Home Assignment

Encourage students to talk with their families about career opportunities connected to the clothing industry. If possible, students should talk to family members, neighbors, and friends connected to the industry. What do they do? What special knowledge/skills do they have?

Also encourage family members to talk about a career in the clothing industry that might be rewarding to pursue (send home copies of Figure 16). What knowledge/skills would be needed? Students should be prepared to share their stories with their classmates.

Dear Parents,

We have been learning about career opportunities connected to the clothing industry. Some of your children voiced interest in these (e.g., owning a clothes boutique, being a model, designing clothes, etc.). We would like you to acquaint your child with individuals you know (if any) who are connected to the clothing industry and discuss clothing-related careers that the child might pursue. Your child might like to draw a picture to represent your conversation.

Sincerely,

FIGURE 16 Model Letter to Parents

Lesson 9

Choice Making

Resources
- Storyboard focusing on choice making
- Questions on strips to be added to storyboard that reveal considerations
- Photos of Ben, Barbara, and Tim (eight-year-olds)
- Price lists for coats and shirts—from catalog, department store, discount store, secondhand store
- Materials for letter writing
- Props: check; cash; credit card; catalog; coat and shirts (with name brands and logos)

General Comments
Prepare and present a storyboard (small board for displaying word and pictures) that depicts choice making. The accompanying scenario should focus on a pair of eight-year-old twins—a boy and girl—who need new coats. Stress that even though weather and climate dictate in part the kinds of clothing that people wear, there are still a lot of opportunities for making personal choices. These include style, type of fabric, how much to spend, where to buy the items, and how to pay for them.

General Purpose or Goals
To develop students' knowledge, skills, and application strategies concerning choices that individuals and families make regarding clothing.

Main Ideas to Develop
- Weather and climate, as well as culture, dictate in part the kinds of clothing people wear, but there are still a lot of opportunities for making personal choices.
- People make clothing choices about style, type of fabric, color, how much to spend given their budget, where to buy the items, and how to pay for them.

Teaching Tips from Barbara
Presenting this lesson with make-believe characters makes it extra fun. At the end of the lesson, I even had one student ask if Ben and Barbara were real people I knew! This is a very authentic real-life application of information from the unit. Don't forget to discuss some less conventional places to acquire clothing: garage sales, thrift stores, hand-me downs,

and consignment shops. For the assessment, we wrote the letter as a whole class first, and then the students all wrote their own. I stressed that no matter what decision is made, you need to be ready to justify it with reasoning and information.

Starting the Lesson

Discuss the home assignment. Encourage students to share their career interests in clothing and the reasons for their choices. Underscore the idea that there are numerous possibilities—and there will be more by the time they are adults. Begin with a storyboard that depicts choice making. Include photos of eight-year-old twins, a boy and a girl (Ben and Barbara) who need new coats. Play the role of the "parent" and, together with the class, decide how to solve the problem. As you lead the class in discussing the situation with Ben and Barbara, address the following questions and issues posted on the storyboard:

- Do they currently have usable coats? If so, why do they need new ones?
- If older siblings or relatives have outgrown coats that would fit Ben and/or Barbara, would that solve the problem? Why or why not?
- If new coats need to be purchased, where should the family go to shop? Catalog? Department store? Discount store? Wait for sale? Secondhand store? Garage sale? [Use drama to offset the need for a perfect picture (e.g., close your eyes and imagine you are at a department store, garage sale, etc.).]
- If purchased now, what sizes, colors, and styles should be selected? Why?
- What trade-offs do different types/styles of coat offer?
- Is a name brand important? Why? Why not?
- Should coats be selected that need dry cleaning, or should they be ones that can be laundered? Advantages? Disadvantages?
- How much can they cost?
- How should the family pay for them? Cash? Check? Credit card? Other? [Use lots of pictures. Post the questions and suggested answers. Include costs at the various places, etc.]

Table Activity

After discussing the choices that Ben and Barbara's family need to make, present another scenario focusing on Tim, an eight-year-old who has a part in a school play or program. His shirts are becoming too small, and the ones that do fit are faded. Have each table decide if Tim's family should purchase a new shirt for him. If so, where? Size? Logo or name brand? Color? Style? Care considerations? Cost? Method of payment?

Post the questions to be considered. Each group should be prepared to present the reasons for its choices. The table leaders should write down on a card what each group decided the family should do regarding Tim's dilemma (buy? not buy? where?). (The responses on the cards should be helpful for the students when they write their own letters giving Tim their recommendations.)

Large-Group Discussion

Conclude the lesson with a large-group discussion that focuses on each table's responses.

Optional   This lesson contains several social action possibilities. Collect unused, outgrown garments that can be contributed to a local service organization. As a class, deliver the clothing. Alternately, you could arrange a garage sale focused on recycling clothing. Open the opportunity to the local community. All proceeds can be donated to a charity of the children's choice—or used to help a local child who currently has a need as the result of a fire, flood, or other disaster. Finally, you might wish to become involved with a local agency or service club that is engaged in a community project that focuses on kids' clothing.

Summarize

- Weather and climate, and sometimes culture, dictate in part the kinds of clothing people wear, but there are still a lot of opportunities for making personal choices.
- People make choices about style, type of fabric, color, how much to spend, where to buy items, and how much to pay for them.

Assessment

Have each student write a letter to Tim's family explaining his or her recommendations regarding the shirt purchase. Students should include reasons for the choices.

Home Assignment

Have each student, with a family member, identify one article of clothing that the student will need in the future, and then discuss the choices that will be made and the reasons for them. Send home copies of Figure 17, which should be used for recording the information.

Name _____

The goal for this family activity is to assist your children in acquiring knowledge, skills, appreciation, and application concerning the choices that need to be made regarding their clothing purchases.

Discuss your child's clothing needs until you agree that very soon your child will need a new _____ (specify article of clothing). Possible considerations: Does an older sibling or relative have one that can be worn by _____ (specify child's name)? Yes/No? Will that be an acceptable choice? Why? _____ Why not? _____ Other considerations? (e.g., style, color, cost, where to buy the item, how to pay for it, etc.)

FIGURE 17 Choice Making

Lesson 10

· ·

Review

Resources

- Time lines
- Graphics (diagrams or charts used during the unit)
- Student work
- Bulletin boards
- Sample articles of clothing
- Large sheets of paper with questions for carousel activity
- Markers (various colors and question sheets for carousel activity—one for each question)
- Letter-writing materials

General Comments

This lesson will focus on a review of the big ideas developed through the unit. The time line, graphics, samples of student work, bulletin boards focusing on clothing, and sample articles of clothing will provide the stimuli for a quick oral review. This will be followed by a carousel activity.

General Purposes or Goals

To develop an overall understanding and appreciation for: (1) why clothing is one of our basic needs; how methods of responding to this need have changed over time; how transportation, communication, and technology have made it possible for people around the world to dress in similar ways on a day-to-day basis, yet dress in unique ways for special occasions; (2) the need to consider climate, culture, cost, and purpose when selecting what to wear; (3) the range of materials (fabrics) that are available for making clothing; and (4) the trade-offs in mass-produced versus creative individual designs.

Main Ideas to Develop

- Clothing is a basic human need.
- Throughout history, individuals have used clothing for protection, communication, decoration, and modesty.
- People in various cultures may dress differently, but on a day-to-day basis, children around the world tend to dress more alike than different.
- People wear special clothing for festivals, to celebrate holidays, to participate in recreational activities, or to perform certain jobs.

- Culture, gender, climate, and economics are all factors related to special types of clothing.
- Clothing has undergone a variety of changes over time.
- Steps or processes that depict the story of wool or cotton are called land-to-hand. They begin with the raw material (i.e., wool from sheep, cotton from a plant). The final step is the manufactured finished product (e.g., wool sweater, cotton jeans).
- Natural fibers come from plants or animals; synthetic fibers are made by chemists from wood, petroleum, or various chemicals.
- Clothing is made from natural or synthetic fibers. Cloth is made by weaving it from threads spun from these fibers.
- The label in a garment identifies the type of material that is used, tells where the garment was made, and explains how it should be cared for.
- There are many careers within the clothing industry. People in the clothing industry with ideas create new products and processes.
- People are responsible for the technology and designs that have resulted in major changes in the clothing industry.
- Today, most clothing is mass-produced from basic patterns, although many are copies of designer originals.
- People make choices about clothing style, type of fabric, color, how much to spend, where to buy the items, and how to pay for them.
- Several changes have occurred in the clothing industry in the past two hundred years.

Teaching Tips from Barbara

During the review lesson, I tried to help students make connections between pieces of information in different lessons. For example, we talked about the role of cost, climate, or culture in many different ways and in different contexts. We talked about the ways clothing has changed over time. We talked about the many types of cloth we have and how each fabric is made.

Starting the Lesson

Ask students to share their home assignment responses regarding future clothing needs with their peers. The lesson will begin near the bulletin boards, timeline, graphics, samples of students' work, and samples of fabrics and articles of clothing. After reviewing highlights of the unit, pose questions in an oral test format. Here are some sample questions, with possible answers in parentheses.

1. Clothing is something that every human being _____ (needs).

2. Throughout history, people have used clothing for _____, _____, _____, _____ (modesty, protection, communication, decoration)

3. People in different cultures may dress _____ (the same or differently).

4. People wear special clothing for _____, _____, _____, _____, _____ (special occasions, parties, funerals, weddings, sports, armed services, proms, etc.).

5. Clothing has undergone lots of _____ (changes) over time.

6. Eight steps to make wool clothes are: _____ (raise sheep) _____ (shear sheep) _____ (clean the fleece) _____ (card the wool) _____ (spin wool into yarn) _____ (weave yarn into cloth) _____ (dye cloth) _____ (make clothes).

7. Eight steps to make cotton clothes are: _____ (plant cotton) _____ (pick cotton) _____ (separate seeds) _____ (wash cotton) _____ (spin yarn) _____ (weave cloth) _____ (dye cloth) _____ (make clothes).

8. Two things you need to have for silk are _____ and _____ (silkworms and mulberry leaves).

9. Clothing is made from either _____ or _____ fibers (synthetic or natural).

10. Some natural fibers are _____, _____, and _____ (cotton, wool, silk, linen).

11. The _____ in your clothes tells what types of material it contains and where it is made (label).

12. There are many _____ in the clothing industry (jobs, careers).

13. When you think about buying clothing, you need to think about _____, _____, _____, _____, _____, _____ (size, style, color, brand, cost, where to buy, how much money to pay).

During this fill-in-the-blank test, read the questions and ask everyone to think carefully. When the students have an idea, they should put their finger on their forehead. (This will give other students more think time.) Then have students pair up and discuss their ideas with a peer.

Finally, return students to their tables and give the directions for the carousel activity. This activity is most effective in the early grades if student mentors—one per group—serve as readers/recorders. Otherwise, name one student at each table to be the scribe for the group. Each scribe has a different-colored marker.

Each group and scribe begins at the site where the question (printed on a large sheet of paper) matches the color of its marker. Designate five minutes for each group to discuss and record its response. Then ask each group to move to its left, keeping its own colored marker. The tasks are to read the new question and the previous group's response, then place a question mark beside any part of that response that this group is unclear about or disagrees with. Then the group will discuss and record additional responses to the question. Continue this procedure until all groups have responded to all of the questions and returned to the sites where they started the activity. At this point, each group should review all of the responses to the question at its station and prepare to expand on the answers during large-group discussion. During the discussion, clarify responses from the carousel activity.

Questions might include:

Why do people wear clothing?

Why do people wear special clothing?

How has clothing changed over time?

How have inventions and designs changed the clothing industry?

What are the steps in creating a woolen garment?

How do people decide what to wear?

Why are we able to have so many different kinds of fabrics for our clothes?

What choices do people make about their clothing?

Summarize

- Clothing is one of our basic needs, but it has changed dramatically over time.
- As with shelter, climate, culture, and cost are among the factors that influence people's choices about clothing.

Assessment

Have students write letters to their upper-grade mentors explaining the most important things they learned about clothing. Encourage their mentors to respond.

Unit 3: Shelter

Introduction

. . . .

As a way to help you think about shelter as a cultural universal and begin to plan your teaching on the topic, we have provided a list of questions that address some of the big ideas developed in our unit plans. The questions focus on what we believe to be important ideas for children to learn about shelter. These include shelter in the past, features of modern homes (including the processes and economics involved in supplying them with heat, light, and running water), the trade-offs and economics involved in renting versus buying shelter, and the students' ideal homes in the future.

To find out what primary-grade students know (or think they know) about these questions, we interviewed more than fifty students in each of Grades K–3. You may want to use some or all of these questions during preunit or prelesson assessments of your students' prior knowledge. For now, though, we recommend that you jot down your own answers to the questions before going on to read about the answers we elicited in our interviews. This will sharpen your awareness of ways in which adults' knowledge about shelter differs from children's knowledge, as well as reduce the likelihood that you will assume that your students already know certain things that seem obvious to you but may need to be spelled out for them. The questions are listed in Figure 1.

If you want to use some of these questions to assess your students' prior knowledge before beginning the unit, you can do this either by interviewing selected students individually or by asking the class as a whole to respond to the questions and recording their answers for future reference. If you take the latter approach, an option would be to embed it within the KWL technique by initially questioning students to determine

1. Do people live in homes just because they want to, or do they need homes? . . . Why?

2. What about in places like Hawaii where it's warm all year? Do people still need homes there? . . . Why?

3. [Show drawing of longhouse and photo of pueblo.] Here are two kinds of homes that different groups of Indians lived in a long time ago. Why do you think that some Native Americans lived in this kind of home [the longhouse] but others lived in this kind of home [the pueblo]?

4. [Show photo of tipi.] Some other Native Americans lived in this kind of home. Do you know what it was called? [Elicit, or if necessary, give the name *tipi*.] Why do you think that they lived in tipis instead of other kinds of homes?

5. [Show drawing of cabin.] Two hundred years ago, the pioneers lived in log cabins. What were those log cabins like back then? . . . How were they different from today's homes?

6. How did people who lived in log cabins get their water?

7. How did they heat up their cabins?

8. What about light? After it was dark, did they have light in their cabins?

9. Let's talk about the homes that people live in today. Some families live in houses, and some live in apartment buildings. Do you think that most people would rather live in a house or in an apartment? . . . Why?

10a. [If child says most people would rather live in a house] If most people would rather live in houses, why do so many people live in apartments? [If answer only mentions lack of money to buy a house] Some people could afford to buy a house but they would rather live in an apartment. Why do you think they want an apartment?

10b. [If child says most people would rather live in an apartment] If most people would rather live in apartments, why do so many people live in houses?

11. Do you live in a house, an apartment, a trailer home, or what?

12. In small towns, most people live in houses or small apartment buildings, but in big cities, many people live in very tall apartment buildings, like this one. [Show photo.] Why do you think they have so many big, tall apartment buildings in big cities?

13. The people who live in apartment buildings—do they have to pay money to live there? . . . Who do they pay? . . . Why do they have to pay?

14. Some people rent a place to live, and some people buy one. What's the difference between renting and buying?

15. Can a family buy a place to live and move into it even if they have only part of the money they need to pay for it?

16. Inside our homes, we use water when we turn on our faucets. Where does that water come from?

17. Our homes are heated when the weather is cold. Where does that heat come from?

18. When we use heat in our homes, do we have to pay for it? . . . Who do we pay? . . . Why do we have to pay?

19. Families light up their homes by turning on lamps or lights. How does that work?

20. Do families have to pay for the lighting in their homes? . . . Who do we pay? . . . Why do we have to pay?

21. When you're grown up and have a family of your own, you might want to buy a place to live. What kind of place would you look for?

22. Is there anything unusual or special about the home you would want?

23. What about the location of the home? . . . Would you want to live near certain things? . . . Would you want to live far away from certain things?

FIGURE 1 (Continued)

what they <u>k</u>now and what they <u>w</u>ant to find out, then later revisiting their answers and recording what they <u>l</u>earned. An alternative to preassessing your students' knowledge about topics developed in the unit as a whole would be to conduct separate preassessments prior to each lesson, using only the questions that apply to that lesson (and perhaps adding others of your own choosing).

Children's Responses to Our Interviews

Students' responses to these questions generally improve as they progress through the K–3 range, especially between first grade and second grade. However, the most interesting findings involved variation in knowledge displayed by the group as a whole in their answers to different questions. Even most kindergartners were able to supply acceptable answers to some questions, but even most third graders were unable to supply acceptable responses to other questions.

Most students understood that people need homes, even in warm places like Hawaii, because we need shelter from the elements and a "home base" for everyday living. However, some students only thought about shelter from cold and snow, not realizing that people also need shelter from the sun and from rain. Also, although most knew that shelter is a basic and universal human need, most were less appreciative of modern homes as controlled environments for comfortable living that cater to a great many of our wants as well as our more basic needs.

Subsequent responses emphasized description over explanation and form over function. That is, students could describe differences in the size, construction materials, durability, and general quality of the shelter provided by various Native American and pioneer homes, but they did not understand much about the historical, geographical, or cultural reasons for these contrasting housing styles. Most were not aware that certain Native American tribes were nomadic societies that moved with the buffalo, so they did not appreciate that portability was a crucial quality of tipis. Most were unable to explain why certain tribes used tipis, or else suggested reasons such as that tipi dwellers were poor people who could not afford better homes, preferred tipis because they could build fires in them and the smoke would discharge through the hole in the top, or needed something to do with leftover animal skins that they didn't want to waste. Most were able to make sensible statements about differences between pueblos and longhouses (e.g., pueblos were made of sand or concrete whereas longhouses were made of trees and branches). However, few mentioned differences in climate or geography as factors contributing to the differences between these two forms of Native American housing. Only about 15 percent of the students, including only 20 percent of the second and third graders, noted that longhouses were built where wood was plentiful whereas pueblos were built in desert landscapes.

Responses concerning log cabins were more accurate and less fanciful than those concerning Native American homes. Even so, misconceptions were common (e.g., that the cabins could collapse easily because the logs were not nailed together). Furthermore, most of the students emphasized deficiencies of log cabins in comparison to modern homes: The cabins were small or cramped, the beds and furniture were primitive, they lacked electricity and modern plumbing, the roofs were leaky, and so on. This tendency to disparage the past by comparing it unfavorably with the present is called *historical presentism*, and it is common among students who have not yet been taught to appreciate the technology of the past as inventive adaptation to time and place. In teaching about log cabins, for example, curriculum and instruction can help students appreciate what the pioneers were able to accomplish, not just what their lives lacked relative to ours. Fireplaces featured stone hearths and chimneys that allowed people to cook in and heat up their cabins without filling them with smoke or burning them down. The cabins were built near an above-ground water source or else a well was dug nearby, so water did not have to be toted very far. The pioneers made their own candles and were able to use these, as well as oil lamps or lanterns, to light their homes after dark. Most furniture and many implements were homemade using relatively simple tools and thus were primitive by our standards, but if taken in the context of their time and place, they can be appreciated as elegantly designed, functional, and often artistic. Wells were not mere holding tanks but means of gaining access to underground water sources. Modern refrigeration was not available, but the pioneers developed creative ways to keep foods cool or preserve them for storing before they could spoil. In these and many other respects, pioneer life can be taught in ways that develop empathy with the people and appreciation for their accomplishments, not just distancing or pity based on the ideas that they lived difficult lives or lacked modern conveniences. Similar goals can be accomplished when teaching about how other people from the past (e.g., Native Americans) or contemporary people living in less developed societies have been inventive in devising ways to meet their shelter needs given the resources available to them.

In thinking about contemporary housing, students focused on what is visible inside and outside the home but did not show much awareness of what is in between the walls or beneath the building. Most of them understood that people have to pay for shelter and that most people prefer homes to apartments. Commonly given explanations emphasized that houses are bigger and provide more living space than apartments, that owning your own house affords greater privacy and avoids the problem of having to live in close quarters with others, that the house is yours to decorate and use as you wish without being constrained by guidelines that renters must follow, and that houses feature extras such as fireplaces, swimming pools, or patios. Many students thought that people live in apartments only when they cannot afford a house or are waiting while their house is being built. Others displayed misconceptions in attempting to explain why some people might prefer apartments, thinking that apartments might be quieter (from students who knew that apartments have rules against noise) or that they offer amenities such as soft-drink and candy machines outside the room and a stocked refrigerator waiting for them inside the room (from students who confused apartments with hotels). Only a few students understood that some people do not want the work of keeping up a house, and even fewer understood that some people take apartments because of their convenient locations.

Students had difficulty explaining what is involved in buying versus renting homes and why people choose these options. More than 90 percent understood that apartment dwellers have to pay to live in their apartments, but most gave only "fact-of-life" explanations: Everyone has to pay for housing, nothing is free, they won't let you stay there if you don't pay, and so on. Fewer than 20 percent understood that rent money is kept by the owner of the building, and most of these thought that all of this money goes to reimburse the owner for building maintenance expenses. No student showed clear understanding that renting is a profit-making business.

Most students understood the difference between renting and buying a place to live, and about two-thirds included the key concept that buying implies home ownership (the rest explained it only in terms of short-term vs. long-term occupancy). However, the students explained home ownership only in terms of being able to use and decorate the home as you wish and to sell it when you decide to move. No student mentioned buildup of equity, appreciation of property value, or other concepts relating to investment or economic assets.

Only about a fourth of the students were aware that a family could buy and move into a house before it had accumulated the full purchase price, and only about 5 percent were able to (partially) explain the basic concept of a mortgage loan. For the vast majority of students, buying versus renting was reduced to paying the full purchase price for a home in a single transaction versus paying much smaller amounts of money periodically to continue living in an apartment. Most knew nothing at all about—and most of the rest could not explain—how mortgage loans make it possible for families to buy and move into a house before they have accumulated the full purchase price. Only two students (third graders) were able to explain the motives and financial arrangements involved in these transactions (i.e., that the bank charges interest and thus makes profits from mortgage loans, but people are willing to pay this interest because it allows them to move into a home much sooner than they would be able to otherwise).

The students showed only limited awareness of the mechanisms through which modern houses are supplied with water, heat, and light. Almost all of them understood that water is piped into the home, but many were vague or incorrect about the source of this water, did not appreciate that it is drawn from fresh- rather than saltwater sources and purified before being sent to homes, and did not realize that it arrives under pressure. Most understood that thermostats are used to adjust heating, but were vague about where the heat comes from or how the system works. Their thinking appeared to progress from believing that a utility company supplies heat (i.e., warm air) directly and the furnace is merely a storage place, to knowing that heat is generated in the furnace but not knowing how, to knowing that the furnace contains a fire that heats air. Only about an eighth of the students clearly understood that furnaces contain fires. A majority knew that electricity is involved in creating light, because they knew that one must throw a switch to allow electricity to enter the bulb. However, they were unable to explain how the arrival of electricity causes the bulb to light up.

Most students did understand that families pay for the water that is piped into their homes, according to how much they use. However, most were unclear or incorrect about payment for heat and light. Few understood that "heat" bills are actually for fuel consumed in fires that create heat in furnaces or that "light" bills are actually for electricity consumed when light bulbs are activated.

Some of the younger students were limited or naive in what they were able to say about their ideal homes, and a few older students playfully depicted mansions equipped with extensive sports or recreation facilities. Most of the students, however, depicted a comfortably large house located in a quiet, family-oriented suburban or semi-rural neighborhood. Many added that this home would be located near those of relatives or friends and close or at least convenient to places to shop and take children, but removed from urban density, crime, traffic, and noise. As far as they went, most students' answers to these questions emphasized themes similar to those that would be emphasized by adults. The major exception to this pattern was that only 6 percent of the students indicated that their ideal home would be located close to their workplace.

Most responses reflected a preference for the familiar (which in this case was middle-class neighborhoods and suburbs in and around Lansing, Michigan). Contrasting responses to some of these questions might be expected from students who live in very different environments (e.g., densely populated and "vertical" areas of large cities or sparsely populated rural areas).

For a detailed technical report of findings from our interviews on shelter, see Brophy and Alleman (1999).

Overview of Shelter Unit
—Barbara Knighton

Shelter is different from food and clothing because most children haven't thought about or paid much attention to their home. I found that my students needed information and guidance before they could come up with useful "I wonder" questions, so I began this unit by discussing with the children where they live and our local neighborhood. I chose to use a neighborhood survey to have the children gather information. We discussed surveys, created graphs and charts, and posted the results. Then we were ready to begin expanding our thinking to the unit lessons.

Photographs are very helpful for this unit. You will want to plan ahead so that you have time to take pictures of housing types and construction stages. My students loved going back to the construction photos and placing them in order.

I found that I needed to review the background information to be sure that I was comfortable before teaching each lesson. This was especially true for the history and global lessons. Remember, don't try to use the information as a script, but be sure to read carefully and highlight or make notes about the big ideas. I often make an outline on a note card to use as I teach. That way I remember to stick to the big ideas.

The home assignments that go with this unit involve lots of family discussions and writing. Therefore, I was thoughtful and prudent about the assignments I chose. You want to be careful about time demands on the families. You might want to consider creating a folder to hold all of the assignments, both home and in-school. Then, when the lesson is over, your students will have a nice record of what they've done and learned.

Finally, be sure to keep the big ideas in mind as you teach. The more often you come back to those ideas in different discussions and in different ways, the more students will begin to internalize them. Don't allow yourself to get overinvolved with the specific details of the lessons and miss the important ideas.

Lesson 1

. . . .

Functions of Shelter

Resources

- Pictures, books, and electronic sources and computer in an interest center focusing on shelter
- Strips of paper with questions related to shelter posted throughout the classroom
- Bulletin board that has been started depicting the functions of shelter
- Photos (exterior and interior) of the teacher's home, illustrating its functions
- A Look at Our Home: Home Assignment Sheet (Figure 2)

Children's Literature

Kalman, B. (1994). *Homes Around the World*. New York: Crabtree.

Morris, A. (1992). *Houses and Homes*. New York: Lothrop, Lee & Shepard.

General Comments

To launch the unit, collect the instructional resources and display visual prompts to generate interest in the topic. Post questions (written on wide strips of paper) around the room and on the bulletin board. Good questions might include:

> What is shelter? Why do we need shelter?
>
> Why do people choose different kinds of homes?
>
> What types of homes do we have in our community?
>
> How do climate and physical features influence the types of homes we have?
>
> Why do people sometimes have portable shelters?
>
> What are some of the decisions people have to make when choosing a home?
>
> Why are there so many different kinds of shelters?

General Purposes or Goals

To help students: (1) become aware of the possible questions to be answered about shelter; (2) understand why people need shelter (it provides protection against the elements, provides a place to keep one's possessions, and is a home base for daily life activities); (3) acquire an appreciation for the diversity that exists in the nature and functions of shelter.

Main Ideas to Develop

- Shelter is a basic need.
- Throughout history, people have needed shelter for protection from the elements (sun in hot weather, cold in cold weather, precipitation, wind, etc.), places to keep their possessions, and places in which to carry out their daily activities.
- There are natural factors that affect the kinds of homes built in an area. These include climatic conditions, building materials found locally in large quantities, and physical features. Physical features refer to the terrain and include hills, mountains, valleys, plains as well as bodies of water such as lakes and rivers.
- There are other human factors that people take into account in deciding the kind of home to build or buy. These include the availability of building materials, economic resources, cultural considerations, and personal preferences.

Teaching Tips from Barbara

Once again, this lesson will set the building blocks for the unit. The book *Homes Around the World* is an excellent way to structure this lesson. Also, you might want to consider organizing the information from this lesson into a concept web with the word *functions* in the middle. I used this idea as a way to review the information from the first lesson before going on to the second lesson.

Starting the Lesson

Pose questions regarding the meaning of shelter and its functions. Sample questions might include: What is shelter? Why do people need shelter? Why are there so many different kinds of shelters? How do climate and physical features influence the types of shelters people have? What types of shelters do we have in our community?

After a preliminary discussion of these questions and an explanation about answering these and other questions as the unit unfolds, show the class a bulletin board that you have begun that focuses on the functions of shelter: (1) protection; (2) place to keep one's belongings; and (3) home base for daily activities. Use your home as an example to illustrate the functions of shelter. Show photos of the exterior and interior of your home as you share "your story," focusing on the three main functions:

Suggested Lesson Discussion

1. *Protection.* People need places to live that provide protection from cold, heat, storms, insects, and animals. Even in warm climates, people need protection from the elements. There is a variety of shelter types that people can choose for protection. In our community, there are houses, apartments, duplexes, and manufactured

homes. A manufactured home is a house built in two sections, each on its own foundation, that sits on a trailer to be hauled to a person's property. It is then put together. They can be quite luxurious, with island kitchens, fireplaces, and master bedroom suites. These manufactured homes have replaced the simple trailer homes of the past. Can you think of others? [Show a photo of your shelter and explain why you chose it. Describe the building materials that were used and why. If available, show samples.]

2. *Places to keep belongings.* The interior of the home is a place to store food, clothes, books, prized possessions, furniture, and other things. [Through photos, take an imaginary walking tour of your home, showing your various belongings and explaining why they need to be kept inside.]

3. *Home base.* The interior of the home is also a place for carrying out your daily activities, such as sleeping, eating, doing school work, watching television, and spending time with family. [Continue the imaginary walking tour of your home, pointing out its uses as a home base.]

Optional   If time permits, organize a walking tour of the immediate neighborhood, pointing out the different kinds of homes—contrasting in many ways, yet all made of building materials suited to the physical features and climate. As you walk, underscore that each of these homes provides protection, a place for one's belongings, and a home base for daily activities. If possible, arrange to tour a home in the neighborhood and illustrate its functions. Explain its similarities to your home.

Share the book entitled *Homes Around the World* with the students (it contains numerous illustrations depicting the functions of homes). Explain that homes vary in size, shape, and type of building materials used, depending on physical features, climatic conditions, available resources, and people's personal choices. However, they all serve the same basic functions.

Activity

At the conclusion of the presentation regarding the functional uses of shelter, ask the students to share in pairs the most interesting ideas they learned. Then, elicit ideas from the pairs and write them on the board. Ask students to indicate other questions that they would like to have answered about the functions (or other aspects) of shelter. Post the questions. Encourage students to peruse the books and electronic resources available in the shelter center in the classroom.

Summarize

- Shelter serves several functions that are universal across time, culture, and place.

- Shelters are made of a variety of building materials, depending on natural and human factors.
- There are many kinds of shelters, such as apartments, duplexes, manufactured homes, and houses, even in our community; however, they all provide protection, a place to store belongings, and a base for daily activities.

Assessment

Have the students brainstorm at their tables the things they have learned about the functions of shelter. Then, as a class, complete a chart focusing on these functions. Encourage the students to give and explain examples. Then have students individually respond to the following open-ended statements. (Use upper-grade mentors or posted word cards reflecting the big ideas, if necessary.)

People need shelters because _____.

My teacher's home protects her from _____.

My teacher's home provides a place for _____.

Day-to-day living activities at my teacher's house include _____, _____, _____, and _____.

If time permits, have students draw pictures to illustrate their responses.

Home Assignment

Encourage the students to share with their families what they learned about the functions of shelter in their neighborhood and around the world, and about their teacher's home (using the open-ended statements as the springboard for the conversation). Also, encourage students to discuss with their families their shelter choices (i.e., why they live where they do) and the functions that their home fulfills for them. Ask families to complete and return the form shown in Figure 2.

Name _____

With a parent or an older brother or sister, look around your home. List examples of how your home functions. For example, the roof, walls, windows, and doors keep out the rain. The roof provides shade from the sun. The locks keep unwanted people from entering. Please attach a photo or drawing of your family's home.

PARTS OF OUR HOME THAT PROVIDE PROTECTION	PARTS OF OUR HOME THAT PROVIDE PLACES TO KEEP BELONGINGS	PARTS OF OUR HOME THAT PROVIDE A BASE FOR DAILY ACTIVITIES

FIGURE 2 A Look at Our Home

©2001 by Janet Alleman and Jere Brophy from *Social Studies Excursions, K–3*. Portsmouth, NH: Heinemann

Lesson 2

Shelter Types in Our Community

Resources
- Pictures and photos of homes in the local community
- Photos of your home
- Local map
- Pictures and photos illustrating shelter types in city, suburb, village/town, and country settings
- Building materials used in the local area (wood, brick, vinyl, aluminum, cement)
- Word cards (factors that contribute to shelter types): culture, physical features, climate, economics, personal preference
- Multiple packets of cards displaying various shelters
- Interview schedule for home assignment

Children's Literature
Kalman, B. (1994). *Homes Around the World*. New York: Crabtree.

Morris, A. (1992). *Houses and Homes*. New York: Lothrup, Lee, & Shepard.

General Comments
Encourage the students to take a careful look around their community as a means of realizing the diversity of shelter types that exist locally. This is a nice segue from their preliminary investigation associated with functions of homes.

General Purposes or Goals
To: (1) stimulate curiosity, build interest, and get students into the habit of actively observing the range of shelter types that exist locally; (2) develop knowledge, understanding, appreciation, and life application regarding shelter considerations and the factors that contribute to people's decisions about shelter.

Main Ideas to Develop
- There is a range of shelter types in our local community.
- Natural factors that contribute to the type of shelters that can be built in an area include climatic conditions, building materials found locally in large quantities, and physical features (terrain, including hills, mountains, valleys, plains, etc., and bodies of water such as lakes and rivers).

- Factors that contribute to family decisions about the type of shelter it will select include location in the community, cost, cultural influences, and personal preferences.

Teaching Tips from Barbara

Photographs are the key to this lesson. You can use a combination of photos of homes in your area as well as copies from books and encyclopedias. A great way to review after this lesson is to use the book *Homes Around the World* and other books that you've collected for this unit. Name a type of shelter and have students look for that type in their book.

Starting the Lesson

Share the results of the home assignment from Lesson 1. Explain that all homes serve the same basic functions; however, they may look quite different. Even in the local community, there is a range of shelter types. Show pictures and photos to illustrate the variety. Then, using a map, compare city, a suburb, and the country (i.e., rural areas).

Suggested Lesson Discussion

Cities have the most people. Some live in houses, duplexes, and manufactured homes. However, there is not enough land for everyone who wants to live in a large city to build a house, so housing tends to be built "up" instead of "out" there. Hundreds of people can live in a large apartment building. High-rises have floors and floors of homes. [Show photos of apartment buildings—exterior and interior. Explain that many of the tall buildings in large cities are apartment buildings, not office buildings, and that very tall apartment buildings are called *high-rises*. You may also wish to explain the difference between hotels and apartment buildings.]

Suburbs are communities that have grown outside cities. Often people who work in the cities choose to live in the suburbs, which tend to be less crowded and where more land is available for housing. [Show photos or pictures of suburban homes, explaining that they often have front and back yards. Some even have swimming pools.]

Some people live in tiny towns and villages in the country. [Show photos or pictures of houses in towns and villages.] They tend to know one another because there are fewer people than in the cities and suburbs. The houses are generally quite close together.

The country has even fewer people. Usually the homes are built on farms or other large parcels of land. The surrounding land is used for growing crops and raising animals.

[Identify whether your students live in a city, a suburb, a rural town or village, or in the country. Then focus on the students' photos of the exteriors of local homes. Explain that their homes are different sizes and shapes because some are houses and others are apartments, condos, manufactured homes, or duplexes. Show a range of photographs that illustrate local housing, and discuss the local geographic features.]

Most of the houses, duplexes, and apartments in Michigan are made of wood. It is a renewable resource that is found in that state and can be easily cut, shaped, and joined on site. Homes can be made entirely of wood, but usually wood is used with other materials. [Show samples of wood, vinyl siding, brick, etc.] One disadvantage of wood as a building material is that it rots. To retard rot, the wood is often treated with chemicals that keep insects and fungus from dampness from destroying it. In four-season communities that have cold winters, hot summers, and quite a bit of moisture, the wood is usually sealed and painted to keep it dry inside.

Some modern apartment buildings are constructed of concrete blocks. Usually the blocks are covered with a layer of cement and sand mixed together with water. Then, the buildings are painted. Manufactured homes are made of some of the same materials as individual family homes but are built on movable frames, allowing them to be transported. Some are now even two-story homes. All of these building materials are good choices for relatively flat land with cold winters and hot summers.

Houses and duplexes are built in many shapes and painted many colors. [Show a montage of photos illustrating the variety.]

People make many decisions about their shelter. First, they decide whether to live in a city, suburb, small town, or rural area. Then they decide whether to live in an apartment, condo, duplex, manufactured home, or house. After they have decided where to look and what type of home to look for, they need to decide whether they can and want to spend a lot of money for their home, whether they want to rent or buy it, and how they will decorate it.

[Underscore the factors that are considered: local geographic features, cost, and cultural influences. Show photos of homes in the local area that show influences of their heritage, such as Japanese architecture or Mexican decorations. Revisit the photos of your home. Now, instead of focusing on functions, emphasize other factors that you considered, such as cost, local geographic features, building materials available, and personal preferences.]

Activity

Use the pictures found in *Homes Around the World* again; however, this time, emphasize types. Ask students to give "thumbs up" if the picture illustrates a type of shelter found in the local community and "thumbs down" if the picture illustrates a type that is not found locally. Ask students to provide reasons for their answers.

Summarize

- There is a range of shelter types in our local community.
- Factors that contribute to the types of shelter that can be constructed in the area include physical features and climatic conditions.
- Factors that affect people's decisions include cultural influences, cost, and personal preferences.

Assessment

Tell the students to imagine that they are local real estate agents familiarizing a newcomer to the types of homes available. Give each student a stack of cards depicting shelter types and ask him or her to identify those that illustrate homes found in the local area. When students have completed the task, conduct a class discussion focusing on their responses and their reasoning. If time permits, have students select one card depicting a shelter type not found in the local area and explain in writing where it would most likely be found and why.

Home Assignment

Have students interview their families about the type of shelter they have selected and why. Ask families to complete and return the form shown in Figure 3.

1. How did our family decide where to live?

_____

_____

_____

2. Describe the building materials used for our home.

_____

_____

_____

3. We have learned that there are many factors that determine the type of shelter that a family selects. These include location in the community, cost, construction materials used, cultural influences, and personal preferences. What was the most important consideration for our family?

_____

Explain.

_____

_____

_____

4. What are the special features of our home? (Encourage the family to take a walking tour to observe yard, decorations, architectural style, etc.)

_____

_____

_____

5. Did you choose between our present home and one or two others? If so, where would we be living today if you had made the other choice(s)? Where would we be going to school?

_____

_____

_____

FIGURE 3 Learning About Your Home: An Interview

Lesson 3

. . . .

Shelter Types Around the World

Resources

- Pictures and photos of homes around the world, including four-season frame house, chalet, igloo, yurt, thatched-roof house, stilt house, houseboat, adobe house, high-rise, Bedouin tent, brightly decorated African clay house, and the interior of a luxury high-rise apartment
- Examples of materials used in building homes in various parts of the world
- Word cards: climate, physical features, availability of building materials, economics, personal preferences, cultural considerations
- Large sheets of paper accompanied by words and pictures that characterize a range of environments in the world (desert, mountains, ice/snow-covered area, tropical rainforest, etc.) and cards with pictures illustrating shelter types

Children's Literature

Boon, K. (1993). *Houses*. Bothell, WA: The Wright Group.

Gibbons, G. (1990). *Up Goes the Skyscraper*. New York: Aladdin.

Jackson, M. (1995). *Homes Around the World*. Austin, TX: Steck-Vaughn.

Kalman, B. (1994). *Houses Around the World*. New York: Crabtree.

Kalman, B. (1995). *Nicola's Floating House*. New York: Crabtree.

Morris, A. (1992). *Houses and Homes*. New York: Lothrop, Lee, & Shepard.

Patrick, S. (1996). *Living in the Sky*. Bothell, WA: The Wright Group.

Scholastic. (1994). *Architecture and Construction*. New York: Author.

Steltzer, U. (1981). *Building an Igloo*. New York: Henry Holt & Co.

Weiss, H. (1988). *Shelters from Tepee to Igloo*. New York: Thomas Y. Crowell Publishers.

General Comments

This lesson focuses on the range of shelter types around the world, showing students that there are many types of shelters besides those with which they are familiar. Emphasize the adaptations that people make to their environment and how their choices are based on geographical features, available resources, economics, culture, and personal preferences.

General Purposes or Goals

To: (1) stimulate curiosity as well as build appreciation for the diversity of shelter types in the world, understood as inventive adaptations to time and place; (2) recognize and explain the types of shelters that would and would not be appropriate in the local environment; and (3) explain how people adapt to their local environment when making choices associated with shelter.

Main Ideas to Develop

- Geographic features, culture, economic resources, and personal preferences are among the factors that figure into people's choices about the type of shelter they will have.
- People all over the world adapt to their environment, and as a result, there are many types of shelters. Until recently, housing construction reflected the availability of local materials. This pattern still exists in some places, but in other places modern transportation has allowed choices to be expanded.

Teaching Tips from Barbara

There are many great books that show types of housing from around the world. Put together a nice collection to support this lesson. As you discuss each type of shelter, use the four basic decision-making factors equally: physical features, climate, economics, and culture. Also, continue to refer back and tie into the functions of shelter. Another great resource for this lesson is the computer program *SimTown*. I used it as a whole-group lesson in which we created a town together. The program offers several different types of shelters to put in the town, including apartments, duplexes, grass shacks, and mobile homes.

Starting the Lesson

Share the results of the home assignment, then begin with a montage of pictures and photos of homes around the world. As you point to each illustration, have the students give a "thumbs up" if you could expect to see the shelter type locally and "thumbs down" if you would find it elsewhere. Elicit reasons for responses and encourage questions about other aspects of the illustrated homes. Explain that this lesson is about homes in other parts of the world: the materials typically used to build them, the special features they include, and how these are affected by local climate and physical features, economic resources, cultural influences, and personal preferences.

Suggested Lesson Discussion

Physical Features   The physical features (land and water forms) of places determine what materials are available to use for building homes. For example, in a mountainous area where there is a lot of rock or stone, we are likely to find a lot of rock or stone houses. In or near forests, however, the materials used will probably be wood and leaves. Where there is a lot of ice and snow—and little else—we might find an igloo (although nowadays, igloos are used only for short periods of time because even in Alaska most people do not live in barren, isolated places for very long. They go there for a few days at a time to fish and hunt, then return to their villages or towns).

Climate   Climate determines what natural elements people need shelter from. In a cold climate, they need a home that is durable against winter weather, seamless or tightly fit to prevent cold winds from blowing through, insulated to retain heat, and capable of delivering sufficient heat to all of its rooms if possible. In a warm climate, they need a shelter that protects from the hot sun, storms, and winds. In places where it rains a lot, they need protection from the moisture. In a four-season climate, they need homes that contain all of these features and are adjustable with the season, through mechanisms such as switching storm windows for screens or a furnace for an air conditioner. [Show picture of a four-season house with screens/storm windows.]

   Some people live in very cold climates because they live in mountainous places. Their homes often have steeply sloped roofs that prevent dangerous accumulation of heavy snowfall on the roof and cause the snow to pile up against the side of the house, where it acts as insulation. Also, some homes are built into the side of a slope (facing the sun) to minimize exposure to the cold and the wind.

   Some places in the world are very cold and barren. Blizzards, endless snow, and extremely cold weather make living conditions very difficult. People who spend short periods of time hunting and fishing in these cold places used to build igloos from snow. First, a circle about ten feet in diameter is marked out; then blocks of snow are used to build a hut. The thickness of the blocks is determined by the kind of snow that is used. Hard-packed snow is preferred, and fluffy snow can't be used at all. An igloo isn't as warm as an apartment or a house, but it stays at a livable temperature because the snow acts as an insulator; it keeps the heat inside and it keeps out the snow and cold air. The body heat from two or three people in an igloo keeps the temperature high enough for comfort, even without a fire [see *Shelters from Tepee to Igloo*, p. 17].

   Another kind of shelter, called a *yurt*, is found in some cold parts of the world and is used by people who are nomadic. Nomadic people periodically pack up and follow the wild animals that they hunt (if they are hunters) or move to new grazing lands for their herds of domestic animals (if they are herders). A yurt is a little like a tipi because both consist of a thick wood frame covered with water-resistant materials. The yurt has a low wall that supports the roof poles. [Show a picture of a yurt in

Shelters from Tepee to Igloo, p. 25.] This wall gives it a low rounded shape that can withstand strong winds. The yurt is self-supporting. It doesn't need ropes or stakes or poles driven into the ground. This is important because where the yurt is used, the ground is often frozen hard as a rock. [See drawing in *Shelters from Tepee to Igloo*, p. 26.] The top of the yurt has a ring called the *crown*. The roof poles are attached to it. The crown is open in the center to let in light and let out smoke from the heating and cooking fire. The yurt is portable like a tent. When the people want to move, they take off the roof cover and bundle it up. Next they take down the roof poles, fold up the walls, and pack everything on the backs of their yaks or camels.

In parts of the world where the climate is hot, people need protection from the sun. In the cities, people live in modern apartment buildings or houses made of concrete or wood. In the rural areas, the people often depend on local building materials. The heat and humidity of tropical climates produce abundant vegetation. There are lush, thick grasses, heavily leafed plants, and often bamboo forests. These materials are all used for building. A tropical house usually has a thatched roof made from long grasses. If the grass is arranged carefully and used in layers, it will keep out even the heaviest rains. The roofs of tropical houses usually have large overhangs so that rain dripping off the edge won't be blown into the house. A large overhang also helps shade the house from direct sunlight.

In some places, these light, open houses are built on poles to raise the floor well above ground. A ladder is used to get into the house. This arrangement keeps the family safe from dangerous animals that may be roaming around in the night (after everybody is home, the ladder is pulled up). Houses raised on poles are also used by people who live on swampy land or on the edges of bays, rivers, or marshes that flood periodically. Rice grows in these flooded places, so most of the people who live in them are rice farmers.

These tropical or jungle shelters are constructed primarily of locally available vines and leaves. Often these areas lack access to modern transportation systems that would bring in materials from other places. The people farm very small pieces of land or hunt or fish for their food. They don't have much money, but even if they did, they probably wouldn't choose to build a house like ours in a jungle setting.

In some tropical areas of the world people live on floating homes. [Show a picture of a sailboat or sampan.] The people don't need protection from the cold but they do need protection from the sun, rain, and stormy conditions. Often their homes are made of wood, leaves, vines, and other materials found in the area. Sometimes people choose to live on boats so they can make a living by catching fish or taking tourists on boat rides. Others do so because they cannot find homes on land that they can afford. Still others can afford to live on land, but they choose to live on water. [You may wish to read *Nicola's Floating House*, a delightful story about an elementary-age child whose family has elected to live on a houseboat and see the world.]

Where the climate is dry—little rain or snow—people often use a clay/mudlike material called *adobe*. [Show photo of an adobe home found in a hot, dry region.] The Pueblo Indians built adobe homes in the Southwestern United States. Often one adobe house was built on top of another to make a many-storied apartment building. [Show illustration.] Originally, Pueblo Indian houses were built close together and even on top of one another to provide better protection against attacks by hostile tribes. If you visit this part of the United States, you can still see some of them, although now you will find other building materials and styles as well.

Economics   Home construction is also influenced by the amount of money a person or family has and the cost of building materials. The building materials that are available locally are usually cheaper, especially if they are plentiful. Modern transportation, however, makes it possible to use almost any building material that is appropriate for the climate. Of course, transporting materials across the nation or world can become very expensive.

In our society, modern construction companies use heavy machinery; factories produce human-made (synthetic) building materials; many types of workers carry out the steps in the construction process; and our homes offer controlled environments featuring luxuries and conveniences. All of these considerations cost money and add to the cost of our homes.

In the United States, especially in the suburbs and rural areas, homes are often spread out because large lots of land can be bought for reasonable prices. On the other hand, in cities there is not much space, and the land that is available costs a lot of money. So, city shelters are built up instead of out. Locally, we have a few fairly tall apartment buildings. In large cities like Chicago or New York, where there's less available land and lots more people, much taller high-rises are built. [Show picture of a high-rise.] Each high-rise contains many individual apartments. Often, there are stores or offices on the lower floors of the building, and a parking lot underneath it.

These high-rise buildings are made of steel and other very sturdy materials that are transported to the construction site. Some of the apartments inside of them are larger than most of our homes. Some have beautiful views of cities, skylines, or oceans. [Show a photo of the interior of a luxury apartment.]

Culture   People's backgrounds, preferences, and personal choices are also factors that determine the types of homes they have. For example, some societies are nomadic, which means that the people move their homes from place to place as they move to new grazing or hunting grounds. The Bedouins of Arabia make their tents out of strong fabric woven from goat or camel hair. [Show a picture of a Bedouin tent.] They can roll up the sides of the tent to let in cooling breezes.

Some West African people use clay as their major building material because it is available in the ground and it keeps houses cool in summer and warm in winter. Often they decorate their homes with brightly colored paints, which is considered a cultural preference. [Show a picture of a decorated home.]

People everywhere need shelters. They build homes that look different, but all provide protection from the elements, give the people places to store their belongings, and provide places for carrying out daily activities.

Activity

Provide each table of students with a large sheet of paper with descriptions of various types of environments (e.g., jungle-like, hot year round; ice/snow terrain; steep, mountainous area; desert). Pictures to illustrate each of these settings will enhance interest and lessen the difficulty of the activity. After adequate explanation to ensure that students can identify and relate to the environments, provide a set of cards depicting shelter types around the world. Have the students match the cards to the environments. Follow with a large-group discussion in which students are asked to provide reasons for their decisions.

Summarize

- Physical features (lay of the land—mountains, plains, flood plains) determine in part the types of building materials that are used and the special conditions to which home building must be adapted. The amount of available space is also a consideration.
- Climate determines what natural elements people need shelter from.
- *Economics* refers to the amount of money people have and the costs associated with housing. Frequently, people have unlimited wants but limited resources. People who have a lot of money are able to fulfill more of their wants (e.g., a four-bedroom house with a marble fireplace). People who have less money may only be able to afford more modest homes built using materials that are plentiful and cost less. People with little or no money may have to build their own shelter using whatever materials they can find.

- *Culture* refers to the traditions, beliefs, and values of people. Every society has traditional forms of housing and ways of decorating. Some people elect to practice them for artistic or religious reasons while others choose to ignore them. Some shelter decisions are related to where people live and how they get their food (e.g., nomads use tents; people in flood plains build stilt houses).
- All shelter types protect people from the elements, provide places for keeping personal possessions, and serve as centers for daily life activities.

Assessment

Have students complete a series of open-ended statements (Figure 4). Consider inviting upper-grade mentors to assist in the student writing. Make sure you model what you expect by completing your own form.

Home Assignment

Have students talk with their families about homes around the world. Encourage students to share their assessment response sheet and, if possible, work on the computer with a family member to see what type of information can be found on the Internet regarding their specific shelter interest.

Then, families should discuss places where they have been in which shelter types were similar to and/or different from those found in the local community. Discussions should include building materials, architectural style, and cultural influences. Encourage students to bring photos of shelter types discussed to share with the class (see Figure 5).

- The shelter type I would like to learn more about is _____ because
  _____
  _____ .

- The things I already know about this shelter type are _____
  _____
  and _____
  _____ .

- The questions I have are _____
  _____
  and _____
  _____ .

- The things this shelter type has in common with my home are _____
  _____
  and _____
  _____ .

FIGURE 4 Assessment Response Sheet

Dear Parents,

We would encourage at least one family member to spend time with your child discussing shelter types found in our community as well as in other places. Include in your conversation ideas about building materials, architectural style, and cultural influences.

If you have a computer, you might search the Internet for information related to your child's specific shelter interest. Information and/or photographs you find about shelter will be very helpful for our class discussion, so please make sure you send it to school.

Sincerely,

FIGURE 5 Model Letter to Parents

Lesson 4
. . . .
Progress in Shelter Construction

Resources

- Time line: Progress in shelter construction
- Pictures or drawings for time line: cave, stone house, longhouse, tipi, log cabin, modern home (range of exteriors and interiors)
- Picture illustrating clearing the land and building a log cabin
- Pictures of notched logs
- Lincoln Logs
- Pictures of interiors and exteriors of log cabins and plank houses
- Picture of heavy equipment used to build a high-rise
- Sample building materials
- Individual time-lines

Children's Literature

Kalman, B. (1982). *The Early Family Home*. New York: Crabtree.

Kalman, B. (1999). *Homes of the West*. New York: Crabtree.

Shamie, B. (1991). *Homes of Hide and Earth*. New York: Tundra Books.

Steele, P. (1994). *House Through the Ages*. Mahway, NJ: Troll Associates.

Weiss, H. (1988). *Shelters from Tepee to Igloo*. New York: Thomas Y. Crowell.

Yve, D., & Yve, D. (1984). *The Tipi*. New York: Alfred A. Knopf.

General Comments

This lesson describes how shelter has changed over time. Until fairly recently, housing construction reflected the availability of local materials. While this pattern still exists in some places, modern transportation has allowed choices to be expanded. In addition, new construction techniques and technological improvements continue to be invented and refined over time. The net result is a level of comfort that people long, long ago and long ago would never have dreamed of realizing.

General Purposes and Goals

To: (1) help students understand and appreciate the types of homes that have been created over time, the changes they have undergone, and the reasons for these changes; (2) engender a positive attitude about history; (3) stimulate students' curiosity regarding shelter types, styles, and building materials; and (4) engender a sense of wonder regarding the range of shelters as home bases for family activities.

Main Ideas to Develop

- Until recently, housing construction reflected the availability of local materials. This pattern still exists in some places, but in other places modern transportation has allowed choices to be expanded.

- New construction techniques and technological improvements get invented and refined over time. Now, besides meeting our needs for protection from the elements, modern homes cater to our wants for a comfortable living space, hot and cold running water, electric lighting, comfortable beds and furniture, and so on.

Teaching Tips from Barbara

The whole-group activity chart is the key to this lesson. Begin by giving students a short narrative explaining housing at each point in time: long, long ago; long ago; and today. I have students use what they have learned to help me construct the information in the chart. I encourage discussion between students before adding information to the chart. By now, they should have enough information to make some educated guesses about unfamiliar things. As you finish, highlight the "today" column as a pre-view to the next lesson.

Starting the Lesson

Share the results of the homework assignment, then begin the lesson by showing pictures or drawings of shelters long, long ago; long ago; and today. Place some of the pictures and drawings on the time line and indi-cate that during the lesson the class will fill in the spaces. An option is to place a large time line on a white board and as you present a storylike narrative, sketch illustrations depicting the various types of shelters and how they have changed over time.

As the lesson unfolds, revisit the functions of shelter. Where appro-priate, mention that shelter is influenced by geographic factors (physical features and climate), culture, money, and level of technology. Allow the students to help decide the chronology of the pictures that have been selected to tell the story of shelter over time.

Suggested Lesson Discussion

Caves   [Show pictures.] Cave people didn't have the skills required for building a sturdy shelter. The best way for them to get protection from the elements and animals was to find an already-existing cave. They kept their cave shelters warm and dry by building fires.

If no cave was available, they would dig a hollow in the ground or build a simple lean-to or hut from branches and animal hides. The shel-ter in the ground was less likely to be blown away by strong winds or seen by other people, often believed to be enemy hunters.

Stone Houses [Show picture or drawing.] Other homes that existed long, long ago were made of stone. In places where there were no trees for lumber, grasses for thatch, or clay for bricks, there often were lots of stones scattered over the barren ground. People built strong, permanent weatherproof shelters out of the stones. These early structures resembled beehives and are called *beehive huts*. They were easy to build because the stones didn't need to be trimmed. There simply had to be some flat ones on the top and bottom. The spaces between the stones were stuffed with dirt to keep out the cold winds and to keep in the heat from the fires built inside. (There were openings at the tops of beehive huts to let out the smoke.) Some of these stone houses had dirt packed on top so grasses and flowers would grow there. Besides being decorative, this served as added protection.

Tipi The tipi was designed by American Indian plains tribes who moved periodically to follow the buffalo they hunted. Buffalo provided food for these Indians and also hides, which were used as coverings for their tipis. A large tipi might need twenty or more hides. They were sewn together and draped over long poles. Smoke flaps were used to create a draft to draw the smoke out from the interior of the tipi. Poles were attached to their corners so they could be adjusted as the direction of the wind changed. When the Indians wanted to move to a new hunting ground, they would fold the cover into a compact bundle and bring it (and the tent poles) with them.

Indians who lived in the other climates and environments had different needs, so they built other kinds of dwellings, such as hogans, pueblos, or longhouses. Only certain Plains tribes lived in tipis (i.e., the nomadic tribes that followed the buffalo).

Log Cabin [Show picture.] In the more recent past, pioneers built log cabins. The only way for the earliest settlers to make a home was to chop down trees to clear an area of the forest, and then build a log cabin.

A log cabin was fairly easy to construct; it didn't require many tools or great skill. The logs didn't have to be sawed into boards or timbers; they just had to be cut to the right length with the branches chopped off. The logs were fitted together with notches, so nails weren't needed. One log fit into another with no chance of slipping. [Illustrate with Lincoln Logs.] The notches provided a rigid and strong means of attachment, and they could be cut with nothing more than a sharp axe. The thick walls acted as a good insulator, keeping a well-built cabin warm in winter and cool in summer.

Most modern homes have wooden frameworks to which walls are attached both inside and outside. The log cabin was much simpler. It didn't require any supporting framework to hold up the walls. The logs were both framework and wall.

The pioneers could mix clay with grass, moss, or straw and jam it between the logs to seal the cracks. The cabins were quite dark inside because they usually had few windows. This was partly on purpose because too many windows would have made it difficult to defend their homes against attacks. Glass wasn't available, so when they did cut a space for a window, they usually covered it with oiled paper. Wooden shutters were used in bad weather. The fireplace provided the heat and most of the light, although they made candles. The pioneers depended on wells for water, and they kept animals and grew their own crops for food. Once they discovered a likely spot for finding water, they would dig a well. A *well* is a tapped underground water source (i.e., not just a holding tank for rain water). The well could be lined on the inside with stones. Sometimes it was covered with a board or stones would be built up around it so no one would fall into it.

Plank House [Show picture.] Later came the plank houses. They were still made of wood but were much more finished than log cabins and usually much larger—with many more rooms. The planks could be cut by hand from squared logs, but this was a lengthy job. Those who could afford to do so would buy planks from a nearby sawmill. Plank houses had wood-burning stoves instead of fireplaces. Stoves didn't let most of the heat escape up the chimney and were easier to use for cooking.

Modern Homes [Show pictures.] As time passed, roads were built, modern means of transportation were developed, and new materials became available for building homes. Usually the most available products (local resources) are the least expensive. If people want other sturdy materials, such as large stone or marble, they can be shipped—although they tend to be very expensive. The cost of a modern home depends on the climate in which the home is built (e.g., how sturdy or insulated it needs to be), the materials used to construct it (local materials are usually cheaper), and personal decisions about the size of the home and what special features will be included. The location of the home and the amount of land that surrounds it also affect its cost.

In the past, people tended to rely on local resources. Also, they we had little technology or highly skilled construction techniques, so buildings were simple. Today we have heavy equipment and lots of modern technology to help us build unique shelters. [Show pictures of heavy equipment, steel beams for construction, and a high-rise apartment building.] We also are able to bring in building materials from other parts of the world.

Now, besides meeting our needs for protection from the elements, modern houses and apartments cater to our wants for comfortable living space, hot and cold running water, electric lighting, and comfortable beds and furniture. During a future lesson, we'll talk more about these conveniences. [Show the interior of a modern house.]

Large-Group Activity

As a group, complete a chart similar to Table 1. Encourage students to use pictures, drawings, and words. See Figure 6 on page 192.

Paired Activity

At the conclusion of the large-group activity, ask the students to study the picture time line in pairs, discuss what they thought was the most interesting change in shelter and why, and then share their responses with the whole class.

Optional Investigate the availability of local resources. For example, take a field trip to a local historical site (such as a log cabin) and help students to observe and appreciate the building materials and the structure—doors, windows, and so forth. Promote a discussion that examines changes since then in construction, technologies, and living conveniences.

Housing has improved over time due to enormous progress in shelter construction. Today we have sturdier and more weather-resistant homes, insulation, electric lights, gas or electric heating and cooling circulated throughout the house, and hot and cold running water.

Summarize

- Shelter has improved in a variety of ways over time.
- Until recently, housing construction relied heavily on local resources.
- New construction techniques and technological improvements continue to add comforts to our shelters (e.g., sturdier and more weather-resistant homes, insulation, hot and cold running water, etc.).

Assessment

Give students individual blank time lines and ask them to show through drawings and words how shelter has progressed over time. If time permits, ask them to write a paragraph explaining which time period they would have most liked to live in because of the type of shelter they would have lived in and why.

Home Assignment

Have students take home a copy of the chart comparing long, long ago, long ago, and today. Ask them to tour their homes with a family member and find other ways that their present house differs from those in earlier time periods. They can add their findings on the back, and return the sheet for class discussion.

	LONG, LONG AGO	LONG AGO	TODAY
Shelter Type	Cave	Tipis, log cabins	Frame houses, apartments
People	Cave dwellers	Native Americans, Pioneers	Us
Construction	Little to none	Low tech	High tech
Light	Fire	Candles	Electric lights
Heat	Fire	Fireplace	Furnace
Water	River	Well	Plumbing
Room Differentiation	None	Minimal	High

TABLE 1 Progress in Shelter Construction

©2001 by Janet Alleman and Jere Brophy from *Social Studies Excursions, K–3*. Portsmouth, NH: Heinemann

Dear Parents,

I have sent home a copy of a chart labeled "Progress in Shelter Construction" that we discussed in class today. Please help your child discover ways in which your present house differs from those of earlier time periods. The responses can be listed on the back. Make sure your child returns the sheet tomorrow so that s/he can share your family's ideas with our class. Thank you.

FIGURE 6 Model Letter to Parents

Lesson 5

Steps in Building a House

Resources
- Word cards—steps in building a house (one set per student)
- Blueprints
- Photos—sequence illustrating the steps in building a house
- Photo album illustrating the story of building a house
- Home video illustrating the story of building a house (secure from a local builder)
- Insulation
- Photos of water/sewer lines (secure from a local builder or photograph a house during construction)
- Photo of sockets, circuit breakers, furnace, carpet layers, painters (secure from a local builder or photograph a house during construction)
- Letter to parents
- Doll house or computer program that provides a virtual home tour

Children's Literature
Barton, B. (1981). *Building a House*. New York: Mulberry.

Gibbons, G. (1990). *How a House Is Built*. New York: Holiday House.

Hamilton-Maclaren, A. (1992). *Houses and Homes*. New York: Bookwright.

Schachtman, T. (1989). *The President Builds a House*. New York: Simon & Schuster.

General Comments
This lesson is designed to help students come to understand and appreciate that construction techniques and technology have been refined over time to the point that modern housing not only meets our shelter needs but provides us with controlled living environments that offer many modern conveniences. As a means of bridging from the previous lesson to this one, begin by asking students to share their home assignment responses about the differences between homes of the past and their homes. [Model by showing and explaining your completed homework.]

General Purposes or Goals
To develop: (1) an understanding and appreciation of progress in shelter construction; (2) some understanding about the steps in building a house

and a range of people who are involved in the project; and (3) under-standing and appreciation for some of the features we currently label as modern conveniences, especially the control of light, heat, and water.

Main Ideas to Develop

- In the past, most housing construction was dependent on the availability of local materials. While this pattern still exists to some extent, modern transportation has allowed choices to be expanded.
- New construction techniques and technological improvements have been invented and refined over time. Now, besides meeting needs to protect people from the elements, modern houses cater to our wants by providing a comfortable range of temperatures, hot and cold running water, and electric lighting.
- Today's homes are planned to take advantage of advances in new designs, technologies, and materials. Many workers are involved to ensure that the plans are realized.

Teaching Tips from Barbara

This was one of the hardest lessons for me to teach. The next time I plan to invite a builder to talk us through the technical parts of the lesson and help students get an understanding of the steps involved as well as the workers needed to build a house. It might be done in two parts; the first part explaining the steps in building and the second part discussing the different systems in the house. All of it was very interesting to my students and generated a whole new list of "I wonder" questions.

Starting the Lesson

Share and discuss the home assignment. If there is a home construction site near the school, a powerful way to engender a sense of curiosity about building a house would be to visit and observe what goes on. Ideally, the building contractor or one of the other workers should conduct the tour of the site and the inside of the house. Provide the resource person with the subject-matter content in your plan, the list of steps in building a house that you intend to discuss with the class, and/or the children's liter-ature books to illustrate what you would like to have explained during the tour. An addition or alternative to the tour (as suggested by Barbara) would be to invite a home builder to the classroom armed with a home video and a host of photos to illustrate and explain the steps.

If a site visit or a presentation by a builder is not possible, you can share "the story" of building a house by using photos, a video that you have made or secured from a local builder, and the children's literature sources suggested. Explain that many types of workers are involved in the process. Using an interactive approach, share the steps.

Suggested Lesson Discussion

First, the builder needs to find a vacant lot on which to build a house. You may have seen a "For Sale" sign on a vacant lot. Once the land is purchased, a set of plans called a *blueprint* is needed. [Show blueprints.] It is a map to scale of what the house will look like. Builders usually build several types of houses to appeal to different buyers. Sometimes families such as yours get involved in the actual planning and building of a new home. If you wanted your house to be *very* different, you would hire an architect, who would develop personalized blueprints to fit your specifications, such as building your house over a waterfall. Then you hire a building contractor. The work begins. A machine digs a very big hole. [Use the book *Building a House* and any relevant photos you can acquire.]

Builders hammer and saw to prepare the frames for the footings for the foundation. *Footings* are projections from the foundation of a house that stabilize and provide additional support for it. A cement mixer pours cement into the wooden frames. The cement will harden and support the foundation for the house. Block layers will lay large blocks for the foundation. Carpenters arrive and make a wooden floor and the wooden frame for the inside of the house. On this framework they add other floors, the walls, and the roof. Then the roofers come and shingle it by putting a covering over the wood and tar paper. A bricklayer builds a chimney (and sometimes a fireplace). The insulators come and put insulation material between the walls. [Show insulation.] It reduces the amount of heating that can pass through a wall, so it keeps the warm air in and the cold air out.

The plumbers put in the pipes and prepare the hookups for water and sewer lines. Water is piped in from a reservoir, a lake, or an underground spring or well. It is usually purified before being sent to your home. It arrives through an underground pipe, under pressure, so that if you turn on a faucet, the water will flow immediately. Some goes directly to the pipes that feed cold-water faucets but some goes to a water heater, fueled by electricity, oil, or gas, which heats the water that goes to the hot-water faucets. Waste water from sinks, showers, baths, and toilets leaves most homes through a drainage pipe before it enters a sewer pipe. It then goes to a sewage treatment plant, which removes all of the impure matter from the water and discharges clean water.

The electrician wires the house. [Show photos of socket, wires, photos of circuit breaker box.] When the task is completed, you can flip a switch and a light comes on or an electrical machine springs into action.

The electricity is generated at a power station and is carried to homes by power lines that are either raised and supported by pylons or poles, or else laid underground. Once in the home, the electricity flows through wires in the walls, floors, and ceilings to lights and outlets. But it first enters a safety device (a circuit breaker box) that cuts off the power if a machine or wire is unsafe.

A heating system is also installed. Fires (in fireplaces) or small heaters can warm individual rooms, but central heating can heat an entire building. A central heating system may have a boiler or a furnace. A boiler uses electricity, gas, oil, or a solid fuel such as coal. The boiler heats water that then circulates through pipes to radiators in rooms. The boiler may also heat water to be used in baths and sinks. Some systems use the sun's rays to heat water inside the solar panels.

Forced-air furnace systems heat air and then blow it through the building. A furnace houses a fire that heats the air that is then circulated through the house (duct work). Heating systems are controlled by timers and thermostats that turn the heat on or off to maintain a set temperature.

Electric heating systems use electricity to heat electrical elements that are sometimes concealed in the floor or ceiling. Other systems rely on baseboard heaters. These become very hot and give off heat that radiates into the room.

The carpenters add doors, windows, and cabinets. Painters paint inside and outside. Light fixtures are added. Carpet and floor coverings are laid. Many workers are involved today in building a house. All of them need to be paid. The result is that houses today cost much more than they did in the past, but they offer many more features that make our lives comfortable. Finally, all of the workers leave, and it's time for someone to move in.

Elicit input from the students. For example, ask, "What was the most surprising thing you learned?" "Would you like to help build a house?" "Why?" "Why not?" "Which part would you like to do?" "Why?"

Activity

Give each student a picture depicting one of the steps in building a house and the corresponding word card. Then, as a class, reconstruct the story of building a house. Discuss the kinds of skills the specific worker would need in order to do his or her job effectively. Underscore the importance of each job and how the net result will affect living in the home.

Activity

Using a miniature (doll) house or a virtual trip via computer, take an imaginary trip through a house. As the "tour leader," pose challenging questions as a means of cementing the main ideas and supportive content of the lesson. Sample questions:

- Where would you expect to find a thermostat? What is its purpose?

- What is the purpose of that gadget on the wall? (thermostat)
- Where do I go to get water? How does the water get to the faucet? Why is it hot?
- Where does the electricity come from? What really happens when I turn on the light switch?
- What's probably behind this wall? What is its purpose/function?
- What was added first—roof, walls, or cabinets?
- Who built the chimney? Do you suppose that work would have been done before or after the furnace was installed? Explain.

Summarize

Using pictures of log cabins and modern homes, indicate that while people often use the resources that are available locally, due to modern transportation and technology, they can get building materials from around the world. Today's building materials are processed and the tools are high-tech (power saws, presses).

The result is that houses today can look a lot different than they did in the past. New materials, inventions, and designs have enabled people to live in housing today that offers better durability, waterproofing, insulation, temperature control, and other "modern conveniences."

Assessment

Using word cards naming the steps in building a house, have each student sequence them. Have the student select the one step and job that she or he might like to do as an adult, and then write a short paragraph explaining the choice. Students can illustrate if time permits. Here are the cards listed in the right order:

1. Purchase the land
2. Blueprints
3. Building contractor
4. Dig a hole
5. Footings and connections for sewer and water
6. Pour cement
7. Block layers build outer walls
8. Carpenters build floors
9. Carpenters build inner structure
10. Carpenters build roof
11. Roofers shingle and carpenters add windows
12. Chimney is built
13. Plumbers put in pipes
14. Insulation
15. Electricians wire
16. Drywall installed

17. Carpenters add door, cupboards
18. Painters paint
19. Light fixtures are added
20. Carpets are laid

Home Assignment

Encourage students to share their paragraph describing what jobs they chose. Send home copies of Figure 7 asking a family member to conduct a home tour that focuses on the modern conveniences that provide a controlled living environment.

Dear Parents,

We have been studying about housing construction and how technology, inventions, and discoveries have enabled people today to live in a comfortable environment. Please assist your child in touring your home, looking for ways that the family has taken advantage of modern conveniences that provide a *controlled* living environment. Encourage your child to list and/or draw pictures to illustrate these conveniences. Focus on heating and cooling, running water, and lighting. As you discuss these conveniences, show your child how they are made available to your home and routed and controlled through pipes, faucets, thermostats, fuses or circuit breakers, switches, etc. Your child needs to bring the list or drawings to class tomorrow so that it can be shared.

Thank you for participating in your child's learning.

Sincerely,

FIGURE 7 Model Letter for Parents

Lesson 6

. . . .

Careers Associated with Shelter

Resources
- Word cards: invention, interdependence
- Pictures or photos illustrating careers related to building a house or an apartment building
- Panel of local people who are working in the housing industry (optional)

Children's Literature
Barton, B. (1981). *Building a House*. New York: Mulberry.
Gibbons, G. (1990). *How a House Is Built*. New York: Holiday House.
Schaachtman, T. (1989). *The President Builds a House*. New York: Simon & Schuster.

General Comments
Show students pictures or photos that depict the range of workers and jobs that are needed in building a house or an apartment. While this constitutes only a sampling of the types of careers related to housing, this seems to be the appropriate scope for exploration, especially since students are already familiar with the steps in building a house. (See Lesson 5.) If a house under construction is within walking distance of the school and the students could spend time with some of the individual workers, a return visit might be appropriate. Otherwise, a panel of individuals engaged in careers associated with housing would be an equally effective resource for this lesson. If neither option is available collect photos and pictures of workers associated with home building. Invite a local individual who does one or more of the jobs to serve as a resource person. Encourage him/her to talk about his/her work. Using pictures/photos of others in the housing industry, discuss their careers as well.

General Purposes or Goals
To develop: (1) knowledge, understanding, and appreciation regarding career opportunities that exist within the home industry; (2) understanding and appreciation for how technology can change the way work is done and how people can change the way homes look; and (3) a sense of efficacy among students—any one of them might invent a machine, a process, or a design that will benefit all of us in the future.

Main Ideas to Develop

- The home industry provides a range of opportunities for individuals to be creative and pursue careers.
- Today, it takes a variety of workers to perform specific steps in building a house or an apartment.
- Many changes have occurred in the home building industry over the past two hundred years.

Teaching Tips from Barbara

One of the keys to this lesson is to make ties to past lessons. The students are able to begin creating a list of careers by reviewing the steps of the shelter construction process (Lesson 5). Actual visitors from the building industry are a bonus, but be sure to prepare both your visitors and your students beforehand. To prepare your students, have them brainstorm questions or topics for the visitors to discuss. I find that it works well to assign questions to specific students to ask, especially those students who might not ask one on their own. That way it isn't the same one or two students asking questions. I also suggest that you chat with your visitors before the visit and share the big ideas for the lesson with them. Enlist their help in making a few points in particular. This will help focus their comments and make the experience much more useful.

Starting the Lesson

Discuss the home assignment. Review the steps in building a house. Then conduct an on-site visit to observe a select group of workers carrying out their jobs (e.g., brick layer, insulation installer, wallpaper hanger, carpenter). Visit with the workers in advance so they are clear about your social studies goals. Underscore the importance of the students observing the job being performed as well as having the opportunity to hear from the worker about what s/he does and why, the importance of possessing a set of skills to do the job effectively, how the skills are related to what s/he learned in elementary school, how the job is paid for, what s/he likes about the job, and what are the most challenging aspects of the career.

An alternative to an on-site visit would be inviting a panel of local people who work in the home building industry to visit your class. Have them respond to questions similar to those identified above. Video clips, photos, drawings, and pictures are encouraged to enhance meaningfulness about careers in home building. Allow ample time for student questions.

Activity

Have the students work in fives to discuss the following: how technology is used by the home building workers they observed, how the work today is different from that done by the pioneers in building their log cabins, and what ideas they have for changing what they might do as designers or builders in the future. You may wish to post the discussion items and invite upper-grade mentors to serve as facilitators or pace the questions and conduct large-group conversation after small-group time.

Assessment

Have each student complete the open-ended statements in Figure 8. Illustrations are optional.

Home Assignment

Encourage students to share their open-ended statements describing what career associated with the home building industry they might like to do as an adult and why. Then, with a family member's help, students should interview one other person who works in the industry. Sample questions include:

What is your job?

What is the most difficult part of your job?

What kinds of special knowledge and skills do you need to be successful at your job?

Are you happy that you have chosen this career? Why? Why not?

The one career I would like to have in the home building industry is _____ .

I think I would like that job because _____

_____

_____

_____

_____

_____

_____

_____

_____ .

The one question I still have about it is _____

_____

_____

_____

_____

_____

_____

_____

_____

_____ .

FIGURE 8 Assessment: A Career in the Home Building Industry

Dear Parents,

We have been learning about careers associated with the building industry. We encourage you to discuss this topic with your child. With a family member's help, we would encourage your child to interview one other person who works in the industry. [See Figure 8.] Sample questions might include:

What is your job?

What is the most difficult part of your job?

What kinds of special knowledge and skills do you need to be successful at your job?

Are you happy that you have chosen this career? Why? Why not?

Please have your child bring the information to school to be used in our next social studies discussion.

Sincerely,

FIGURE 9 Model Letter to Parents

Lesson 7

. . . .

Costs Associated with Your Shelter

Resources
- Parents or volunteers for the role-play
- Mortgage payment book
- Water bill
- Electric bill
- Heating bill
- Tax statement
- 3-D cutouts or photos and stations representing a house, an apartment, a bank, the apartment manager's office, a utility office, and a township or city office
- Word cards—paying a mortgage, paying rent, paying utilities, paying taxes

General Comments
Students tend to have many misconceptions about costs associated with housing, and what is involved in renting and buying. They may know that families pay for utilities, but they are likely to have little idea about what is being paid for (i.e., electricity, oil, or natural gas used to create heat).

General Purposes or Goals
To develop: (1) an understanding of and appreciation for the need to pay for a shelter/home and for modern conveniences such as purified water, energy/electricity, and fuel delivered to our homes; and (2) an understanding of basic principles and options involved in buying or renting shelter.

Main Ideas to Develop
- You can buy a house before you have the full purchase price, although you can lose it if you don't continue to make your payments.
- Some people choose to live in an apartment temporarily while they save enough money for a down payment. Others choose apartments as permanent residences for other reasons such as convenience, fewer maintenance responsibilities, and so on.
- Banks (and sometimes private individuals) lend people the money to buy a house. The people have to pay back the amount of the loan plus interest. That's how banks make money.
- People have to pay to live in apartments. The rent money is kept by the owner of the building. Renting is a profit-making business.

- Whether you live in a house or an apartment, you pay utility companies for heat (fuel), water, and light (electricity).
- You pay money to the government (taxes) to maintain roads, provide police protection and fire protection, and operate schools. (If you are buying your home, you pay taxes directly to the government. If you are renting, some of the money you pay to the apartment building owner goes to the government for these services.)
- A large part of the family income goes for buying or renting and maintaining the property.

Teaching Tips from Barbara

This lesson brings out a great deal of information about the economics of shelter. Some of the information is beyond the students' personal experiences. Many of my students had never heard of mortgages, taxes, or utility bills before this lesson. Go slow and spend most of your time on the role-playing (rather than the chart at the beginning). The home assignment encouraged some interesting discussions between students and their parents. One parent even reported that her son became very vigilant with the family's utility use once he found out that electricity and water must be paid for!

Starting the Lesson

Encourage students to share pictures and stories regarding what they observed on their personal home tours (Home Assignment). Talk briefly about how the same functions were accomplished in the past.

PRESENT	PAST
Furnace	Fireplace, coal stove
Air conditioner	Fan
Sink	Tub, basin
Toilet	Outhouse
Thermostat	Add more wood or coal to fire; open windows to cool house
Lamp	Kerosene lantern
Refrigerator	Ice box

Remind students that things in the United States are very different from the past. All of these conveniences are available, although not all people can afford all of them and some people choose not to have some of them (e.g., the Amish).

Suggested Lesson Discussion

These conveniences aren't available for many people in other parts of the world who do not have access to needed technology or who cannot pay the costs. All of these things cost money. Today we are going to talk about the costs involved in owning or renting a home—and whom your parents have to pay for what. Have you ever heard someone in your family say, "It's the first of the month already. We have to pay the rent (or mortgage) again" "Oh, we just got another water bill" or "Our taxes went up again"?

There are many costs in owning a home or in renting an apartment. These include: land, home, electricity, water, heat, and taxes.

The entire lesson will be carried out in a role-play manner. Use 3-D cutouts of buildings and/or pictures at stations that illustrate the following: house, apartment, bank, apartment manager's office, utility office, and township or city office for collecting taxes. Invite parents or other volunteers to serve in the various roles: homeowner, renter, banker, apartment manager, utility company service desk clerk, and township service desk clerk.

As the teacher, play the role of homeowner or renter, depending on your actual status. Prepare "scripts" as needed. Go over the goals and major understandings with the role players and practice in advance of the lesson.

Set the stage. It's the first of the month and it's time to pay bills. Have the homeowner and renter seated at kitchen tables in their respective homes. They will describe how the money is distributed, explain what it pays for, and why it is an ongoing process.

Here are some ideas for their interactive narratives:

Homeowner   Our family has decided to live in this area for a long time (indefinitely) so we bought a home. We saved some of our money so we could put a down payment on a house, and we pay a certain amount every month. Most people who buy a house do not have all of the money they need to pay for it, so bankers make mortgage loans available. This allows the people to take possession of the house even though they have not paid the full price for it. A bank lends a family the money it needs to buy the house (the price minus down payment). Some of you may have heard of a thirty-year mortgage or a fifteen-year mortgage. It means that you have that many years to pay the bank for your loan. Every month you make a mortgage payment to the bank. Some of this money goes to pay back the loan, but some goes to pay interest, which is money that the bank charges you for the loan (you have to pay back what you borrowed plus interest). Banks are businesses and make money from their loans. They charge you interest for using (borrowing) their money. If the family is not able to keep up its mortgage payments, it has to move out of the house. The house will be sold and some of the money will go to the bank and some to the family (the equity that the family has built up—down payment plus payment on principal).

[Write a check—*show mortgage amount*. Walk the check to the "bank" station. The banker will underscore the key points about loans, interest, and businesses that make money.]

Renter   Our family has decided to live in an apartment (either to save money for down payment on a house, or for convenience and fewer responsibilities). We have to pay to live in the apartment. The money goes to the owner of the apartment building. He uses some of it to maintain the building (cut grass, paint, fix the staircase, etc.) and keeps some of it as profit. Renting is a profit-making business. If you don't pay the rent, you will have to leave the apartment. Renting an apartment is different from staying in a hotel. You rent an apartment for a long period of time, whereas you usually stay in a hotel for one or just a few nights. Hotels usually have restaurants and swimming pools. Apartments are more private. You decorate them with your own things, and you usually plan to stay for a long while. [Walk to the "apartment manager" station. The apartment manager will underscore the key points about paying rent every month, what happens when you don't pay, and how the money is used (i.e., maintenance, profit). (Taxes will be explained later.)]

[Note: For the next part, alternate conversations between homeowner and renter. Each will explain that whether you live in a house or an apartment, you have to pay for utilities—heat (fuel), water, and light (electricity). After each, explain that these bills have to be paid and why. Walk to the "utility" station with the checks. The utility office staff will underscore the key points of paying utilities.]

Utilities   You also have to pay for services that you get each month— heat, light, water. The utility companies that you pay own the equipment and provide the services. For example, we get our electricity from the [name local power company]. The generators at the power station produce electricity, which is then sent to our homes through power lines. The power line that feeds our home flows through a meter that shows how much electricity we use each month, and we are billed for that amount. We use electricity whenever we run our furnace or air conditioner, turn on a light, or use a radio, television, or other appliance that is plugged into a wall socket. [Write check.] Our local water company [give name] collects fresh water from [name the local river, lake, reservoir, or underground source], filters it to remove impurities, and then sends it up into the water tower. From the water tower, it flows down through pipes, under pressure, to our homes. As it enters our homes, it flows through a water meter provided by the water company to indicate how much water we use. We pay for that as well. [Write check.]

Many of us have natural gas furnaces. We get our gas from [name the local gas company.] It is piped underground into our house and to the furnace. In the furnace, there's a pilot light burning gas. [Illustrate using a grill lighter.] We use a thermostat to regulate the activity of the furnace. When the temperature in the house drops below a set level, the thermostat activates the furnace. Gas flows into a burner near the pilot light, and a much bigger fire flames up. You can hear the "whoosh" if you are near the furnace when it flames up. A fan blows the warmed air out of the furnace and through the heat ducts that go into the rooms. We pay for the amount of gas we burn when we run our furnace. There's an outdoor meter that keeps track of our usage and is read monthly by the company to determine how much we need to pay. [Write check.]

[Note that some homes have electrical, solar, or steam heat. Explain key elements of any of these heating systems that may be used in some of your students' homes (e.g., fire in boiler heats water that then is piped to radiators in rooms).]

Utility companies supply us with water, gas, and electricity and they come out to fix problems such as a fallen power line after a storm.

Taxes   [Homeowner speaks again.] "We just got another bill! This time it's for the property taxes. In addition to paying for utilities (gas, electricity, and water), people who own buildings have to pay property taxes. The money is used for public services such as roads and schools. [Show a tax bill. Write a check and deliver it to the local government office, which is the "township" or "city" station. The desk clerk underscores the key ideas associated with taxes.]

[Renter speaks again.] "I wonder why I didn't get a tax bill? Maybe I don't have to pay taxes!" [Role-play calling the township or city offices to find out. The clerk says that yes, you do pay taxes, even though you don't get a tax bill. The taxes are included in your monthly rent. The person who owns the apartment uses part of your rent check to pay the property taxes on the building (if there were no such taxes, your rent would be lower). [The apartment manager writes a check and walks it to the "township or city" station and pays the taxes. The clerk underscores the key points regarding taxes paid by renters and how the tax money is used.]

Activity
Have students replace the volunteer role-players and re-enact the story, focusing on costs associated with shelter. Then lead an interactive discussion to cement the major understandings.

Summarize
If your family is buying a home, a big portion of the family income goes to *paying off the mortgage loan, paying utility bills,* and *paying taxes.* Once the mortgage loan is paid off, the family owns the home and doesn't have to keep paying the bank, but it still must pay for utilities and taxes.

Some people do not own a home and rent instead. However, they still have to pay for the water, light, and heat they use, and some of their rent money is used by the building owner to pay taxes.

During another lesson, we'll talk about the decisions involved in renting a home versus buying one.

Assessment

Have students write paragraphs focusing on costs associated with buying and renting. If time permits, students could draw and label their responses.

Home Assignment

Encourage students to share with their families their explanations about buying and renting and why both take so much money. Then families should discuss which alternatives they have selected and why. Send home copies of the letter shown in Figure 11.

Why does buying a house take so much money? Write a short paragraph answering this question.

_____

_____

_____

_____

_____

_____

_____

Why does renting an apartment take so much money? Write a short paragraph answering this question.

_____

_____

_____

_____

_____

_____

_____

FIGURE 10 Assessment: Shelter Costs

Dear Parents,

Your child has been learning about the costs associated with owning or renting a home. Please take a few minutes to allow your child to share his or her learning. We encourage you to have a conversation with your child about the choice you have made (to rent or buy) and why. We hope that you will be willing to have your child share the response during an upcoming class discussion.

Sincerely,

FIGURE 11 Model Letter to Parents

Lesson 8

. . . .

Choice Making

Resources

- Photos or pictures of Brandi and her family and of Rosie and her family
- Map of area
- Pictures of housing types—apartment, house
- Word cards: location, renting, buying, cost, size

General Comments

Students rarely have the opportunity to think about, examine, and discuss the multiple issues that families face when relocating. This lesson is intended to promote lots of conversation and to examine the trade-offs that need to be considered in making decisions about relocating.

General Purposes or Goals

To: (1) enhance students' understanding regarding the forms of shelter that are available; (2) develop an appreciation for the opportunities that people may have to exercise choice in meeting their shelter needs/wants; (3) enhance students' understanding and appreciation regarding major choices that need to be made early in the decision-making process—namely location and whether to rent or buy.

Main Ideas to Develop

- One of the choices people have to make is location—where they will live.
- Another choice is whether to rent or buy.
- Other choices concern such issues as the size of the place.

Teaching Tips from Barbara

I made this lesson more meaningful for my students by sharing my personal experience with a recent home purchase. Once again, I tied this lesson to the information on the functions and types of shelter from previous lessons. After we talked about my real-life choice making, we used an imaginary student and her family for the students to discuss. They enjoyed "helping" the student's family make a decision. In fact, some of my students had a difficult time believing that the imaginary family wasn't real.

Starting the Lesson

After discussing the family responses regarding the expenses associated with housing (Home Assignment), reveal that this lesson will focus on the decisions related to relocating. Ask the students if their families have ever moved. What challenges did the family face? After they have responded, explain that often people have to move because a family member's job changes. Make a list of what some of the other reasons people move. Then, set the stage for Brandi's family dilemma (which is hypothetical). If personal circumstances dictate that you need to move because of your spouse's job, or if a child is joining or leaving your class due to a move, by all means use that example too.

Suggested Lesson Discussion

As a class, we will work together to help Brandi and her family make decisions about their move. At the end of our lesson, each of you will have a chance to write to Brandi and give her recommendations and reasons. [Set the stage for Brandi and her family, who will be moving from out of town into your area due to her mom's promotion. Show the mom's new work-site on a map.] This family has to make a lot of decisions.

1. Where should they live—city or suburb? Should it be close to her mother's job? Close to a particular school? Close to the interstate?
2. The family will have to decide whether to rent or buy.

In order to buy a house, you can take out a mortgage (loan) from a bank with a promise to pay the money back over an extended period of time, but you need to have money in the bank for a down payment. Brandi's family has to sell its present home, so it will have money for the down payment. If the family can't sell the home before it moves, it may have to rent a place to live. Sometimes you can rent a house, but often you rent an apartment. *Renting* means that you are paying to live in a place that someone else owns—you are not buying it, so it doesn't become yours eventually. You can rent a place for several months or even years. You also can rent a hotel room to stay in for a couple of nights, but this isn't the same as renting a place to live.

Some people have enough money saved to buy a house, but they choose to rent instead. Often such a decision is due to a limited stay in an area, uncertainty about where to buy, a desire to save the money, or not wanting homeowner responsibilities such as upkeep or redecoration.

Besides deciding about renting or buying, the family needs to decide where it wants to live. Choices include but are not limited to: Should the home be in the city or the suburbs? Does it need to be near a particular school? Does it need to be close to the airport or train station (if a family member does a lot of traveling)? Should it be near a park? Expressway? Shopping center?

Location is a major factor in deciding where to live. *Size* of the home and amount of land (open space) is another very important consideration.

Cost is a third very important consideration. Large homes, homes that include a lot of land, and homes located where many people want to live tend to be more expensive. For example, some of the most expensive homes are found in very tall buildings that overlook beautiful parks, lakes, or other bodies of water.

Some people want to spend a lot of their money on housing. Other people would rather buy other things, such as expensive cars or airline tickets to places around the world. Still others want to save some of their money.

Renting is usually less expensive than buying, so many people rent for that reason. Some plan to rent only until they save enough money for a down payment, then buy a home. Others plan to rent an apartment permanently, maybe because they travel a lot and don't want to worry about a lawn to mow or snow to shovel. When people decide to rent an apartment, they must choose the size of the apartment and decide if they want entertainment and exercise facilities or laundry facilities. Note that conveniences and "extras" cost the renter extra money.

Optional   Review this segment if students still seem confused about renting—see Lesson 6. Explain that apartment buildings usually are owned by companies (groups of investors) that operate them to make money. The apartment manager is hired to supervise the complex. The families who occupy the apartments pay monthly rent to the manager—or someone in the office who handles the money. The building owner uses this money to pay off money that was borrowed from the bank to build or buy the apartment complex, as well as to pay taxes, maintain the building, and pay for any extras (laundry facilities, cleaning the hallways, outdoor lighting, etc.). Whatever money is left over then goes to the owners as profit.

Activity

After you share pictures and narrative, carry out a large-group discussion regarding the range of possibilities and issues associated with moving. Assign each table the task of preparing a group response for Brandi's family. What recommendations does the group have for Brandi's family, and why? Encourage each table to brainstorm ideas first, then decide by consensus what to recommend. Select a recorder for each group (upper-grade mentors or volunteers could also serve as recorders).

Activity

Provide the class with a second scenario. This one involves Rosie's family and its future move. Assign roles to family members and a real estate agent. During the enactment, give the other members of the class the task

of deciding whether they agree or disagree with the family's decisions.
Why? Why not? Use further enactments if appropriate.

The scenario: Rosie, her parents, and two younger brothers (school age) are moving to the area because Rosie's father has been transferred again. Her father's company manager has said the family should expect several more moves over the next two years because of the nature of Rosie's father's job. The family has a house to sell and it owns one car. Rosie's dad would like to move the family to a quiet rural community outside the city and suburbs so that it could do some gardening and raise animals. Is this a good time to be looking for housing in such an area? Why? Why not? What factors should Rosie's family consider as it chooses a new place to live? If it selects a house, where should it be located and why? What features should it have? Should the family rent or buy? Why? If it selects an apartment, where should it be? Why? What features should it have? Why?

Summarize

- People make choices about their shelters. Among them are whether to rent or buy.
- A major factor in deciding on a home is its location.
- Other choices include size, conveniences, and "extras" such as garages, laundry rooms, swimming pools.
- Families must pay for the choices they make. The more conveniences and extras, the more a home costs. Not all people choose to spend their money on things beyond the basics. (They may decide to save their money or to spend it on other things such as new cars, travel, education, etc.).

Assessment

Have each student complete the questioning exercise focusing on choice making. You may wish to invite upper-grade mentors or adult volunteers to serve as recorders. Optional: If time permits, have students role-play their plan for questions associated with family choice making.

If, in the future, our family needs to move, we should ask several questions before we make a final decision about where we will live. Questions we need to ask—and be able to answer—include:

1. Why are we moving?
2. Do we have a house to sell? (If we do, we probably can't buy another until we sell the one we own now.)
3. Do we need to be near our parents' work?
4. Does our family have its own means of transportation?
5. Do we need to be near the schools? Interstate? Airport? Other? Why?

Home Assignment

Encourage students to discuss with their parents the choices they made regarding where they live, the type of shelter they have selected, and the reasons why. Send home a copy of the letter in Figure 12. Ask them to be prepared to share their responses with the class.

Dear Parents,

We have been talking about the choices that people make regarding the types of homes they select, whether they should rent or buy, where the home should be located, what features it should include, and so forth. Please spend a few minutes discussing the choices your family has made. For example, why did you decide to live where you do? What other alternatives were considered? We will ask the children to share their responses with the class tomorrow.

Sincerely,

FIGURE 12 Model Letter to Parents

Lesson 9

. . . .

Portable Shelters

Resources
- Pictures or photos of portable shelters, including tipi, covered wagon, yurt, Bedouin tent, modern tent for camping, travel trailer, RV
- Maps of the local area, the United States, and the world

Children's Literature
McGovern, A. (1974). *If You Lived with the Sioux Indians*. New York: Scholastic.

Shemie, B. (1991). *Houses of Hide and Earth*. Toronto: Tundra Books.

Smith, A. (1999). *Homes and Houses Then and Now*. London: Usborne.

Weiss, H. (1988). *Shelters from Tepee to Igloo*. New York: Thomas Y. Crowell.

General Comments
Students will be familiar with some of the ideas from a previous lesson on shelter types (e.g., tipi, yurt). The intent of this lesson is that students will realize that portable shelters range from being a necessity to being simply for pleasure.

General Purposes or Goals
To develop an understanding and appreciation: (1) that portable shelters are intended and designed for portability; (2) that some people depend solely on portable shelters because they are nomadic, while others use them for short periods of time to satisfy their short-term needs (e.g., hunting, recreation, etc.).

Main Ideas to Develop
- Portable shelters are built out of a variety of materials, take many forms, and are used for a variety of reasons.
- Especially in the past, portable shelters have been used by nomadic societies.
- Today, portable shelters range from being primarily recreational in our area to being a necessity in a few places.

Teaching Tips from Barbara
One of the nice things about this lesson is that you can review past information about function, building materials, types, and cost, and look at shelter from an entirely different perspective at the same time. Also, this

lesson lends itself well to an art connection by having several groups of students paint, draw, or sculpt different portable shelters and match them with facts. This home assignment was a popular one and garnered many interesting responses.

Starting the Lesson

Begin the lesson by reviewing the home assignment, then show the students a series of pictures illustrating portable shelters—yurt, tipi, covered wagon, Bedouin tent, travel trailer, and RV. Ask, "What do these forms of shelter have in common?"

Explain that portable shelters have existed for many years. They are built out of a range of materials and they take many shapes. They have been used by people who move often or who need temporary shelter during a trip away from their permanent home.

Suggested Lesson Discussion

Long ago, the Plains Indians made tipis out of buffalo hides. To build a tipi, they first built a tripod. Three young trees were trimmed of their branches to make long poles. Two of the three poles were cut to a point at the top and the other was forked. The bottom ends were stuck into the ground and tilted inward to meet at the top. More straight, lightweight poles were stuck in the ground to form the conical tipi shape. A frame was made and covered with buffalo skins sewn together by women. The tipi was an ideal home for some Indians (Sioux) because it was sturdy enough to withstand the harsh winds of the Great Plains, yet light enough to be taken apart in minutes.

Often the Sioux painted their tipi coverings with scenes from their daily lives. [Show picture of painted tipi.] Plants, animals, and other aspects of nature were common in their artwork. Tipis made of skins usually did not last for more than a year—and each time a new one was constructed, it was a community project. When trade with settlers made canvas available to the Indians, that material was used instead of buffalo hides. Canvas covers were easier to make, the material was lighter and more easily transported, and canvas tipis could be larger. Tipis were pitched frequently because the Great Plains Indians followed the buffalo when they moved to new grazing grounds.

The pioneers used the covered wagon as their portable shelter as they crossed the United States in search of land and a place to settle. A whole family would live in the covered wagon during the journey. Everything the family owned would be placed in the covered wagon. The wagon was made of wood and the cover was made of canvas. The wagon was pulled by oxen. The journey was slow. Usually the family would be on the move all day. Typically, the family members would take turns walking because the wagon was very crowded. At night the family would stop for eating and sleeping. This was also a time to give the oxen some food and rest.

Today, some groups of people still use portable shelters. [Show picture of yurt.] A *yurt* is a circular tent with a felt covering—felt is a cloth made by pressing sheep or camel wool into layers. The felt is attached to a wooden frame with leather or horsehair thongs. Yurts are used mostly by shepherds in parts of Russia, Mongolia, and Siberia. [Point out these places on a globe.] The shepherds raise sheep and goats. When the grazing land is used up, the shepherds must move their camps and find new pastures.

Another type of shelter is the Bedouin tent. In many parts of northern Africa and Asia, and especially in the deserts of Arab countries, there are people called *Bedouins* who have no permanent dwellings. The land that these nomads wander through is very dry. There is not enough rain to make farming possible. The livelihood of these people is provided by the sheep, goats, and camels they raise and the trading they do.

Most people in the world live in more permanent shelters, although they may have portable shelters to use for recreation. For example, families can live in tents at camp sites for short periods while they enjoy nature, fish, hunt, or hike. In fact, tents are a common portable shelter used by vacationers. [Show picture of modern tent.]

Another type of portable shelter is a recreational vehicle. People who own or rent RVs travel in them for fun, not to hunt food.

Some people live in travel trailers. They are constructed on wheels and can be pulled by a truck. Frequently, they are chosen by people who have more than one home (e.g., people who use them as summer cottages or people who go to a warm place for a few months in the winter).

Activity

Have a series of large pictures or drawings of portable shelters on display. As you describe a given shelter or explain the need for a particular portable shelter, have the students give a "thumbs up" when they are ready to identify the specific portable shelter that should be selected. Use maps to locate the places being described. Students should be prepared to give reasons for their responses. Examples of descriptions and explanations follow:

RV. The family is planning a road trip to the west coast of the United States. It doesn't want to stay in motels yet it wants the conveniences of a home. Which type of portable shelter should it select?

Yurt. The family lives on the cold desert in Siberia. When the animals use up the grasses, the family must move with its animals in search of new pastures. It needs a shelter that is self-supporting and doesn't need stakes driven into the ground because the ground is often frozen. The frame of the shelter is covered with felt to keep the people warm inside. What is the name of the shelter being described?

Bedouin tent. The family moves with other families from place to place in search of food. It has no permanent home. It needs a portable shelter that can be carried from place to place by the camels. This portable shelter is usually made of goat hair. Ropes and poles are used to anchor the shelter. The ropes are tied to bushes and buried in the sand. What is the name of this shelter?

Tipi. This portable shelter was used long ago by the American Plains Indians. The buffalo provided food for the people and hides for the coverings of their homes. The hides were sewn together and draped over long poles. What is the name of this shelter?

Modern tent. The family wants to go fishing and wants to stay in a campsite near the lake. They will cook outside and sleep inside this shelter—probably in sleeping bags. Today these shelters are usually made of canvas or nylon. What is the name of this shelter?

Travel trailer. The family plans to travel across the United States and has decided they'd like to be able to cook inside their shelter. They plan to pull their shelter behind their truck. They will make reservations in advance so they can park at designated campsites. What is the name of this shelter?

Covered wagon. The family traveled across the United States long ago in this shelter. It was made of wood and canvas. It was usually pulled by oxen. This shelter stored all of the family's personal possessions. What was it?

Activity

Have students work as table groups. Ask each group to imagine that it would have an opportunity to spend a week in a portable shelter. Which portable shelter would it find most desirable? Least desirable? Give reasons for their choices.

Summarize

Portable shelters have been built out of a range of materials, and they take on many shapes. A few people in the world live in portable shelters out of necessity. However, today most people use portable shelters primarily for recreation.

Assessment

Have each student complete an individual journal entry based on the questions in Figure 13.

Home Assignment

Encourage students to discuss with parents why they would or would not like to use a portable shelter on their next vacation. Families should complete and return the form shown in Figure 15. Share the results in social studies class the following day.

I learned that portable shelters _____

_____

_____

_____

_____

_____

_____

The most interesting portable shelter type to me is _____

because _____

_____

_____

_____

Questions I have about the most interesting portable shelter include:

_____

_____

_____

_____

FIGURE 13 Portable Shelter Journal Entry

Dear Parents,

We have been discussing portable shelters in our social studies class. We would like you to discuss with your child why, as a family, you would or would not like to use a portable shelter (tent, camper, RV) on your next vacation. Tomorrow, your child will be asked to record a yes or no and discuss the pros and cons for portable shelters.

Sincerely,

FIGURE 14 Model Letter to Parents

Our family would like to use a portable shelter (tent, camper, RV) on our next vacation.

_____ Yes   _____ No

Reasons For   Reasons Against

1. _____   _____

2. _____   _____

3. _____   _____

4. _____   _____

5. _____   _____

6. _____   _____

7. _____   _____

FIGURE 15 Portable Shelter Survey Form

Lesson 10

. . . .

Design Your Ideal Future Home

Resources
- Local real estate multiple listings book
- Pictures of a range of home types
- Pictures of house features: garage, deck, air conditioning, fireplace, porch, hot tub
- Decision-making data sheet

Children's Literature
Hewitt, S., & Rowe, J. (1997). *Have You Noticed? The Homes We Live in Today*. Austin, TX: Raintree, Steck, Vaughn.

General Comments
This lesson will probably be most successful if older students could work in a tutorial situation with your class. Students are to project ahead as adults (thirty to forty years of age) and be realistic. They shouldn't plan for things that cost millions of dollars unless they also have a plan for making large amounts of money.

General Purposes or Goals
To: (1) draw on acquired knowledge and appreciation regarding shelter in order to "design" an ideal home; and (2) develop an appreciation regarding the range of considerations that need to be addressed when deciding on the ideal home.

Main Ideas to Develop
- Location, climatic conditions, availability of materials, cost, family size, and composition are among the factors to consider when attempting to identify and "design" the ideal home.
- Individual tastes and preferences enter into the decision-making process.

Teaching Tips from Barbara
This was a very difficult lesson for my students. Despite all their prior and newly developed knowledge, they tended to emphasize fanciful choices instead of reasonable and practical ones. When doing this lesson again, I plan to do more modeling before asking students to answer the questions themselves. Also, having an adult pull each child individually would be ideal. I borrowed a copy of a real estate listing book to help

with this activity. I was able to bring them much closer to reality by showing specific houses and their features as well as the actual costs.

Starting the Lesson

Discuss the responses from the home assignment. Revisit the idea that the class has been studying about shelters past and present and how they have changed over time and have been built out of a range of building materials. Review some of the choices people make about shelters (such as whether to rent or buy, where to live, and type of home). Refer to the range of pictures and photos that are displayed throughout the classroom. Explain that students will have the opportunity to design on paper their ideal homes. Each student will do his or her own because no one's ideas about the ideal home probably will be exactly the same as anyone else's. (Alternatively, explain that students will do so in partnership with a mentor who will help them clarify and write down their ideas.)

Many factors, such as climate, cost, location, and family size, need to be considered. Decision making is also influenced by one's family background and culture, personal taste/preferences, and personal experiences. Show pictures (refer to the local real estate multiple listings book) that illustrate a range of building sites, types of homes, and types of home features that need to be considered when creating one's ideal house.

Remind students that, in general, the more land they have, the more space they have, and the more conveniences they choose, the more expensive their home will be.

Introduce the decision-making data sheet (Figure 16) and provide class time for the students to *individually* make decisions about their ideal homes and share their reasoning with their peers. They may draw or construct the structure. If construction is selected, the work will need to be done at home, during free time at school, or as an art project (if it matches the arts goals).

Home Assignment

Encourage students to talk to their families about the choices they made in their school assignment regarding their ideal home. Send home the completed sheet and a blank sheet, along with a copy of the letter shown in Figure 17. Then, as a family, design an ideal home on paper. Encourage students to bring their family's ideal home plan to school to share with a peer, noting reasons for their choices. The major understanding to be drawn from the activity is that there are many considerations that come into play when deciding what the ideal home would look like, and the decisions that will be made involve numerous trade-offs.

Describe the number of members in the family, ages of the children, pets, etc.

_____

_____

Describe the number of vehicles the family owns.

_____

_____

Describe the location of the home

    City, country, suburb, etc. _____

    Climatic conditions _____

    Physical features nearby _____ woods _____ lakes _____ mountains _____ other

What building materials will be used?

_____

_____

Type of structure

    Ranch _____

    Two-storey colonial _____

    Other (describe) _____

How many rooms will your ideal home have and how will each be used?

_____

_____

What special features will your home have? (air conditioning, fireplace, sauna, etc.) Why?

_____

_____

What special outside features will your home have?

_____

How much will it cost? _____

Other:

_____

_____

FIGURE 16 Decision-Making Data Sheet for Designing Your Ideal Home

Assessment

Ask students to talk into a tape recorder to explain their ideal homes. Have students write down three things they considered when attempting to design their ideal homes.

Dear Parents,

Your child has been learning about the range of choices and factors such as cost, climate, and location that need to be considered when thinking about your ideal home. Your child has created an ideal home on paper. We would like to encourage you, as a family, to use the enclosed decision-making sheet for designing your ideal home. Feel free to use cutout pictures or drawings, or do some construction to illustrate your choices. Finally, as a family, prepare a paragraph that describes what guests might notice on the first visit to your ideal home. What would they see as they walked up the sidewalk, drove into the driveway, looked out the back door, etc.? Describe four things you would want your guests to see.

Thank you.

Sincerely,

FIGURE 17 Model Letter to Parents

Lesson 11

Homelessness

Resources
- Map of local area illustrating sites where people can get help in the event they become homeless
- Newspaper articles focusing on disasters that result in homelessness

Children's Literature
Bunting, E. (1991). *Fly Away Home*. New York: Clarion.
DiSalvo-Ryan, D. (1991). *Uncle Willie and the Soup Kitchen*. New York: Morrow Junior.

General Comments
The intent of this lesson is to create a social awareness regarding homelessness, being careful not to frighten or worry the students. They should come to realize that while lack of income is the major cause, many people suffer temporary homelessness due to disasters. As citizens, we want to help others in ways that are appropriate.

General Purposes or Goals
To help students: (1) understand that in extreme cases people are unable to pay for shelter and may become homeless; and (2) acquire a sensitivity for homeless people and a desire to practice citizenship as it relates to assisting others in need.

Main Ideas to Develop
- Sometimes people cannot pay for shelter and utilities due to unemployment or underemployment, and some become homeless. Often these circumstances are due to illness, fire, flooding, loss of jobs, or accumulation of bills.
- People who are homeless can secure help from community organizations (e.g., the United Way, Rescue Mission, Salvation Army, religious organizations, etc.).
- As members of the community, we can contribute to organizations that assist people in need by donating time, food, money, or clothing.

Teaching Tips from Barbara
Keep this lesson simple. It's especially helpful if you've already done the food unit's lesson on hunger. Use the books to help keep the discussion

focused. Keep your comments and your students' comments nonjudgmental. I also made sure that I spent equal time on solutions, citizenship, and helping others.

Starting the Lesson

Begin the lesson by reviewing the home assignment. Explain that it will probably take more than one evening to do, therefore an expanded discussion will take place at the end of the unit. Pose questions regarding homelessness. Sample questions might include: What do you know about homelessness? Why does it occur? Have you ever had contact with a person who was homeless? Have you ever had a glimpse of the life of a homeless person?

Introduce the children to *Fly Away Home* by Eve Bunting—a story of Andrew and his father, who live at the airport. Ask children to imagine they are Andrew, and after listening to the story, to share their feelings with the class. Read the story. Stop at appropriate points to acknowledge students' comments and answer or reflect on their questions.

Points to emphasize:

- Fear, uncertainty, frustration, anger, and sadness are among the feelings associated with homelessness.
- The airport was selected by Andrew and his father as a temporary shelter because it's a place where there's lots of activity—everybody is on the move—and they wouldn't be easily noticed or singled out (public buildings cannot legally be used as temporary shelters).
- Andrew has hope of having a home again. As a young boy, he doesn't quite understand why other people have homes and he doesn't.

After reading the story, share with the children some of the reasons for homelessness. These include tornados, floods, earthquakes, illness, and loss of jobs. Also, share newspaper articles that reveal disasters—times when people are left without homes. Be alert to appropriate local news stories that might be used.

As a class, discuss what could be done to provide assistance for members of our community who find themselves in a crisis. (*Uncle Willie and the Soup Kitchen* is an excellent children's book for setting the stage for discussing volunteerism in the community.) Using a local map, point out places where people in need can go to get help. Use photographs of the local community agencies.

Activity

Explain that for a few minutes you want students to imagine that Andrew is a member of their school community. What can the class do to help Andrew? Have students discuss this change in triads for five minutes and then share their ideas with the whole class.

Summarize

- Homelessness may result from extremely unfortunate circumstances.
- Communities have organizations that provide assistance to people in need.
- One way of practicing good citizenship is helping others.

Assessment

Have students respond to three open-ended statements:

1. Reasons people might become homeless include _____ ,
   _____ and _____
   _____ .

2. Our community helps homeless people by _____
   _____
   _____ .

3. I can help homeless people by _____
   _____
   _____ .

Home Assignment

Encourage students to share with their families what they have learned about homelessness and what the class has decided to do to assist people who are experiencing unfortunate circumstances. Ask for family involvement in the activity (e.g., donating articles of clothing, money, or food). If relevant, connect with other school initiatives that engender positive citizenry.

Lesson 12

Review

Resources
- Bulletin board displays that were developed around shelter
- Artifacts from the unit (e.g., journal entries, student responses to activities, blueprints, home assignment responses, charts, diagrams, photos, pictures, etc.)
- Parent or community volunteers to serve as guides for the shelter fair

Children's Literature
Dorros, A. (1992). *This Is My House*. New York: Scholastic.

General Comments
This lesson will be most successful if the students are allowed to move around the room and revisit their work, which should be displayed on bulletin boards, in centers, and on charts. The artifacts should serve as prompts for the class discussion.

General Purposes or Goals
To: (1) draw on prior knowledge, understanding, appreciation, and applications conducted in school and at home that collectively will enhance meaningfulness and continued curiosity in learning about shelter; and (2) revisit and reflect on the big ideas developed about shelter.

Main Ideas Developed Throughout the Unit
- Shelter is a basic need.
- Throughout history, people have needed shelter for protection from the elements (sun in hot weather, cold in cold weather, precipitation, wind, etc.), places to keep their possessions, and places in which to carry out their daily activities.
- There are many different forms of shelters due to personal wants and needs, climate, physical features, available building materials, economic resources, and cultural considerations.
- There is a range of shelter types in our local community.
- Factors that contribute to the types of shelter people choose include physical features and climatic conditions of the local area, building materials available, cost, cultural influences, and personal preferences.

- Geographic features, culture, economic resources, and personal preferences are among the factors that figure into people's choices about the type of shelter they will have.
- People all over the world adapt to their environment, and as a result, there are many types of shelters.
- Until recently, housing construction reflected the availability of local materials. This pattern still exists in some places, but in other places modern transportation has allowed choices to be expanded.
- New construction techniques and technological improvements get invented and refined over time. Now, besides meeting our needs for protection from the elements, modern homes cater to our wants for a comfortable living space, hot and cold running water, electric lighting, and comfortable beds and furniture.
- Today's homes are planned to take advantage of advances in new designs, technologies, and new materials. Many workers are involved to ensure that the plans are realized.
- You can buy a house before you have the full purchase price, although you can lose it if you don't continue to make your payments.
- Some people choose to live in an apartment while they save enough money for a down payment. Others choose apartments for other reasons, such as convenience and fewer responsibilities, such as maintenance.
- Banks (and sometimes private individuals) lend people the money to buy a house. The people have to pay the bank the amount of the loan plus interest. That's how banks make money.
- People have to pay to live in apartments. The rent money is kept by the owner of the building. Renting is a profit-making business.
- Whether you live in a house or an apartment, you pay utility companies for heat (fuel), water, and light (electricity).
- You pay money to the government (taxes) to maintain roads, provide police protection and fire protection, and operate schools. (If you are buying your home, you pay some money directly to the government. If you are renting, some of the money you pay to the apartment building owner goes to the government for these services.)
- A large part of the family income goes for buying or renting and maintaining the property.
- One of the choices people have to make is location—where they will live.
- Another choice is whether to rent or buy.

- Other choices concern such issues as the size of the place.
- Portable shelters are built out of a variety of materials, take many forms, and are used for a variety of reasons.
- Especially in the past, portable shelters have been used by nomadic societies.
- Today portable shelters range from being primarily recreational in our area to being a necessity in a few instances.
- The home industry provides a range of opportunities for individuals to be creative and pursue careers.
- Today, it takes a variety of workers to perform specific steps in building a house or apartment.
- Several changes have occurred in the home building industry over the past two hundred years.
- Location, climatic conditions, availability of materials, cost, and family size and composition are among the factors to consider when attempting to identify and "design" the ideal home.
- Individual tastes and preferences enter into the decision-making process.
- Sometimes people cannot pay for shelter and utilities due to unemployment or underemployment, and some become homeless. Often these circumstances are due to illness, fire, flooding, loss of jobs, or accumulation of bills.
- People who are homeless can secure help from community organizations (e.g., the United Way, Rescue Mission, Salvation Army, religious organizations, etc.).
- As members of the community, we can contribute to organizations that assist people in need by donating time, food, money, or clothing.

Teaching Tips from Barbara

This review is an excellent way for you to go back and highlight the big ideas one more time. You can also focus on anything that your students struggled with the first time around. An alternative ending to this unit would be to give a group of students an imaginary family complete with needs and location. The students' job would be to decide and create (paint, draw, computer illustrate, sculpt, etc.) the shelter. As a finale, the groups would share their shelters with each other.

Starting the Lesson

Discuss the home assignment. Remind the class that is has been learning about shelters from the past and present, how they have changed over time, the kinds of building materials that are used, the steps in building a house today, and the choices people make, such as where to live and whether to rent or buy.

Review other features of the unit, including costs associated in having a home; an opportunity to dream about your ideal home—and perhaps begin thinking about what you'll need to do to achieve your dreams; an opportunity to talk to your families about your ideas as well as become more familiar with your own homes and others in the community; and a chance to begin investigating how things work—such as how your homes are equipped with heat, lighting, and running water. As you grow up, you will be making lots of decisions about your lives, including where to live and what kind of home to have.

Explain that this lesson involves going back to look at what we've been learning and sharing our thoughts and opinions about shelter before we move to the next unit. Recognize that some students still have some unfinished business—and that's fine too. For example, a student and a parent might be redoing a doll house—and thinking a lot about costs. They are using catalogs to secure prices—to try to figure out what their dreams would really cost if they were creating and decorating their house today. Set up a corner for ongoing shelter projects. Make books and materials available. Periodically, check on progress and ask those who are doing shelter projects to share.

At this juncture, explain to the class that in groups with their volunteer guides, they will revisit the shelter sites and review the key ideas acquired during the unit. This will be called a "shelter fair." (Prior to the lesson, provide the volunteers with a list of key ideas and conduct a walk-through in an effort to familiarize them with the goals and content. Establish a time limit for each site visit.)

Optional   Provide each volunteer with a key question for discussion that's reflective of the material displayed at the site. The questions will vary depending on the displays. Sample questions include:

- Why do people need shelters?
- Why are there so many different kinds of homes around the world?
- Why are homes today different from those in the past?
- Why do most homes today cost so much?
- What are some of the choices you have to make about your shelter?
- What are the costs related to living in a home or an apartment?
- What did you learn about portable shelters?
- Why are some people homeless?

Large-Group Discussion and Activity
After every group has visited each of the sites, return to the large group and write an entry for the class journal summarizing the highlights of the shelter unit.

Individual Assessment Activity

Give each student a copy of Figure 18, and read each statement to the class. Model the directions by doing one as a class. Items 1, 2, 5, 7, and 8 are true.

Place a T by each statement that is correct. After you have marked all of the T statements, draw pictures to explain why you believe they are correct.

_____ 1. Not all types of portable shelter exist in our community. (Draw one that does not.)

_____ 2. In the early days, housing construction reflected the availability of local materials.

_____ 3. Only some people need shelter.

_____ 4. All of the shelters in our community look the same.

_____ 5. Climate and culture influence the types of shelters people have.

_____ 6. People who own houses don't have to pay for water, heat, or electricity.

_____ 7. There are many kinds of portable shelters.

_____ 8. A large part of the family income goes for paying for shelter and maintaining it.

FIGURE 18 Individual Assessment Sheet: If True, Illustrate!

©2001 by Janet Alleman and Jere Brophy from *Social Studies Excursions, K–3.* Portsmouth, NH: Heinemann

Reflecting Back, Moving Forward

Why do I eat the things I do? Is it because somebody has placed the food in front of me or advertised it on TV? Or do I have better reasons? Why does our family live where it does? What factors contributed to the decision? Might my preference for sleeping in bunk beds in my older brother's room change my parents' plan to sell our house and buy a bigger one? Might my ideas about clothing choices save my family some money?

Self-efficacy is a sense of empowerment, of being able to make a difference in one's life by using what has been learned. It is a state of mind that says, "I can do it! I can contribute. I can decide. I can figure it out." Our experiences with these units have involved not only children but also their families. We have been gratified with their response to the home assignments. In our interviews with parents, reports of their children's "I can" statements was an overarching theme. We attribute this to four principles associated with self-efficacy that we threaded throughout the units.

1. The content should be emotionally and intellectually comfortable for students so as to provide good places to start. (All children have prior experience with cultural universals, so no student is disenfranchised because of culture, socioeconomic background, or achievement level.)
2. The content should have potential for immediate application outside of school.
3. Home assignments should support students' transition from egocentrism to social engagement with family members and other children and adults.

4. The content and learning opportunities should develop students' awareness of their geographical and cultural contexts.

One parent shared the story of her daughter who wanted french fries every night for dinner until the food unit was taught at school. Then she gradually shifted from "I want French fries" to "Our family needs potatoes and baked ones would probably be better." Suddenly first and second graders were having some say in the menus. One mother related that their child was very observant during her cooking, wanted to be a part of it, and chastised her about putting sugar in baked beans, explaining that sugar comes from the EAT LESS category.

The clothing unit has obvious connections to students' sense of efficacy given that most children have definite ideas about what they prefer to wear and have at least some say in choosing their daily outfits. Students were eager to talk with their parents about the changes that have taken place since their parents were young, and they became excited when asked to think about possible careers in the clothing field that they might like to pursue as adults. One second grader mapped out a plan that included designing, modeling, and ultimately owning a boutique. Another said he was now more hopeful about his family's upcoming move to California—he suspected that becoming a designer would be easier there.

Shelter seems, at least initially, to be a domain for adult decision making. However, students learned that their families made choices within limits defined by resources like money, time, and information, and they began to understand and appreciate the cost of providing shelter—both for the dwelling itself and for the modern conveniences within such as heat, light, and running water. Parents reported that their children were concerned about their families' ability to pay the costs of living. In one case, a child suddenly became more thrifty with her allowance. She had always been a planner, but after discussing housing costs in class, she realized that she had better start saving for her future home. Another student, more concerned with the here and now, was overheard scolding her older brother for using too much hot water: "Nick, you'd better cut that shower short; that water costs a lot of money."

Other parental reports included:

- "It made my son think—and realize things. For example, he thought his dream house would cost a dollar. He was amazed at how many dollars it might be. He learned to distinguish between modern conveniences and basics (e.g., dishwasher vs. floors). The assignment regarding how much it costs was eye-opening for him, even if he couldn't grasp all the terms."

- "My daughter was eager to complete the assignments, had a good understanding of what was expected, and grasped all of the new ideas and terms. She began to pay attention to things around her such as the bill paying process—and the huge amounts it takes to live in a house. She was equally impressed—and at times a bit overwhelmed—with all the variables that need to be considered about buying clothes."

- "Our son talked about things we had no idea he knew anything about. The assignments produced a lot of interesting discussions."

- "We can't go anywhere now without our child saying something like, 'Now there's a duplex made of brick—and there's an apartment. I bet many people live in that building.' One day we were at K-Mart and out of the blue my son read a shirt label and said, 'See, this is silk—and silkworms are needed to make shirts like that.'"

- "The assignments were thought-provoking. It's good for them to realize that mom and dad's job is the way we pay for shelter."

- "In our discussions, we brought to light different reasons why someone might be homeless—as well as in need of clothing. My son exhibited insight and empathy plus an understanding of other lifestyles. He developed an appreciation for his blessings and has expressed an interest in donating time, money, and clothing to area shelters."

Parents appreciated advance communication about completion dates for home assignments as well as specific directions about expected amounts of input. (One student insisted that her family inventory every closet to determine fabric types.) A few parents also voiced a desire for more about the rationales underlying home assignments, to help guide them in expanding their discussions with their children.

Personal efficacy, family impact, and constructing meaningful understandings have been the hallmarks of our experiences with the units. We encourage you to frequently revisit the big ideas drawn from the units to help your students explain life experiences and develop habits of higher order conversations about the world around them. Provide parents with the lists of big ideas so that they too may experience the luxury of helping their children make connections between real life and book learning, for example, by applying what they learned in school to a television program, retrieving data from the Internet to enhance a lesson, or discussing "how things work" at home and in the community.

References

Chapter 1

Brophy, J., & Alleman, J. (1996). *Powerful Social Studies for Elementary Students*. Fort Worth: Harcourt Brace.

Egan, K. (1988). *Primary Understanding: Education in Early Childhood*. New York: Routledge.

Evans, R., & Saxe, D. (Eds.). (1996). *Handbook on Teaching Social Issues*. Washington, DC: National Council for the Social Studies.

Good, T., & Brophy, J. (2000). *Looking in Classrooms* (8th ed.). New York: Longman.

Haas, M., & Laughlin, M. (Eds.). (1997). *Meeting the Standards: Social Studies Readings for K–6 Educators*. Washington, DC: National Council for the Social Studies.

Harris, D., & Yocum, M. (1999). *Powerful and Authentic Social Studies: A Professional Development Program for Teachers*. Washington, DC: National Council for the Social Studies.

Hirsch, E. D., Jr. (1988). *Cultural Literacy: What Every American Needs to Know*. New York: Vintage.

Krey, D. (1988). *Children's Literature in Social Studies: Teaching to the Standards*. (Bulletin No. 95). Waldorf, MD: National Council for the Social Studies.

Larkins, A., Hawkins, M., & Gilmore, A. (1987). Trivial and noninformative content of elementary social studies: A review of primary texts in four series. *Theory and Research in Social Education, 15,* 299–311.

National Council for the Social Studies. (1993). A vision of powerful teaching and learning in the social studies: Building social understanding and civic efficacy. *Social Education, 57,* 213–223. [Also included in the NCSS, 1994 Bulletin on Curriculum Standards for Social Studies]

National Council for the Social Studies. (1994). *Curriculum standards for social studies: Expectations of excellence* (Bulletin No. 89). Washington, DC: Author.

Ravitch, D. (1987). Tot sociology or what happened to history in the grade schools. *American Scholar, 56,* 343–353.

Roth, K. (1996). Making learners and concepts central: A conceptual change approach to learner-centered, fifth-grade American history planning and teaching. In J. Brophy (Ed.), *Advances in research on teaching. Volume 6: Teaching and learning history* (pp. 115–182). Greenwich, CT: JAI Press.

Chapter Two

Alleman, J., & Brophy, J. (1999). The changing nature and purpose of assessment in the social studies classroom. *Social Education, 65,* 334–337.

Alleman, J., & Brophy, J. (1997). Elementary social studies: Instruments, activities, and standards. In G. Phye (Ed.), *Handbook of Classroom Assessment* (pp. 321–357). San Diego: Academic Press.

Alleman, J., & Brophy, J. (1994). Taking advantage of out-of-school opportunities for meaningful social studies learning. *Social Studies, 85,* 262–267.

Brophy, J., & Alleman, J. (1991). Activities as instructional tools: A framework for analysis and evaluation. *Educational Researcher, 20* (4), 9–23.

Hoberman, M. (1978). *A house is a House for Me.* New York: Penguin Books.

Introduction to Shelter Unit

Brophy, J., & Alleman, J. (1999). *Primary-Grade Students' Knowledge and Thinking About Shelter as a Cultural Universal.* Bloomington, IN: ERIC Clearinghouse for Social Studies/Social Science Education (Document No. ED 437 311).

Introduction to Clothing Unit

Brophy, J., & Alleman, J. (1999). *Primary-Grade Students' Knowledge and Thinking About Clothing as a Cultural Universal.* Bloomington, IN: ERIC Clearinghouse for Social Studies/Social Science Education. ERIC Document Reproduction Service Number ED 439 072.